W9-BYX-047

BY THE SAME AUTHOR

BIOGRAPHY
The Emperor Alexander II

AUTOBIOGRAPHY
Tomorrow Will Come

FOR CHILDREN
Frossia
The Knights of the Golden Table

ALEXANDER I

EMPRESS ELIZABETH

THE
EMPEROR
ALEXANDER I

E. M. ALMEDINGEN

NEW YORK

THE VANGUARD PRESS, INC.

WINGATE COLLEGE LIBRARY
WINGATE, N. C.

FOR

JOHN AND FANNY SIMMONS

IN FRIENDSHIP AND AFFECTION

Library of Congress Catalog Card Number: 66–16979
Copyright, ©, mcmlxiv, by E. M. Almedingen
*No portion of this book may be reproduced in any
form or by any mechanical means, including dupli-
cating machine, or tape recorder, without the written
permission of the publisher, except by a reviewer who
may wish to quote brief passages in connection with
a review for a newspaper, magazine, radio, or tele-
vision.*
Manufactured in the United States of America

CONTENTS

33560

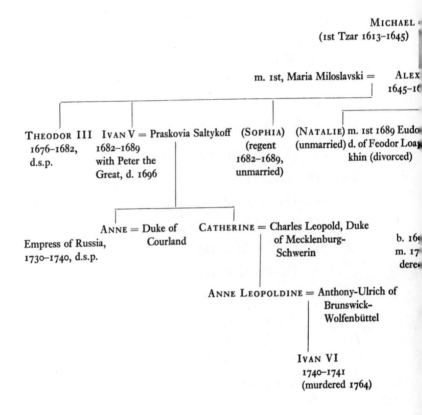

MICHAEL
(1st Tzar 1613–1645)

m. 1st, Maria Miloslavski = ALEX
1645–1(

THEODOR III
1676–1682,
d.s.p.

IVAN V = Praskovia Saltykoff
1682–1689
with Peter the
Great, d. 1696

(SOPHIA)
(regent
1682–1689,
unmarried)

(NATALIE) m. 1st 1689 Eudo
(unmarried) d. of Feodor Loa
khin (divorced)

ANNE = Duke of
Courland
Empress of Russia,
1730–1740, d.s.p.

CATHERINE = Charles Leopold, Duke
of Mecklenburg-
Schwerin

b. 16
m. 17
dere

ANNE LEOPOLDINE = Anthony-Ulrich of
Brunswick-
Wolfenbüttel

IVAN VI
1740–1741
(murdered 1764)

YNASTY

, Maria Dolgorouki
divorced)
d, Eudoxia Streshnieva

m. 2nd, Nathalie Naryshkin

PETER THE GREAT = m. 2nd, 1707, Martha Skavronsky (Livonian)
1682–1689 with (crowned by Peter the Great as Empress)
Ivan V, 1689– 1725–1727 as Catherine I
1725 alone

EXIS = Charlotte of   ANNE = Duke of   ELIZABETH (unmarried)
1718,   Brunswick-   Holstein   Empress, 1741–1762
ur-   Wolfenbüttel   (took the throne from Ivan VI)

TER II (unmarried)   CHARLES PETER ULRICH = Sophia-Augusta-Frederica of
1727–1730)   Jan. 1762–July 1762,   Anhalt-Zerbst, 'Catherine
as Peter III   the Great', 1762–1796

m. 1st, Wilhelmina of Hesse = PAUL I, born 1754 = m. 2nd, Sophia-Augusta-
(1796–1801)   Dorothea of Württem-
(murdered)   berg (Marie)

ALEXANDER I
(1777)
1801–1825

A PREFATORY NOTE

THIS BOOK is a portrait. It does not claim to be a definitive biography of Alexander I. Archives being inaccessible, I have had to limit my research to printed books. A short bibliography will be found at the end of the book. Conjecture and guesswork are twin pitfalls in the path of any biographer. In the present instance, the danger is heightened because of the contradictions in the Emperor's character. I have tried to avoid the danger as much as in me lay and I would ask the reader's indulgence for any conclusions of mine which may run counter to the earlier accepted ideas.

It is my pleasant duty to acknowledge my deep indebtedness to Mr John S. G. Simmons, MA, Oxford, for his invaluable help with the Bibliography, to Madame de Watteville of Cologny, Switzerland, for the generous loan of her own notes, to Mrs L. V. Dickins and Miss F. M. Pilkington for their great help with the Index, to the Librarian, R.U.C., Central Library, London, and to the Branch Librarian, County Library, Shepton Mallet, Somerset, for their patience and help in obtaining books not easily procurable in this country.

Brookleaze,   E. M. Almedingen
Nettlebridge, near Bath

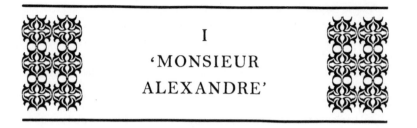

I

'MONSIEUR ALEXANDRE'

BY THE will of the nation a Romanov was elected to the throne of Muscovy in 1613, but to the very end of the eighteenth century the dynasty stood in jeopardy of extinction. On the accession of Catherine the Great in 1762, the imperial family consisted of herself, her husband, the deposed Emperor Peter III, and their only child, Paul, born in 1754.

In the spring of 1776, the young Grand Duke was a widower, his wife, Grand Duchess Nathalie (born Princess Wilhelmina of Hesse), having died in childbirth. So unusual were the circumstances that the Empress Catherine ordered a post mortem to be held. It revealed that the Grand Duchess could never have given birth to a living child. The period of mourning was callously brief, the Empress at once busying herself to find another bride for her son. She looked for neither wealth, beauty, nor intellect. Royal blood and good physique were the only essentials needed for her future daughter-in-law. Catherine's choice fell on a Württemberg princess, and Paul was presented with a *fait accompli* as soon as the girl's parents had given their consent. In the autumn of 1776 Paul was married to his seventeen-year-old bride, who had been received into the Greek Church on her betrothal and given the name of Marie.

In May 1777 the young Grand Duchess was known to be pregnant, and every precaution, both necessary and futile, was taken, though her health gave no cause for any anxiety. The sex of the baby to be born gave the Empress many a troubled hour. She must have a grandson. Science being then unable to set her mind at rest and she having but small use for astrological fantasies, Catherine must needs wait, and she confessed herself grateful to Nature that the appointed months did not exceed the number of nine.

13

WINGATE COLLEGE LIBRARY
WINGATE N C

Marie carried him, but it was the grandmother who created his character—and that before his birth—endowed him with genius, and mapped out his future paths. She knew that she had a goodly heritage to bestow: an Empire greatly enlarged by her, a society which—for all the leaven of corruption—had something to offer to the world, and a power far more absolute than that of any other European sovereign.

All through the summer and autumn of 1777 Catherine's thoughts were busy with that creation of hers—the grandson as yet unborn was to be her successor, he would further and perfect much begun by her, he would govern in wisdom bequeathed to him by God and in glory created by his grandmother.

All of it may seem rather strange when we remember that the heir to the throne of Russia was still Grand Duke Paul, the only child Catherine had borne in wedlock.

It should be explained that mother and son were strangers to each other, Paul having been claimed at birth by his great-aunt, the Empress Elizabeth. By 1776, the cleavage, however screened by the demands of etiquette and common courtesy, had taken deep root. It was an open secret that the two courts stood in opposition to each other. The son was denied the least important share in the mother's government. There was bitterness on one side. There were impatience and contempt on the other. To Paul, his mother's foreign policy was insane, her liberalism spelt the future ruin of the Empire, and her educational and judiciary reforms provoked him to mordant mockery. To Catherine, her son's inept criticism of her government, his absorption in military minutiae and his undisguised worship at the Potsdam shrine, his inability to distinguish the general from the particular, all of it together brought back echoes of his unfortunate father's lack of stability and good judgment. The gulf between mother and son, however unremarked by the masses, coloured every occurrence at court, entered the diplomatic correspondence, and caused many a statesman in Europe to ponder over the landscape likely to open after Catherine's death.

On 23rd December 1777 the young Grand Duchess had her first-born at the Winter Palace in St Petersburg. Two days later the Empress wrote to her faithful friend, Melchior Grimm: 'I could wager that you do not know *Monsieur Alexandre*, not Alexander the Great—but a very, very small Alexander,' and many eyewitnesses set on record that the Empress wept for joy at the christening. She shed tears seldom enough and hardly ever in public.

Practically all that is known of Alexander's early days has come to us from Catherine's voluminous correspondence with Grimm. All the festivities in connection with the birth and the christening were centred round her and the infant. She it was who chose the sponsors, the Emperor Joseph II of Austria being one of them, but she made an amiable gesture in allowing her son to name Frederick the Great as the second sponsor, and she left Paul free to choose the name. None the less, the young parents were at once made to feel that their first-born primarily belonged to the Empire, in more immediate terms to his grandmother.

Catherine did not entirely echo the cruelties meted out to herself by the Empress Elizabeth. Little Alexander was not torn away from his mother within a few minutes after his birth, nor were Paul and Marie debarred from seeing him every day, but from the very beginning all the child's small courses were appointed for him by the Empress.

'Your dear wife,' she is supposed to have said to Grand Duke Paul, 'is much too young to carry heavy responsibilities. What can a girl of eighteen know about a child's upbringing?'

Alexander's father might well have retorted that if his wife was too young, his mother was far too busy to spare much time for her grandson.

And busy Catherine was indeed but, all the government cares notwithstanding, she found time to arrange the furnishing of the nurseries, to determine Alexander's diet, even to design his clothes and to make toys for him. 'There is nothing much for me to tell you,' she wrote to Grimm in March 1778, '. . . [Alexander] has so far not given us the least anxiety. He is so healthy a prince. . . .'

Here, as elsewhere, the use of the word 'nous' is significant. Catherine had firmly convinced herself that, far from monopolizing the child, she shared him with the parents. Neither Paul nor Marie would have endorsed the use of that 'nous'. The Empress's insistence on physical hardihoods scared and angered the parents. Alexander's windows were constantly kept open, he slept on a flat leather mattress laid on an iron bedstead with no curtains to it. He was washed in cold water and wore comfortably loose clothes designed for him by his loving 'bábushka'. His first nurse, inevitably chosen by her, was an Englishwoman, one Pauline Hessler, wife of a footman in the household. 'A woman of rare merits,' the Empress wrote to Grimm. . . . 'She is tidy, clean, simple and sensible . . . I feel sure that if *Monsieur Alexandre* had a son of his own brought up by the same Englishwoman, the throne would stand secure for more than a century to come . . .'

In May 1779 Grand Duchess Marie gave birth to her second son, Constantine, the name chosen by the Empress, who, in the proud flush of her victories over Turkey, dreamt about Constantinople falling to her armies and of her second grandson ascending the throne of a magically resuscitated Byzantium, its fortunes interwoven with and dependent upon the Russian Empire. From the luxury of such dreams Catherine turned to everyday realities, and a Greek nurse was installed at the Winter Palace, but the future '*Basileus*' did not thrive rapidly. 'He looks a weakling compared with his brother', the Empress wrote rather plaintively to Grimm.

The brothers remained under her care, their winters spent in St Petersburg, their summers at Tsarskoe Selo. Meanwhile, the cleavage between Catherine and Paul deepened still further, and the Empress's palaces echoed with the rumours of her intention formally to disinherit her son. In the summer, the Grand Ducal pair lived in the neighbourhood of Tsarskoe Selo. Paul's acid comments about his mother were carried by the zeal of the servants from one palace to another.

In the nurseries, Pauline Hessler remained in command, her loyalty and good sense beyond question, but there were many occasions when she must needs delegate her authority, and her Russian underlings do not seem to have been chosen with any particular care. Gossip from the palace backstairs travelled freely enough. Thus, from his earliest childhood Alexander heard about a wall between his parents and his grandmother. For a time, its significance beyond his understanding, it could hardly be said to interfere with his peace. Probably he was the happiest little prince in the Europe of his day, Catherine's care and affection lighting up all his conscious moments. None the less, the painful conflict in the palace and beyond was there from the beginning. That happy, carefree childhood carried the seeds of deep misery in the future.

At that time, the Academy of Sciences was ordered to print the Empress's 'Elementary Instruction for the Upbringing of Children'.

Having utterly failed as mother, Catherine may well be considered an ideal grandmother.[1]

It is a matter for wonder that such a busy woman should have found time to embody her thoughts in a piece of writing, its basic ideas far beyond the educational methods of the day. '. . . You should never make fun of a child . . . Much can be learned about a child's imagination if he is watched at play—so long as he is allowed to play by himself or with the friends of his own age . . . No child should ever be afraid of his elders—such an attitude engenders cowardice and mendacity . . . A child should always be busy either at work or play . . . If you do not know the right answer to a child's question, do not lose your patience and above all do not deceive him . . . Reflect carefully on the consequences of any punishment before you inflict it . . . Self-respect and compassion should be developed as early as possible . . . Every child, however exalted his rank, should be told that he comes into the world naked and in precisely the same manner as the offspring of the lowest-born parents . . .'

Imperial writings did not easily lend themselves to candid criticism, and much fulsome flattery was showered by the contemporaries on Catherine's comedies and essays. She was far too shrewd to accept it for truly minted coin. But the case was different with 'The Elementary Instruction'. The ideas were revolutionary in 1782, and the great majority of the Empress's subjects had not even heard of Rousseau, not that the booklet was wholly an adaptation of his. 'The Instruction' ended by being something of a minor bestseller.

Yet Catherine's enlightened intimates would surely have read irony into a marginal note made by her in her copy of Fénélon's 'Télemaque'—'que jamais de misérables principes, de mauvaises finesses ne trouvent entrée dans son coeur. Les duplicités sont inconnues aux grands hommes: ils en méprisent les bassesses.' Such was the

---

[1] Paul was Catherine's only legitimate child. She had a son and two daughters by Gregory Orlov, and a daughter by Poniatovsky, who died in infancy. Orlov's son, created Count Bobrinsky, had an estate settled on him, and the arrangement marked the beginning and the end of the Empress's concern for him. The two daughters were brought up by a retired lady-in-waiting. Having made a more or less adequate provision for them, Catherine took no further notice of her daughters, whose names never appear in any of her writings. It might be said that the shock of having had her first-born taken from her within a few minutes after his birth crippled all her maternal instincts for ever.

cornerstone of all her hopes for '*Monsieur Alexandre*', who, on first hearing about the Macedonian, wished to be introduced to him and 'was very unhappy on being told that such an introduction was impossible', as the Empress wrote to Grimm shortly before the boy's fifth birthday.

Her hopes ran high and ever higher, but the unconscious irony of the marginal note cannot be denied when we remember Catherine's own genius for duplicity in dealing alike with friend and foe, and it should not be forgotten that all her achievements and all the splendours of her court could not cancel out the obverse side of the medal: the poverty of the Empire, the venality of a bureaucracy which battened on the ignorance and the helplessness of a yoked nation, and the poison of court factions. All those were there—one day to form part of Alexander's inheritance, and so much of what Catherine most passionately desired to bestow on him did not lie within her power of bestowal.

In appearance at least those early years were halcyon. The Empress spared time for lessons, herself plunging into a study of history the better to satisfy her grandson's curiosity. Her letters carry many details about his numerous interests, his visits to paper and glass factories, the share taken in the harvest at the home farm at Tsarskoe Selo, his attempts to paint a summer house under the guidance of an expert Scotsman, and always his passion for reading. The Empress quoted from her conversations with him, commented on the boy's affectionate nature, his exquisite manners, his concern for the aged, the poor and the sick.

Catherine made hardly any mention of the shadowy family background, its streaks of ugly jealousy, its climate of tortuous uncertainty. Paul, entrenched at his miniature Potsdam created at Gatchina, kept wondering if his mother truly meant to disinherit him. Marie fought her husband's battles with ineptly chosen and clumsily used weapons. Their court never wearied of ridiculing Catherine's habits, her lovers, her mode of governing, and her victories. At the Winter Palace and at Tsarskoe they mocked at 'the Prussian sergeant-major of Gatchina' and dismissed him for a fool.

Born in one of the loveliest cities in the world, Alexander lived in a palace which Catherine's prodigality was gradually turning into a rich museum. Painted canvas, sculptured marble, rare mosaics, priceless collections of books, coins and cameos, and a variety of most exquisite '*objets de vertu*,' gathered from all the corners of Europe, were his to look at and to learn from. Intaglios began finding their way into the schoolroom. Things carved of amethyst and malachite, quarried in the Urals, stood on the Empress's tables side by side with state papers. The art of governing appeared to harmonize with other arts, and so good were Alexander's manners that he escaped banishment when the Empress received statesmen and diplomats in private audience.

The two brothers grew close together, no signs of jealousy between them. Alexander was an Adonis with his fair silken hair, 'enchanting' blue eyes, an exquisite mouth, and an obvious readiness to please and to be pleased. Constantine was as uncouth 'as a small Vulcan', with a bear cub's uneasy stare and a tiger's temper, ugly of face and clumsy of movement. For all her ambition to see him crowned at Constantinople, Catherine never referred to him as '*Monsieur Constantin*'.

At the end of 1783 the Empress decided that Alexander's nursery days must end. She was not at fault there, but she stumbled curiously and badly in her choice of the tutor-in-chief to her grandsons. General Saltykov knew how to live at court; he did whatever his wife told him to do, and he signed unread any papers his secretary brought to him. For the rest, he was a man to whom servility came as easily as a well-fitting glove to the hand. Determined to remain in the Empress's good graces, Saltykov was adroit enough so to steer his course as to win her son's favour as well. The Grand Duke and his wife were pleased with an appointment in which they had had no voice.

Saltykov was styled 'tutor' by exaggerated courtesy. In reality, to quote a contemporary's words, the General's duties consisted in superintending the digestion of the young Grand Dukes and in seeing that their apartments were kept clean and their wardrobes in fair order. But Saltykov's activities went further than that. He was born for the role of a human buffer, and he played it to perfection, and the Empress never suspected the latent peril of such an accomplishment where Alexander was concerned.

The Grand Duke and his wife now lived wholly at Gatchina some fifty miles to the west of the capital and near enough to Tsarskoe Selo for fruity gossip to travel backwards and forwards. Little by little, Alexander—more so than Constantine—acquired the consciousness of two worlds, both very close to him, each at enmity with the other. The boys' visits to Gatchina were sanctioned by Catherine, herself most scrupulous in avoiding the least allusion to the family discord. But neither Paul nor Marie thought of hiding their grievances from their small sons, and early enough Saltykov made it plain that anything heard at Gatchina must not be repeated under the grandmother's roof. It was a dangerous climate for a young and impressionable mind to grow up in.

Catherine suspected none of it, and Saltykov's adroitness went a long way to screen his part of a buffer between the two courts. Yet, if the Empress did misread the man's character, she was soon enough convinced of his pedagogical limitations, and Saltykov's unquestioned supremacy in the grand-ducal apartments lasted less than a year. Catherine wished to find 'the very best brains in Europe'. Saltykov and his underlings might have done for Constantine, not for Alexander.

The Empress appealed to Grimm to find 'a teacher of high integrity, liberal views, and a proved proficiency in history, geography, mathematics and philosophy'. 'None such' she added sadly, 'are to be found in the Russian Empire.'

They were in 1784. The terrible Pougachev mutiny had certainly shaken Catherine's liberalism, but 1789, which would altogether entomb it, was still five years distant.

Grimm recommended—and that in most flaming terms— Frederick Caesar La Harpe, a Swiss of republican principles and a brilliant scholar, whose merit, according to Grimm, was still awaiting the recognition it called for. The Empress trusted her friend's judgment implicitly, and she invited La Harpe to Russia to undertake the education of her grandsons, the elder of whom, she was secretly determined, would succeed her one day. At that time, succession in Russia was governed by a law passed by Peter the Great in 1722. That law gave the sovereign the utmost liberty in choosing his or her successor, and Catherine would have been within her rights in preferring Alexander to Paul.

There was anger at Gatchina when La Harpe's appointment became public. There was much mockery in St Petersburg and sullen discontent in Moscow. A wit was heard saying that the Swiss tutor would turn Grand Duke Alexander into a Marcus Aurelius whilst the Empire was in dire need of a Tiberius. Krylov wrote a fable where the upbringing of a lion cub was entrusted to an eagle—with appalling consequences for the animal kingdom, its young sovereign having been instructed in nothing but the building of eyries.

Much of the criticism reached Catherine, but she stood firm, and La Harpe reached Russia in the summer of 1784, with a carefully detailed curriculum among his papers. 'History,' so he wrote to the Empress, 'must be studied with particular care and great discernment. . . . We should never forget that Alexander the Great, for all his genius, ravaged Asia . . . solely in his desire to follow in the steps of Homer's heroes . . .'

Catherine approved of the man and his programme. Yet she did not do what she should have done—i.e. define clearly La Harpe's authority and dismiss Saltykov.

There were four other tutors: a Frenchman, Masson; the chaplain; and two Russians—Mouraviev and Protassov. Among them, Mouraviev, who taught Russian grammar, seems to have been alone in carrying out his task with such absorption that jealousies left him untouched. Masson was openly envious of La Harpe's intellectual superiority. Saltykov mistrusted both La Harpe and Masson. Protassov, despising Saltykov and disliking La Harpe, grudged the time devoted to classics and to what he termed 'ideas', i.e. philosophy. Saltykov kept sending highly coloured reports to Gatchina, and even at the Winter Palace there were many who jeered at a programme which included Demosthenes, Plutarch, Tacitus, Caesar, Machiavelli, Locke and Gibbon.

Apart from the Empress, La Harpe's only supporter was the chaplain, Andrew Samborsky, whose own appointment came under heavy fire both from church and from society. Born of a poor clerical family, Samborsky was educated at the Kiev Theological Academy. In 1763 his name headed the list sent to Catherine for 'special promotion'. To the dismay of the hierarchy, she sent Samborsky to England there to learn agriculture. Five years later he married a Miss Fielding and was given the charge of the Russian Embassy church in London. In 1783 the Empress recalled him to Russia. She permitted him to wear lay clothes and to remain clean-shaven. To Grand Duke Paul, the very appearance of 'that unpriestly priest', suspected of heresy by most of the bishops, suggested sulphur and smoke. Samborsky taught the young Grand Dukes catechism and English. When the court went to Tsarskoe Selo, he encouraged the boys to spend their leisure in the fields, and taught them the use of harrow, plough and scythe.

La Harpe and Samborsky were mistrusted by all the other tutors. The gulf between the imperial and the grand-ducal courts was repeated in little in the children's apartments.

La Harpe came prepared to find factions and rivalries but unable to tell one drift from another. It is unlikely that Grimm would have enlightened him about the tension between the Empress and her son and still more improbable that La Harpe would have been given thumbnail sketches of his colleagues before his arrival. He was no linguist; the little Grand Dukes had spoken English from their earliest days but they knew no French and the linguistic barrier must be broken before La Harpe could begin his work. A lesser man would have recoiled from the difficulties of such a post. An ambitious man might have accepted it as a means of gilding his own future purposes. La Harpe considered his appointment in terms of a total dedication. To prepare a boy for the throne of the most autocratic country in Europe certainly suggests a paradox when we remember that La Harpe was a republican. However vilified by his enemies, he succeeded in teaching Alexander that the varied modes of government could all be considered under a humanist's lens. Without attacking the cardinal principles of autocracy, La Harpe made his pupil see that even an autocratic form of government need not be denied qualities essential to an enlightened rule.

He never betrayed the Empress's trust in him, though the difficulties of steering such a course must have been Herculean, yet the fact of Alexander being a most rewarding pupil must have smoothed many a hard edge. '*Une justesse d'idée*', which La Harpe discovered in the boy, laid the foundations of a friendship that was to last almost to the end of Alexander's life. On his own admission, he owed everything to this tutor. For his part, La Harpe could honestly claim that he had not wholly failed in his task. In the sparsely furnished classroom, he soon enough established a supreme court of appeal—that of conscience and sound judgment.

The years went by, each one bringing more and more clashes between Catherine and her son. The annexation of the Crimea, the disaster and the ultimate triumph of the Second Turkish War and, finally, the events of 1789—all these created more and more misunderstandings between Catherine and Paul. The rupture was more or less absolute when Catherine refused to enter the coalition against France, telling her son that ideas could not be fought with guns. Soon after, a matter hitherto kept within the privacy of her study began to be whispered about not only in her palaces but beyond. It concerned the Empress's intention to bequeath the crown to Alexander, and Paul had no doubt that she would do so.

At thirteen, Alexander was keenly aware of his own position between a devoted, if slightly demanding, grandmother and his frustrated, perpetually fretting parents.

Detested by Grand Duke Paul and disliked by the Grand Duchess, La Harpe kept telling his pupil that his duty lay at Gatchina as well as in St Petersburg. La Harpe could not expect to arrive at a fair apportioning of his brilliant pupil's loyalties, but he considered it essential for him to try and narrow the gulf between the parents and the son without in the least lessening his responsibility towards the Empress, who had appointed him, who trusted him, and whose purse supplied his salary.

A letter written by Catherine to Grimm in 1790 offers something of a key to those difficult formative years of Alexander's life. Unhappily, the key was not of a metal to satisfy La Harpe.

'Ce garçon-là,' wrote Catherine about Alexander, 'est la réunion de quantité de contradictions.'

The background considered, some of the contradictions appear inevitable, but not all. Enthusiasm replaced by boredom, candour by secretiveness, kindness by harshness, generosity by spurts of miserliness, a passion for solitude neighboured by a hunger for companionship, a friend's opinion accepted and rejected within a few hours. . . . Yet contradictions alone do not explain Alexander's character. To wear a mask continually would have been hard enough for an adult. In the case of a boy as imaginative and sensitive as Alexander, the resulting harm could scarcely be exaggerated. For all his tutor's fiery eloquence about 'la judiciaire', Alexander decided that it was far more comfortable to seem at his ease both in St Petersburg and at Gatchina than to be ravaged by the unhappy consequences of imprudent candour at either place. Thus the Empress, for all she duly remarked her grandson's contradictions, remained calmly assured of his loyalty, whilst at Gatchina the parents began lulling themselves into the belief that their elder son was no longer a stranger to them.

Much light is thrown upon those years by General Protassov, Saltykov's assistant, whose diary may well be regarded as one of the best contemporary records of Alexander's development.[1]

Protassov's remarks about court life make it obvious that he did not relish the young Grand Duke's growing preoccupation with courtly functions. Protassov was a soldier, but the journal he kept gives many hints that he might not have been a failure as diplomat. It was none of his business to share with Saltykov the unrewarding task of steering a middle course between the two courts. Protassov, concerned with the boy's moral development, gained his confidence early enough. In Protassov's eyes, Alexander was first and foremost the heir to the throne, and the hard art of government could not be learned in a ballroom, and who was there to teach him? 'How can a foreigner do it?' asked Protassov. Saltykov, too, was of no use. 'Courtly lore,' said Protassov, 'is one thing and statesmanship quite another.'

By 1790 Alexander, still spending many hours in the schoolroom, had begun making his public appearances. The Empress's brilliant circle of soldiers, statesmen, diplomats and '*messieurs en titre*', to say nothing of court ladies, all confessed themselves 'captivated' by him. At thirteen, Alexander appeared at his ease in his grandmother's audience chamber, the banqueting hall and the ballroom. Catherine is supposed to have said that she had fears for her grandson's future: not a woman or a girl at court but felt they were enmeshed in his charm. There was grace in all his movements, a peculiar warmth of manner, and his smile made people think of the April skies. Generous to sheer prodigality, the Empress indulged his passion for clothes: embroidered waistcoats, the finest silken hose from Vienna, the most delicate lace from Italy and the Low Countries, gaily coloured velvet and brocade coats and smalls filled the wardrobe rooms. At fourteen Alexander was a dandy for the golden youth of St Petersburg to admire and to imitate.

But the exquisite Adonis of the state apartments did not shine quite so gloriously in his own rooms. Protassov complained that he

---

[1] cf. N. K. Schilder, *Life and Reign of the Emperor Alexander I*, Vol. I, 229 et seq.

had few supporters in his efforts to make the young Grand Duke mend his ways. The General would have had La Harpe's support for the asking, but the Russian and the Swiss were on terms of armed neutrality, and Protassov blamed La Harpe for Alexander's poor knowledge of Russian history. The accusation was unfair: it did not lie in La Harpe's province to teach Russian history. Still less could he be expected to acquaint his pupil with the contemporary conditions in the Empire. That part of Alexander's education was entrusted to Russian tutors, of whom Protassov was one.

Many a page of the journal was covered with entries illustrating the young Grand Duke's vanity, cunning and stubbornness. '. . . he has much innate kindness . . . and is brilliantly gifted, but so idle. . . . He does not care to learn about things happening in his own country. . . . He wants to enjoy himself continually. . . .'

The strictures about Alexander's idleness must be accepted with caution. Protassov slept in a room next to the boy's and probably knew more about his habits than anyone else in the Palace. On the other hand, Protassov did not spend his time in the classroom where La Harpe exercised his continually disputed sovereignty. That Alexander was ignorant of Russian contemporary conditions may well be true. That he was inching his way into the complicated pattern of European affairs is clear enough from La Harpe's record and from diplomats' letters. Again and again La Harpe speaks of his pupil's hunger for more and more knowledge and of his astonishingly firm grasp of historical issues. All secretly there were many hours filched from sleep to pore over books and maps. But in a different sense Protassov's record is not fabled: he wrote about the self which Alexander permitted him to see. Vanity, cunning, a certain readiness to keep all hard and unpleasing matters at a distance, were all there in Alexander's boyhood. They lived side by side with far more attractive qualities. All in all, it suggests almost a reconciliation of the irreconcilables brought about by the stress made by the family background on a pliant and supersensitive nature.

An entry during 1791 says bluntly: 'Physical desires are coming to the fore. . . . That is evident from his talk. . . . He sometimes tells me about his dreams. . . .' A little later Protassov lost his temper over a foible of Alexander's: '. . . he will waste so much of his leisure in criticizing his household and mimicking their speech and their oddnesses of manner . . . [he] is courteous and honest . . . in his dealings, but he must learn not to toy with decisions—however trifling they be—once they are made. . . .'

La Harpe came to Russia in the summer of 1784 when Alexander was not yet seven. Catherine had invited the Swiss 'to educate the Grand Duke for the throne.' La Harpe should have been permitted to continue with his work until 1795, or even a little later. Alexander's education could hardly be considered complete at the age of sixteen, and yet such was the case.

By 1791 Catherine's enthusiasm for Grimm's nominee had begun burning low; the reason could be sought in the effect the French Revolution had upon her mind. For all the Empress would not enter the coalition against France, her earlier liberalism fell into a deep grave. The young Grand Duchess and Empress, who had dreamt of a constitutional government and abolition of serfdom in her dominions, gave way to an aging, disenchanted woman who now began persecuting the least liberal expression in her own Empire. Many of the reforms projected in the seventies and the eighties were shelved. The Turkish campaigns were over, but all the successes of her 'eagles' had not given Constantinople to Catherine. There was trouble with Sweden, and her troops were also engaged in the west—forcing a dismembered Poland into an acceptance of the alien yoke. The Empire seemed established firmly enough, but the brilliant results of Catherine's foreign policy had a converse effect on home conditions. Her reactionary mood naturally led her to mistrust a man known all over Europe for his unswerving republican faith.

And there was yet another reason why Alexander's education came to be cut off at a most critical moment of his development. Grand Duchess Marie, having borne two sons, kept having one daughter after another[1] and the hopes of the dynasty were concentrated on the two young Grand Dukes. By 1792, Catherine began nursing a vision of herself at the threshold of the nineteenth century—with great-grandchildren in the Palace nurseries. She had her own plans for Alexander's future, and La Harpe's hopes for an extended curriculum did not enter into those plans.

The extension of the programme meant much to La Harpe. He hoped for at least two more years to make Alexander at home in

---

[1] She would have six in all, and two more sons would be born to her: Nicholas, the future Emperor Nicholas I, in 1796, and Michael in 1798.

matters which stood closer than history or geography. La Harpe's task was not to turn his pupil into a scholar but shape him into a man, his mind adequately furnished to grapple with the problems of a sovereignty one day to be under his hand. Such a task could not possibly come to an end when the pupil was barely sixteen. Whole reaches of intellectual effort were left untouched, and those lacunae would hamper Alexander for the rest of his life. In a certain sense, the results of La Harpe's tuition rather elude judgment.

None the less, many precepts taught by him had been absorbed by Alexander—the dignity of man, the sacredness of freedom, the need for civic and personal integrity, and the inviolability of justice. By 1792 those themes could no longer be discussed with the imperial grandmother, in whose mind liberty had become synonymous with savage licence, nor were there any men at her court to whom the young Grand Duke might open his mind.

In the autumn of 1792 the Empress sent Countess Shuvalova abroad to fetch two of the five daughters of the Crown Prince of Baden: the elder, Louise, having just passed her fourteenth birthday, and Frederika, two years her junior. There had been much preliminary correspondence between St Petersburg and Baden, and the court knew perfectly well the purpose of the Shuvalova mission. Gossip insisted that the Empress meant to proclaim Alexander her heir on his wedding day.

The children (for the sisters could hardly be called anything else) reached St Petersburg in October, and both were presented to the bridegroom-to-be, himself a child, however well developed for his fifteen years, and, according to General Protassov, 'wholly unprepared for the delights and the pitfalls of married life'. Nor did Alexander appear at all ready to be pleased with his grandmother's decision to endow him with a bride. He looked sullen in his own rooms, and did not smile much when he met the sisters in the Empress's apartments. In fact, '[le Grand Duc] me regardait d'un air hostile,' wrote Princess Louise in her journal that same evening.[1]

She was almost at once preferred to her younger sister, Frederika,

[1] cf., Grand Duke Nicholas, The Empress Elizabeth, 3 vols., St Petersburg, 1908, I, p. 120. All the subsequent quotations from the journal and the letters are taken from the same source.

and Alexander was apparently soon enough reconciled to the idea that his schoolroom days were ending. Just before Christmas Louise answered a note of his in most passionate terms: '*Mon cher ami, vous me dites que j'ai le bonheur d'une certaine personne en main. Ah, si c'est vrai, son bonheur est assuré à jamais. Vous pouvez être certain que je vous aime au delà de toute expression,*' and the girl from Baden would prove those words to be true to the very end. A dryly contractual matter, which was not expected to speak to the heart, was by her turned into a life-long devotion. That, unhappily, could not be said of Alexander.

The court, obedient to the cue given by the Empress, approved her choice. 'Even her walk is pleasant,' Protassov wrote in his diary, 'she is beautiful and gentle, her voice is lovely, her modesty quite remarkable.'

If St Petersburg at first admired Louise, she could not be said to admire St Petersburg. She respected the Empress and had fallen head over ears in love with her boy bridegroom. But there was also the court, then reputed to outshine even Versailles. The blinding splendour, the bewildering weave of rival factions, the buzz of gossip up and down the palace stairs, novel customs, strange food and language, all of it together scared and repelled Louise. Within the first few days, the gulf between Gatchina and St Petersburg was made known to her. It deepened her confusion. Louise came from a closely knit family, its members brought up in a healthy and enlightened climate, and there she had felt herself grafted into the family. Intelligent, affectionate, deeply cherishing home values, she now found herself facing a future fretted with problems almost beyond her strength. She tried to discuss it with Alexander, and found much sympathy and very little understanding. She looked around and guessed that any frankness on her part would meet with neither sympathy nor understanding from the members of the household. Louise began finding refuge in reserve.

The first enthusiasms grown slightly dusty, society delivered its verdict. '*Son abord est froid, mais poli. Elle est très peu communicative, ce qui fait que très peu de monde la connaît,*' says a contemporary.

To read her letters is to focus a brilliant lantern on much that was happening in those days. She had come from a family linked together by blood, affection, habit and shared interests. She came to Russia prepared to learn a slightly different pattern under different skies, and she found none such to learn. Her future parents-in-law had not been consulted about the Empress's choice of a bride for Alexander. Their consent, demanded by Church and by law, was commanded rather than asked for. Grand Duchess Marie, herself a Princess of Württemberg, a house known for its slavish adoration of Prussia, had small use for qualities and opinions acquired at Baden where the Prussian policy came under the fire of well-informed criticism. Grand Duke Paul, according to the Empress, 'would have found fault with an angel from heaven summoned by me'. Louise drove out to Gatchina to receive a welcome in strict conformity to etiquette and thus shorn of all warmth. It is doubtful if Alexander could have helped her to steer her way in and out of the countless cross-currents between the two courts.

The contrast between the rigidity of Gatchina, where life was regulated by drum and trumpet, and the uninhibited rhythm at the Winter Palace would have troubled even a mature mind. She grasped the main issue and behaved accordingly. However revolted by all seen and heard at Gatchina, she remembered that Grand Duke Paul was still considered to be his mother's heir and that his children's courses would one day be directed by him. The prospect spoke of a winter to come, but the girl's intelligence fully matched her courage. She had her boy bridegroom and his grandmother whose liberality and kindness seemed doubly rewarding after the first visit to Gatchina.

The formal betrothal took place in May 1793 when Louise, received into the Orthodox Church, became Grand Duchess Elizabeth, her name and titles entering the liturgy. There followed a spate of fatiguing festivities, and Derzhavin marked the occasion by a starchily pompous ode. The Empress wrote to the Crown Princess at Baden and to Grimm at Darmstadt that 'the dear children looked as happy as angels'.

It was a grimly accurate description. Two children, virtual strangers to each other, were entered together upon a solemn life-long engagement. It is true that Louise was deeply in love. It is also true that at Easter Alexander admitted to Protassov that he had begun 'having a special feeling for the Princess, and that the feeling heightened whenever she came into the room, or when he happened to stand near her'. But none of it was enough. The betrothal and the wedding were disastrously premature, and those who censured the

Empress for haste were right. She longed to see herself a great-grandmother and hoped to anchor and regularize his sexual life at the earliest possible moment, but the blessing of the Church would in no way secure Alexander's fidelity and a nature like his considered any anchorage a prison.

The general confusion in the palace did not fail to reach the grand-ducal apartments. Alexander's studies, already interrupted now and again since the autumn of 1792, came to be virtually given up during the summer of 1793, its months crowded with the preparations for the wedding in September. The Russian tutors, with the exception of Protassov, accepted the condition as inevitable. La Harpe protested, and he alone succeeded in engaging Alexander's attention for a few hours a week, but there could be no question of any serious and consecutive studies. As the summer drew on, even those occasions grew fewer and fewer.

The Empress and her court were at Tsarskoe Selo. Grand Duke Paul and his wife moved to Pavlovsk from Gatchina. Intrigues thickened. The Empress, overhearing rumours, either snapped her fingers at them or acted rapidly, asking no one's advice about her decisions. In July Princess Frederika returned to Baden—a mere two months before her sister's wedding. No reasons were given for the sudden departure. There were stories that Platon Zubov, '*monsieur en titre*' of the day, had danced with the girl rather too often. There were wisps of tales about silly little extravagances and a few debts. But nothing came to light. The day after, Elizabeth wrote bitterly enough to her mother: '. . . *je serai seule, absolument seule, sans avoir personne à qui communiquer mes petites pensées. . . .*' The remark at first suggests a contradiction: Elizabeth had her Grand Duke. But there was no contradiction. Frederika's departure cut the last thread. The '*petites pensées*' were of a colour unfamiliar to Alexander, little cameos of lovingly shared memories—anything from a cake at a birthday party to a new pair of dancing slippers. Alexander would have listened to it—but he could not have imagined the decoration on the cake or remembered the tiny buckles on the slippers.

Not a year had passed since the girl's arrival in Russia when she was moved to make a poignant confession to her mother. She loved Alexander and was resolved to be his wife, but— '*quand on le connaît de bien près, on remarque de petits riens, vraiment des riens où on peut dire c'est selon les goûts, et il y a quelques peu de ces riens qui ne sont pas de mon goût et ont détruit la manière excéssive dont je l'aimais. Je l'aime encore beaucoup mais d'une autre manière. Ces riens-là ne sont pas dans le caractère, car de ce côté-là sûrement je crois q'il n'y a rien à lui reprocher, mais dans les manières, je ne sais quoi dans l'extérieur. . . .'*

Many of those *'riens'* found their way into Protassov's diary: touches of unkind irony, extravagances in the choice of clothes, in the use of scent, little exaggerated stresses laid on the shape of cravats and the jewels for shoe buckles, occasional, always brief, revelations of boredom at a concert. But it was hardly a *'rien'* for Alexander to appear equally affable at his grandmother's court and among the rough set of his father's intimates at Gatchina. Elizabeth allowed that Alexander owed duty to his parents and to the Empress, but something elusively troubling in his relations to his father already haunted her, and she was still a child, incapable of deciphering motives below the surface.

Calumny did not spare her even before her marriage. Her reserve with the Russian ladies in attendance on her led to consequences, some of which were unhappy and others just absurd. One story left Russia for abroad and eventually reached the palace at Baden. The tale was supposed to start at Pavlovsk. A Princess Trubetzkoy, maid-of-honour to Grand Duchess Marie, had heard it from a cousin at the Empress's court, and the Grand Duchess mentioned it to a diplomat's wife. We cannot tell if the Empress ever heard of it. If she had, she would have shrugged it away: she believed in Elizabeth's good sense and in her grandson's honour. But the Crown Princess of Baden heard it and did not shrug. She placed no faith in it, but she felt outraged that such things should have been said about her daughter. In August 1793 Elizabeth wrote, grief and indignation playing havoc with her style:

'Chère Maman, qui vous a dit que je faisais entrer le Grand Duc Alexandre par la fenêtre. Je ne l'ai jamais fait. Je lui parle bien souvent de la fenêtre, je lui donne la main par la fenêtre, mais jamais il n'est entré par la fenêtre. . . .'

They were married on 9th October 1793, among customary and wearying splendours. The Empress showered gifts and honours on all the members of the Grand Duke's household, La Harpe alone being unrewarded—to the great pleasure of Alexander's father. An illness of Elizabeth's father prevented her parents from coming, but presents and fulsome letters from Catherine went to Baden. She wrote that 'it looked like a marriage between an Apollo and a Psyche, and the dearest children were so happy. . . .'

Psyche was certainly in love with her Apollo at the time. Was he with her? Opinions differ, but all the available evidence suggests that his feeling for her had not really taken deep root until a few years later.

All the precepts of his English governess and of La Harpe could not alter Alexander's views on sex. He had to marry a girl of blood royal and to assure the continuity of the dynasty, and he thought that by so doing he conformed to the terms of his marriage contract. At the time, religion meant hardly anything to him beyond the appointed observances which he often found boring. He slept with his bride because it was his duty to do so, but he also slept with many other women some time before Marie Naryshkina was to catch him into her web. Sex to him was a many-roomed mansion, and to possess another woman meant nothing derogatory to his marriage vows. His grandmother's court teemed with men and women who turned the seventh commandment into an unprintable joke and to whom immorality was of as much account as a white lie. His grandmother, a widow since her thirty-third year, had one lover after another. At Gatchina, a maid-of-honour was known to be one of the Grand Duke Paul's mistresses. In broad terms, conjugal fidelity in Russia at the time was considered an oddity. Grand Duchess Marie, herself scrupulous in her observance of marriage vows, was dubbed a fool by some of her husband's intimates and at the court of the Empress. Young Elizabeth learned soon enough that all the solemnities of her wedding day meant little more than a chaplet of old symbols to society.

Immediately after the wedding the second grand-ducal court was formed by the Empress. Count Golovin became its marshal; there were three chamberlains, three equerries, and three ladies for Elizabeth. Some of the appointments were unfortunate. Countess Shuvalova, 'the titled scavenger', became mistress of the robes—in spite of Golovin's protests. Saltykov retired with many unmerited honours and a diamond snuffbox, but La Harpe remained, and so did Protassov, who continued his diary: ' . . . the Grand Duke will talk too much to young dandies at every ball . . . [he] has begun to acquire a taste for wine . . . [he] thinks it does not hurt him so long as he does not get really drunk . . . his love of constant pleasure grows day by day . . .' Apparently, La Harpe still gave occasional lessons, but these were often interrupted by court functions, and 'nothing Russian is taught any more'. In March 1794 Alexander 'is all taken up with a new toy—a dolls' theatre . . . so absorbed is he that he has taken to neglect the Grand Duchess. . . . It is shameful to see. . . .' wrote Protassov, and Count Rostopchin in a letter to Simon Voronzov in London complained that the Grand Duke was hardly ever seen occupied with a book. '. . . *toute sa cour est composée de polissons et de sots,*' and he added that the Grand Duchess was dying of boredom. '. . . *elle aime son mari, mais il est trop jeune pour l'occuper entièrement. . . .*'

Rostopchin's letter is full of exaggerations and even Protassov thickens the colours too much. No contemporaries allowed for the fact that marriage and schoolroom made odd neighbours. The situation was grotesque. Alexander had his own court but, with the exception of Saltykov, his tutors remained. Inevitably, hostility came to colour the relations between courtiers and preceptors. To make the general situation slightly more difficult, ugly intrigues broke out among the courtiers. Golovin and his wife were outraged by Countess Shuvalova's vulgarities. Neutrality might have answered Alexander's purposes much better, but he hated Shuvalova's ugliness, gluttony and smutty conversation, and he openly called her '*un diable incarné avec ses éternelles intrigues*'. The woman welcomed a chance of revenge. Elizabeth's marked preference for Countess Golovina, a pleasant and intelligent woman, was soon painted in the colours of 'a most unwholesome friendship,' and the Countess was dismissed. The young Grand Duchess wrote to Baden:

'. . . *une chose terrible pour moi est que je n'ose jamais me livrer entres les personnes qui m'entourent. . . . Sans mon mari qui seul me rend heureuse ici, je serais morte mille fois. . . . Si je trouve quelqu'une d'aimable comme il y a quelques dames, surtout une certaine Comtesse Golovina . . . je n'ose pas la faire paraître, car le public est insupportable ici. . . .*'

In the summer of 1794, spent according to custom at Tsarskoe

Selo, all the ladies at the three courts began wondering about 'God's blessing' in the near future. At last Shuvalova made brazenly frank inquiries. Maids in the Grand Duchess's service and the women employed in the Palace laundries gave disappointingly negative replies. Shuvalova carried the report to the Empress, whose reply was that the child being so young, there was plenty of time in the future. At Gatchina, Grand Duchess Marie by-passed all the rumours by a point-blank question. Her son replied that he could not tell. 'But it is your duty to know if your wife is pregnant or not,' retorted his mother.

Elizabeth was not. As the summer drew on, she began feeling conscious of a certain embarrassment in her husband's manner. Shuvalova felt that the time had come for a direct attack, and questions were put to Elizabeth which made her blush when her ladies were in the room and break into tears when she found herself alone. She felt that every detail of her life with Alexander was being spied upon. It nauseated and angered her.

In a letter written in the autumn of 1794 she mentioned a certain Countess Gynlai. '*Cela m'étonne qu'elle n'aît pas été embarrassée le lendemain de son mariage. Elle est naturellement timide. . . . Pour moi, j'ai été si tourmentée par le Grand Duc père et par la Grande Duchesse que j'ai cru tomber sous terre. . . .*'

None the less, they were happy together. La Harpe's teaching was not altogether wasted. For all the strictures passed by Count Rostopchin, they were not all fools and scoundrels who came into daily contact with the young Grand Duke and his wife. Prince Alexander Golitzin was certainly a *bon viveur*, but he had a mind above the average. There were certainly ways of escaping the deadly trivialities of the court. Young Victor Kotchubey, Count Paul Strogonov, Novossilzev were all men of promise, and so were the Czartorizky brothers, the Princes Adam and Constantine. They could dance and gamble. They could also read and talk in a way which enlarged Alexander's horizon. The state of Europe, the destiny of mankind, the sacredness of human rights, all the lessons of La Harpe were echoed by these enthusiasts, who had not been taught by La Harpe but had reached many disturbing conclusions by themselves. Such discussions were not particularly safe during the last years of Catherine's reign. The young people were glad of the vast reaches of the park at Tsarskoe where the most perilous theme might be taken up, such as, for instance, the intolerable evil of serfdom or the dismemberment of Poland.

Little by little, Alexander grew acquainted with a manuscript never shown him by his tutors, and that was the book of Russia. Great weariness, exhausted finances, the grip of venal bureaucracy, the curse of serfdom, the terrible cost of territorial expansion—such were some of the chapters, shame and glory interwoven on every page, but in Alexander's eyes the shame cancelled out the glory. Where, he would ask himself, were all the promises of the earlier years of his grandmother's reign? At the cost of two bloody wars Russia had won her right to the Black Sea; the Crimea was hers, and so were the northern footholds of the Caucasus and the Baltic coast. But the reforms undertaken so ardently were not completed. Much indeed had been done to further education, but none of those measures concerned the masses, still left in their midnight ignorance. The abolition of slavery was as remote as ever and those who ventured to speak of it were imprisoned.

Catherine, as her grandson knew, had further plans of expansion. She had fought two wars against Turkey, and she was determined to fight another and win her way through to the Straits. Potemkin, Golitzin and Roumiantzev were dead and Suvorov had reached his evening, but a brilliant pupil of theirs, one Michael Kutuzov, was still there, and the Empress had great hopes of him. She would sometimes open her mind to Alexander, and he listened, his own thoughts known only to himself.

Her desire to alter the order of succession was no secret. Grand Duke Paul was convinced that she meant to disinherit him. Her words 'my son would turn the Russian Empire into a province of Prussia' were reported to Paul. Her refusal to join the coalition against France infuriated him. Her obstinacy in not allowing him a voice in her government was another notch in the tally against her. Paul's uncontrolled imagination began running riot when he heard reports of secret conferences at the Winter Palace. He trusted none of his mother's intimates. Would he be imprisoned, exiled, or murdered? He wondered if he had better escape somewhere abroad, but there did not seem any place for a Russian Grand Duke to hide himself in. The King of Sweden had insulted him; none of the German potentates would welcome him for fear of Catherine's displeasure, France was, naturally, out of the question, and Italy promised neither safety nor tranquillity.

Paul's fantasies were many and varied, but it was true that his mother had resolved to name Alexander as her successor, and she tried to enlist La Harpe's help to prepare her grandson's mind for the decision, but La Harpe refused and was dismissed about Christmas 1794—to Alexander's great sorrow. His letters to his tutor[1] offer many glimpses of his mental state during those crucial years:

'. . . [*je*] *vous dois tout hormis le jour* . . . *et maintenant je suis seul à cette cour que j'abhore, destiné à une condition dont la seule idée me fait frémir*. . . .' The Grand Duke did not dare to entrust his correspondence to normal channels: he must wait for 'an occasion' when a proven friend was about to leave Russia for abroad, his social status ensuring the immunity of his luggage. In these circumstances, Alexander's candour can be understood. He informed La Harpe of his firm intention '*de me défaire de ma charge* . . . *ici tout le monde pille, on ne recontre presque pas d'honnête homme* . . . *c'est affreux* . . . *mais je suis assez heureux avec ma femme*. . . .' At eighteen, Alexander was busily building his castles in Spain. He would go and settle somewhere in a hamlet on the banks of the Rhine, or, better still, in some corner of North America, learn an honest handicraft, earn his keep by the sweat of his brow, forget all about crowns and thrones and European turmoils, and he added that his wife shared his wishes in all things.

About Easter 1795 Alexander told La Harpe that he was very busy. What was he busy at? La Harpe had left him long lists of books which Alexander must read so as not to allow any rust to creep into his mind. But the Grand Duke's 'occupation' had nothing to do with the mind. He and his brother, Constantine, were now at Gatchina, learning their father's military pattern in all its details, and they were there at the Empress's wish. She had convinced herself that the Gatchina experience would prove to Alexander his father's unfitness to reign, and the Empress's judgment was most fatally at fault there. Once at Gatchina, Alexander fell under his mother's influence. Now whole days were passed in an atmosphere

---

[1] cf. Schilder, op. cit., Vol. I, 103 *et seq.*, and Grand Duke Nicholas, *The Emperor Alexander I*, St Petersburg, 1912, 2 vols. I, 193 *et seq.*

of open hostility to Catherine and her court. The criticisms he heard certainly differed from those expressed by his young friends: Alexander would not have learned much about the sacredness of human rights under his father's roof, but Paul's strictures on the course of the foreign policy certainly found an echo in the son's mind.

The Gatchina experience hardened Alexander.[1] Conversely, it evoked deep compassion for his father. Paul was not always angry, cruel, suspicious and revengeful. He could be gentle and generous. The earlier unguessed-at qualities in his father captured Alexander, who felt that Paul had indeed been denied his rights, and when the Grand Duke expressed his anger and disgust at the partitions of Poland, Alexander's heart beat to a hope he dared not express.

His grandmother never suspected the change in him. 'The bundle of contradictions', as she had called Alexander in his boyhood, was well accustomed to wear a mask.

Paul's kindly moods, however, were not particularly frequent. It was at Gatchina that Alexander met a certain artillery officer, earlier dismissed from a staff post for his bestial cruelty to his subordinates and welcomed by Paul as a most valuable second-in-command in that eighteenth-century version of a concentration camp where the use of whip and stick was the great essential of army training. On the parade ground and at the daily reviews Paul showed himself as ruthless to his sons as to all the others. Many a time the gunner, now raised to the rank of colonel in the Gatchina corps, would act as a buffer between father and son. The name of that gunner was Alexis Arakcheev.

---

[1] It may not be out of place here to remember Prince Adam Czartorizky's comment on the Gatchina experience. 'Les minutiés du service militaire et l'habitude d'y attacher une extrême importance faussèrent l'esprit du Grand Duc. Il prit à Gatchina le goût dont il ne put se guérir. Il fut atteint pendant tout son règne de la paradomanie qui fit perdre un temps précieux lorsqu'il fut sur le trône, et l'empêcha pendant sa jeunesse de travailler utilement et d'acquérir de connaissances indispensables.' (cf. Schilder, op. cit., footnotes to Vol. 1.) The judgment certainly errs on the side of severity, but it is true that Alexander's proneness to 'le soldatesque' dated from that period.

II

THE INTERLUDE
OF TERROR

ON A day in late September 1796 Count Bezborodko, Catherine's
Secretary of State, brought his usual report to the Winter Palace,
but he had no audience with the Empress, her ladies telling him
that their mistress was indisposed.

She had had a slight stroke in the night, but the ominous word
was studiously avoided, and Rogerson, the physician-in-chief,
assured everybody in turn that they need not be anxious. Platon
Zoubov, Catherine's *'monsieur en titre'* of the day, was already
making plans for the Empress's second journey to the Crimea in the
spring of 1797. There was good news from General Kamensky's
headquarters at the Persian front, and the atmosphere at the Palace
was tranquil enough except for the ripples of indignation at the
rudeness of the King of Sweden, who had dared to jilt Catherine's
eldest granddaughter, Grand Duchess Alexandra.

Within a few days the Empress was writing to her faithful Grimm
to tell him, among other things, that she was 'as busy as a bird'.

None the less, they were anxious at Gatchina, and Paul seized the
pretext of his daughter's broken engagement to visit his mother.
The polite fiction of Paul's solicitude for her health did not deceive
Catherine. She was distantly pleasant and no more. But the Grand
Duke went back to Gatchina and told his wife that all his enemies
at the Winter Palace, led by Platon Zoubov, had looked at him in a
most peculiar manner. Paul added that he was convinced the
Empress meant to have him either killed or imprisoned. When
Grand Duchess Marie pointed out that their eldest son would
never consent to disregard his father's rights, Paul retorted that he
could place no trust in a pupil of La Harpe's.

Meanwhile, that pupil had all in secret determined his own
future. Far from wishing to oust his father, Alexander meant to

38

relinquish what rights were his. Elizabeth, Constantine and his wife, Anna, and a few friends were in Alexander's confidence. The news of the Empress's indisposition made him feel that he was approaching an important cross-roads.

He was not his own master at Gatchina. Nothing but a summons from the Winter Palace could free him from garrison duties even for the space of a day. Such a summons came quite unexpectedly one October morning, and it threw Paul into a panic, but Alexander remained calm. He left for St Petersburg at once, and was closeted with the Empress the entire afternoon, not a single witness being present in the room. In the evening, Catherine is supposed to have told Platon Zoubov that she had made up her mind to exercise her rights in the naming of her successor without delay. Such was one variant of the story. There were others. From the palace the rumours ran all over the capital. There were expectations of a manifesto to be published on New Year's Day 1797.

Catherine had not a single suspicion that the grandson brought up by her since his earliest infancy had long since ceased to respect her way of governing. Nor did she know anything of his desire to make dust of his rank and dignities and to hide himself in some deep forest of the New World, forgetting Europe and by her forgotten. The habitual clarity of her judgment curiously blurred in this instance; the Empress never paused to consider that La Harpe's liberal ideas could not but have left an impress on Alexander's mind and that her own abandonment of such ideas so eagerly professed at the beginning of her reign was bound to create some revulsion in his thoughts. But, however blunted Catherine's judgment, Alexander's power of dissimulation was very well developed. He played his part to perfection.

He found his grandmother slightly hampered in her movements, but her speech rang clear and her mind seemed as vigorous as he had ever known it to be. She was in her sixty-seventh year and the young Grand Duke had no reason to doubt that she would enter the nineteenth century, her hand still on the reins.

It has already been mentioned that nobody was present at the very long interview. Whatever confidences Alexander made to his wife remain unrecorded, and Paul's frenzied anxiety about his own future, a state in which he would remain until his mother's death in November, makes it obvious that he was kept in the dark about his son's intentions. But there does exist one document, at once illuminating and ambiguous: Alexander's letter to the Empress.[1]

He was not yet nineteen; he captivated everybody by his physical beauty and the charm of his manner. He fired his intimates by his ardour, his thirst for justice, his hatred of tyranny. Even those who censured his indolence and dandyism could not deny Alexander a quality possessed by so few in that generation: a charm which attracted, reconciled, and made people think of other things than their stomachs and the pleasures of the card table. Those who knew him best were certain of the great promise still latent in Alexander. He had a child-wife whose devotion and loyalty deepened with every month she spent in Russia, in whose eyes he remained a shy and desirable bridegroom, some inner grace enabling him to move easily from schoolroom to audience chamber and banqueting hall. It is true that his father mistrusted him, but Paul would have mistrusted a fly on the window pane. Alexander's mother was serenely certain of his loyalty to his parents. His grandmother was as sure of his devotion to her.

But there were so many Alexanders within that slim and supple body. There was the respectfully affectionate grandson, who hid his true opinions most adroitly; the apparently submissive son, whose pliancy was born of fear lest his father's anger should fall on him again; the well-trained soldier who appeared to embrace whole-heartedly the Gatchina régime, whilst all within him was sickened by the monotony and the brutality of it. There was the adoring husband, who—in a few brief years—would feel no compunction at deserting his wife for a most unworthy mistress. There was the friend who never weighed his words and the courtier whose least important remark was the fruit of careful deliberation. Finally, there was the dreamer, whose inner sanctuary was never entered by any among his contemporaries and whose true signature remains unread to this day. In the final reckoning, Catherine need not be judged too harshly for having misread Alexander at the end.

The letter he wrote soon after the interview might well serve for a model of ambiguity. It carries Alexander's signature and a date, but it might well have been written by Machiavelli and won the approval of Talleyrand and Metternich. Yet, all its ambiguities apart, it is clear enough on one point: Alexander must have been

[1] Full text in Schilder, op. cit., I, p. 279.

asked to give his consent to a matter of primary importance and he had given it.

He began by confessing himself incapable of expressing his gratitude for the Empress's confidence in him. He went on to thank her for '*la bonté que Votre Majesté a daigné avoir faire de sa main un écrit servant d'intelligence aux autres papiers.*' The piece of writing in Catherine's own hand has not come down to us, nor can any details be given about 'the other papers' left so carefully unspecified in the letter. That they concerned matters of state importance is self-evident and that the Empress believed Alexander to be of one accord with her is also obvious. '*J'espère que Votre Majesté verra, par mon zèle, à mériter ses précieuses bontés, que j'en sens tout le prix.*' 'By my zeal . . .' Alexander was then living at Gatchina, and he had daily opportunities to see his father's anxiety about the future, but in the Empress's eyes it was no matter of a choice between father and son: it was the question of an Empire being governed or misgoverned.

'*Je ne pourrai, il est vrai, jamais assez payer même de mon sang tout ce que [Votre Majesté] a daigné et veut bien encore faire pour moi.*' There was no question here of gifts. They were not closeted together the entire afternoon to discuss a pink diamond necklace for Elizabeth or a new palace to be built in St Petersburg for Alexander. Nor could there be any allusion to loosened purse strings to pay his debts. He had many extravagances, all of them sanctioned by Catherine, but he had an ample income and not a single purveyor to the grand-ducal court ever had a bad debt.

It need not be a wild conjecture that 'the confidence', so humbly and gratefully acknowledged by Alexander, came out of Catherine's proud conviction that he alone, brought up by her and trained by a man of her choice, was fit to succeed her. Again be it remembered that the Empress knew nothing about Alexander's changed feelings towards his parents. As to his dreams of sinking his identity in some obscure corner of the world, the Empress would not have given it credence even if she heard it from Alexander's own lips. To her, it would have been little more than a joke in rather doubtful taste.

Some historians have suggested that the letter came to be written not only with Paul's knowledge but at his dictation. Yet the closing paragraph, once its background is carefully considered, demolishes all such surmises. '*Ces papiers confirment évidemment toutes les réflexions que Votre Majesté a bien voulu me communiquer tantôt et qui, s'il m'est permis de le dire, ne peuvent être plus justes.'*

Catherine had no maternal feelings for Paul, but she would never criticize the father's personal qualities in his son's presence. Moreover, she could be icily objective when the matter in hand demanded such an approach. For more than twenty years she had been irritated, pained and amused by Paul's strictures about her foreign policy, her administration, her tentative reforms. Some of those evidences of his attitude reached her by word of mouth. Quite a number of them came to her in writing. The head and front of her determination to disinherit Paul lay in his inability to govern.

No other meetings of moment took place between the Empress and Alexander. Her health continued to improve. She spent as many hours as usual at her desk. Her letters to Grimm carried many amusing references to her youngest grandson, Nicholas, bórn the previous summer. She gave audiences and entertained at the Hermitage. Observing a rigid neutrality, she keenly watched the progress of the coalition against France. Her own goal was still Constantinople and the Straits. She looked at the maps in her study and thought that she must see her armies penetrate still more deeply into the Caucasus. Comparatively few home matters engaged Catherine's attention at the time except for the ever-increasing urge to stamp out 'the dangerous ideas' in her Empire.

And there was nobody to tell her that her most beloved grandson did not share in her grandiose plans about a resurrected Byzantium and that he, endorsing her own earlier policy, hoped for a most daring implementation of all her reforms. Catherine had long since ceased to concern herself with emancipation. To Alexander, the uprooting of serfdom meant immeasurably more than any expanded frontiers. But such a task, as he saw it in 1796, was not for him to shoulder.

On a morning in mid-November, the Empress had another stroke. Late that evening, without recovering consciousness, she died. No succession manifesto had been signed by her. At the age of forty-two, having nearly despaired of his inheritance, Paul became emperor.

There was not even one hour of transition between one reign and another. Paul's rule came in with an abruptness without parallel in Russian history. Overnight, the Winter Palace became a barracks crowded with the Gatchina battalions dressed in the obsolete and cumbersome Prussian uniforms. All the splendours of a court unrivalled in Europe died in the thick fog of one man's will, whose reasoning none dared to probe and whose sanity came to be doubted soon enough. From the first hour of his succession, the Emperor began translating the Gatchina pattern into imperial terms. Through the whole of that night he dictated '*ukazes*', putting an end to one liberty after another.

That November night Alexander was virtually reduced to a sergeant's status. He was his father's subject far more than his heir. His young wife had followed him from Gatchina, but Alexander dared not spend any time with her. His father's summonses came one after another.

In the small hours Arakcheev arrived, and Alexander welcomed him with tears. The bully had often shielded him at Gatchina. Now Arakcheev's services were needed more than ever with the petty tyrant of 'little Potsdam' become the Autocrat of All the Russias. Contemporaries mention that, Arakcheev having brought no luggage with him, a clean shirt was brought from the Grand Duke's rooms. Alexander would have parted with his entire wardrobe to give pleasure to his friend and he would never know that on arrival Arakcheev received an order from the Emperor 'to watch over the grandmother's spoilt pet' and to report on anything 'curious' said or done by him. Arakcheev was Paul's loyal servant. None the less, that order was never obeyed.

Twice during that night, which brought triumph to many and despair to many more, Alexander succeeded in seeing his wife for a moment. At dawn, he went in, wearing the Gatchina uniform never before seen at the Winter Palace, and Elizabeth burst into tears. He could not stay to comfort her. He was charged with the duty of having sentry boxes placed every few yards along all the walls of the palace.

By early morning, Catherine's home looked like a beleaguered fortress, with armed sentries mounted on guard along all the walls and at every entrance. Passers-by stared in dumb bewilderment at the unfamiliar sight. No enemy force was menacing the capital. What could the danger be from which the new sovereign must be guarded? Such questions were not asked in public. If they had been, no answers would have been given.

Since the days of Peter the Great, three members of the Romanov family had indeed been murdered. Alexis, Peter's first-born son, was killed at his father's orders in 1718. Peter III met his end in 1762—certainly with the connivance of his wife, Catherine the Great; and Ivan VI was killed during a mutiny at Schüsselburg in 1764. Conspiracies had indeed been a feature of the century, but their heartbeat came from the court and the guards regiments, and none had happened during the thirty-four years of Catherine's reign. It was with the accession of her son Paul that elaborate precautionary measures to ensure the sovereign's safety rather than the peace of the Empire began weaving their insidious pattern across the entire Russian landscape.

That grimly guarded fortress of a palace housed two very young and frightened Grand Duchesses, Elizabeth and Anne, wife of Grand Duke Constantine. Not until January 1797 did an opportunity come to Elizabeth to share her burdens with her mother at Baden. That letter, if intercepted by Paul's myrmidons, might well have meant prison, if not worse, for the Grand Duchess. She had so much to tell her mother, but she must needs wait for an opportunity offered by a diplomat's kindness, since all normal ways of communication with abroad were closed even to the members of the imperial family. At Paul's order, no letters were to leave Russia without passing the censors' scrutiny.

'*Vous n'avez pas d'idée,*' wrote Elizabeth, '*comment tout jusqu'aux plus petites choses est totalement renversé.*' She did not exaggerate, and her use of the word '*renversé*' in preference to a simpler '*changé*' speaks volumes. They were upheavals rather than changes. The most trivial details of his subjects' daily lives fell under the Emperor's control. Catherine had governed, her mistakes and all, superbly *en grand*. Her son started by bemusing the people's consciousness by *ukazes* which determined the shape of a hat, the cut of a collar, the depth of a curtsey, the number of guests to be invited to a private party. Catherine had persecuted men like Raditchev and Novikov for the ideas she considered dangerous. Paul banned all imports of foreign books and placed what few booksellers there were in Moscow and St Petersburg under rigid police surveillance. Catherine had striven to avoid all interference by bureaucracy so long as the law was obeyed. Paul placed police interference above the law.

'*Cela m'a fait un si vilain effet que je ne me reconnaissais presque moi-même. . . .*' Except for the members of the imperial household and the ranks of 'Gatchina men', these words would have been echoed by everybody in the capital. They no longer knew who or what they were, or what was expected of them. The spate of imperial orders continued day in, day out. People found themselves arrested and manhandled for disobeying an order as yet known to none except the Emperor's secretaries and the police. In the palace Alexander would have been wholly wrenched off his moorings if it had not been for Elizabeth and also for the help given him by Arakcheev.

The Grand Duchess's letter spoke of the first months of the reign. All described by her would change from bad to worse during the four years to come.

'*Anne était ma seule consolation, comme moi la sienne . . . nos maris n'étaient presque jamais à la maison. . . .*' And how could the Grand Dukes have any leisure for their wives? The Emperor having brought the Gatchina climate to the capital, the court life was put on a barracks footing. From dawn till late at night Alexander and Constantine were preoccupied with the monotonous round of regimental minutiae. Constantine would have been reconciled to it if it had not been for the Emperor's uncertain temper. But Alexander suffered from spells of insomnia, lost his appetite and, when alone with Elizabeth, plunged into silences which were far more eloquent than any complaints would have been.

'*Anne et moi,*' continued the Grand Duchess, '*nous ne pouvions pas nous occuper.*' Everybody's time at the palace now belonged to the sovereign and his consort. The young daughters-in-law found themselves at the beck and call of the Empress Marie to perform services which her ladies might have done and even to run errands which should have been entrusted to footmen and to maids. The Grand Duchesses' dress, coiffures and what attempts at conversation they ventured to make, all were subject to most mordant criticism. Constantine, already out of conceit with his young bride, mocked at her distress and added to it by his own unkindnesses. Alexander met his wife's tears with his own. At night only, they could pour their hearts out to each other—always in most careful whispers, 'surveillance' having reached their apartments early enough.

'. . . *Vous n'avez pas idée d'un vide affreux qu'il y a.* . . .'

To Elizabeth, that environment must indeed have become a void. Her mother might no longer send her the latest books from Leipzig and Stuttgart. Her husband and she might no longer converse with the ministers accredited to Paul's court. Look where they would, nothing could be attempted, still less done, unless the plan were approved by a man whose moods were unpredictable and whose anger fell like a flail upon anyone daring to differ or to contradict. The Grand Duchess talked about the general depression: '*Tout le monde est triste* . . ?' adding '*excepté les nouvelles Majestés*'. The irony of the adjective needs no comment.

Catherine had wrested her sovereignty by chicanery and established it at the cost of a crime, but she had tried to use it for the benefit of the Empire and worn her purple with the ease of one born to the dignity. Paul came to the throne by right of inheritance, but he wore the imperial mantle much in the manner of an upstart who had reached the height by a sordid trick he dared anyone to remember. Peter III had been a buffoon, but even his coarse grotesqueness had not quite the vulgarity which stamped so many of his son's gestures. '*Les nouvelles Majestés*' appeared well-nigh drunk with their exalted position. Elizabeth confessed herself shocked by the Emperor's attitude to his mother's memory. He had his father's body exhumed from its tomb at the Alexander Abbey, had it lying in state side by side with Catherine's coffin, and had them both buried at the Cathedral of SS Peter and Paul. '. . . *pas un mot de sa mère, excepté pour la blâmer et de désapprouver tout ce qui s'était fait de son temps.* . . .' But the mother-in-law was even worse. '[*elle*] *se conduit dans toutes les occasions un peu serieuses sans aucun sens juste. . . . Il faut voir mon mari dans ces occasions dans quelle colère elle se met. "Quelles bêtises Maman fait. Elle ne sait pas se conduire du tout. . . ."* C'*est entre nous deux* . . . *qu'il dit de ces choses.* . . .'

'*Entre nous deux.* . . .' Those four and a half years would have been unbearable for the young people but for the happiness they found in each other. They stood shoulder to shoulder in all their hopes and fears. The hours of complete privacy were few, since all too often Alexander had duties in the guardroom which kept him away even at night, but they learned how to use those brief spells creatively, and the child-wife grew to her maturity and was able to help her bewildered and tormented young husband on many an occasion when a more experienced woman would have adjudged the situation beyond remedy.

For all the horrors and the humiliations, those were their happiest years together. They helped each other in all the innocent little conspiracies shaped in order to filch an hour of privacy, to look for a chance of smuggling a dangerously candid letter abroad, to seek ways and means to ease the fate of someone among Paul's numberless victims. The rooms which were allotted to their use became a gracious and tranquil island—in spite of the Empress's interference with the furniture and the carpets.

Paul's coronation took place in Moscow in May 1797. On the morning of the great day, as is recorded in Countess Golovina's Memoirs, the Grand Duchess, 'following an impulse of her artistic nature, decided to pin some lovely pale pink rosebuds to the diamond buckle of her sash.' Her ladies having finished dressing her, Elizabeth must needs present herself to her mother-in-law to have her toilette approved. '[The Empress] looked at her and, without saying a word, pulled roughly at the roses and threw them down on the floor. Then she said acidly: "*Cela ne convient pas.*" ' The Grand Duchess blushed crimson at the humiliation. Alexander, who happened to be in the room, looked upset. Such was the felicitous beginning of a most tiring day.

The Empress Marie was indeed in a sour humour. It was whispered on all sides that '*les nouvelles Majestés*' had expected a far more tumultuous welcome than that accorded by Moscow. Somehow the customary delegations from all the estates in the realm were in no hurry to pay their homage at the Kremlin, and Marie was heard to complain she did not consider her hand was kissed often enough.

When the festivities finished, Elizabeth must accompany her mother-in-law to St Petersburg, and the Emperor began his coronation tour of the country, his two sons accompanying him. Alexander wrote fairly often to his wife. The excursion gave him no pleasure and the separation from his '*chère amie*' cost him dear. '. . . [il] *désire aussi fort de retourner vu la gêne où il est, couchant toujours dans la même chambre que l'Empereur.*' On Alexander's return to the north, they were 'madly' glad of each other. '. . . *j'eus beaucoup de plaisir de revoir mon mari . . . j'étais singulièrement émue en l'embrassant.*'

Alexander's education had been upset by his marriage. His father's accession all but crippled his home life. The comfortable apartments at Tsarskoe Selo had to be abandoned. No member of the family might live at Tsarskoe during Paul's reign. The palace was shut up, the great park and the pleasure grounds neglected at the Emperor's orders—so keen was he on obliterating every landmark cherished by his mother. In the summer, the court went either to Gatchina or to Pavlovsk in the vicinity. Gatchina, its creator become Emperor, was more of a prison than even before. The rest of the year must needs be spent at the Winter Palace since there was no other imperial residence in St Petersburg. Paul hated it, and towards the end of his reign he would begin building a home designed to offer utmost protection to a man who feared the least unfamiliar flavour in a sauce.

Having, at his accession, formally declared to the diplomatic corps that peace was to be the cornerstone of his policy, Paul laboured day and night to place his Empire on a military footing, and Europe could not but be puzzled by the contradiction.

Neither at Gatchina nor in St Petersburg could the young people belong to themselves. The Grand Duke's respectful behaviour and his zeal in fulfilling his duties did nothing to remove Paul's suspicion that 'the grandmother's spoiled pet' was a Jacobin at heart. One by one, the few trusted intimates of Alexander were dismissed from court service or sent into exile. Koutaissov, Paul's favourite, once a barber and now a courtier, lost little time in poisoning the Emperor's mind against Count Golovin and his wife, the first to be sent away. Peter Tolstoy, Victor Kotchubey, Prince Volkonsky, Alexander Golitzin, Paul Strogonov and Novossilzev, to say nothing of Adam and Constantine Czartorizky, all of them vanished from the court. Even Arakcheev was not spared. A suspicion that 'his right hand' occasionally screened Alexander's lapses from the daily regimen was enough to send Arakcheev into the country. Tension heightened when Elizabeth's sister, Princess Frederika of Baden, was betrothed to the King of Sweden, who had a little earlier jilted Paul's eldest daughter, Alexandra. The Empress's anger descended on Elizabeth, who found herself accused of an intrigue designed to humiliate her husband's family. Elizabeth protested that she had not heard a word about any preliminaries, but Marie would not believe it. No letters of congratulation were sent to Stockholm, and Alexander and his wife were forbidden to mention the matter when writing to Baden, nor were they able to send any presents. Meals at the palace became purgatorial. They must needs appear at them since Paul would not permit any food to be eaten anywhere except in the dining hall. For a long time after Frederika's betrothal, her sister found herself ostracized at table. The Emperor scowled at her and the Empress indulged in acid remarks at the expense of Elizabeth's family.

In Paul's immediate neighbourhood, nobody knew, on rising in the morning, where they would lay their head in the evening, and the uncertainty did not exclude the heir to the Empire. The recital of dignities conferred on him reads impressively enough: he was member of the Senate, State Councillor, Governor General of the Capital, and honorary chief of several regiments. But all those high distinctions were hollow. Neither Senate nor Council of State had the least liberty of action, nor had Alexander any time to attend their sessions. His day began and ended with a detailed report on 'the general security' made to the Emperor. The Grand Duke was just a cog in a vast military machine, all his duties governed by an implicit obedience to the Emperor's orders.

Paul's outbursts of temper were diabolical and nobody could foretell what might provoke them. He would fly into a rage at a footman's slow pace or a courtier's hurried step. He would shout himself hoarse, stamp his feet, use his fists, his cane, or a whip. With Arakcheev exiled into the country, Alexander found himself wholly helpless. Terror shackled him in the Emperor's presence. He would stutter, go ashen pale, and his hands were seen to shake. Time and again Elizabeth would tell her mother that it was impossible for her husband to ask anything from his father—'ils sont très mal ensemble'.

A lesser man would have been ground to dust by such treatment. It certainly damaged Alexander. Conversely, it helped him to realize his own responsibility to his country. Scarcely a year after Catherine's death we find him well acquainted with Russian conditions. 'The accident of birth' he had once cursed now appeared in a different light. All the romantic dreams about a rose-wreathed cottage on the banks of the Rhine or in some deep American forest were dismissed for the nonsense they were. Out of much mental torment came a determination to remain true to his name and to work for the restoration of peace and for the beginning of happiness in the Empire. More daringly than his grandmother at the dawn of her reign, Alexander held that the realization of those aims was impossible unless a constitution were granted to the nation. When a chance offered itself to have a letter smuggled abroad, Alexander shared his inmost thoughts with La Harpe.[1]

He began by describing the chaos in the Empire created within the first few months of his father's accession.

'*On ordonne aujourd'hui ce qu'un mois après on contremande. . . . Le bonheur de l'Etat n'y entre pour rien . . . n'y a qu'un pouvoir absolu qui fait tout à tort et à travers. . . . Ma pauvre patrie est dans un état indéfinissable. . . .*' Alexander went on to give the details of his ordinary day . . . '*perdant tout mon temps à des devoirs de bas-officiers, n'ayant pas même un instant à donner à mes études. . . .*' This last sentence may well have been written for the purpose of pleasing La Harpe: Alexander had not greatly occupied himself with any studies between 1794 and 1796—much to Elizabeth's disappointment. None the less, the general tone of the letter speaks of a painful awakening. Alexander's conscience could not rest. For him to seek purely personal happiness now seemed the most unworthy *raison d'être* of existence.

'*Je ferai beaucoup mieux de travailler à rendre mon pays libre et à le prevenir dans l'avenir de servir de jouet à des insensés. . . . Cela serait le meilleur genre de révolution étant opéré par un pouvoir légal qui cesserait de l'être aussitôt que la constitution serait achevée et que la nation aurait de représentants. . . .*' Once such an aim was achieved, Alexander thought he could retire into obscurity and live contented in his country's happiness.

That, too, was a dream, but a dream with far more substance to it than a rosily painted landscape, with Elizabeth, a peasant's cloak on her shoulders, stirring the supper stew and him chopping the wood. It was a dream hammered out of the iron realities Alexander saw round about him. He firmly believed he would achieve it one day and thus safeguard his dear country for ever from '*des atteintes du déspotisme et de la tyrannie. . . .*' He declared himself determined not to count the cost of the sacrifice needed to reach '*ce but si cher pour moi. . . .*'

All the statesmen then in exile might well have endorsed Alex-

[1] Full text of the letter in Schilder, op. cit., Vol. I, 280 et seq.

ander's words. He was twenty at the time. Everything La Harpe had taught him seemed all the more desirable when considered against a background where a man's dignity had become a meaningless sound and the mere spelling of the word 'liberty' was taken for an act of *lèse-majesté*.

Before leaving Russia, La Harpe had furnished Alexander with a list of books for him to study by himself. It is unlikely that the Grand Duke read many of them, but his father's reign certainly proved a school to him.

In May 1799 a daughter was born to him and Elizabeth. To Paul, who had changed the Succession Act of 1722 by another whereby the crown was heritable to males only in strict descent from the sovereign, the birth of a granddaughter meant little enough. The young parents were happy. Unfortunately, the child, born delicate, died in little more than a year, and Elizabeth confessed that her grief would have been unbearable without Alexander's understanding and help. They mourned alone—except for Grand Duchess Anna and Princess Nathalie Shakhovskoy, Elizabeth's lady-in-waiting, whose devotion could not have been remarked by the Empress Marie, otherwise Nathalie Shakhovskoy would have found herself dismissed with ignominy.

It used to be customary for ambassadors to be received in audience by the heir as soon as they had paid respects to the sovereign. But the custom now fell into disuse. Alexander gave no audiences. He even avoided speaking to diplomats unless the Emperor happened to be within earshot. Rostopchin wrote: 'It is dangerous for the Grand Duke not only to form friendships with foreigners but to take any special notice of them at court—so suspicious is the Emperor of his eldest son.' Alexander had his seat in the Council hall, but on the few occasions that he attended he did so as an onlooker who had no voice. He dared not offer his opinion on any subject—however trivial—because of the possibility of his words being twisted out of their meaning and thus reported to Paul. For the same reason, the Grand Duke must keep aloof from his father's ministers. Panin, the Vice Chancellor, might well have offered him valuable advice. Alexander could not afford to take it. His public appearances grew fewer, his caution increased, and he was conscious that the least sign of his popularity spelt danger.

Cheers in his honour would be immediately reported to the Emperor and lead to a stormy scene when accusations of disloyalty and treason ended by stunning Alexander into silence.

'*Nous sommes si accoûtumés à tout nous dire, à ne rien nous cacher . . .*' so wrote the Grand Duchess in a letter to the Margravine of Baden. The constant sense of peril and of mutual need, rather than passion, had drawn him to Elizabeth. She was his only anchor through those years, halcyon for their married life and fateful in another sense. The natural gift of dissimulation, regretted by his tutors, now developed most alarmingly. The Grand Duke had learned how to mask his reactions, feelings and preferences, and he wore the mask continually except for those occasions when he found himself alone with his wife.

During those four and a half years, the course adopted by Russia pursued a wildly zigzagged path. Paul made no distinction between the particular and the general. When the Margrave of Baden concluded a treaty with France, the Emperor of Russia replied by persecuting the Margrave's daughter. Since Elizabeth was expected to become Empress one day, Paul decreed that on all occasions the Dowager Empress was to take precedence over her successor.[1]

He had formally pledged himself to keep peace, and the war with Persia ended immediately on his accession. He had also expressed his contempt for the late Empress's expansionist policy, and told every ambassador in turn that he had no intention of either enlarging his own dominions or of interfering with European affairs.

But Paul's decisions melted as rapidly as snow in April. Adroitly enough Great Britain and Austria began coaxing him to enter the coalition against France. They had failed to persuade Catherine. They succeeded with her son. Flattery always answered with Paul, and he at once saw himself as a saviour of Europe, his particular mission being to restore the Bourbons to their inheritance and to crush the revolutionary hydra. Louis XVIII, then living at Mittau Castle in Courland, had his pension increased tenfold, and the

---

[1] Paul's Act remained in force till the end of the dynasty. It is difficult to see why it was never repealed. In hard practice, it led to a number of awkward situations. Not only did the Dowager have precedence, but the most important heirlooms were hers to use. The only Empress of Russia who was not subjected to humiliations at the hands of a mother-in-law was Marie, wife of Alexander III (1881-84), her husband's mother having died a year before his accession.

Emperor ordered that full royal honours were to be paid to him. He then proceeded to break with Prussia because of her neutrality. Russian troops, led by Suvorov, went to Italy to help the Austrians, and Kamensky was sent to the frontiers of Prussia. The peaceful interlude ended in a manner none could have expected.

There followed a rupture with Austria on the pretext that the Austrian government had not honoured their obligations to the Russian army in Italy, and Suvorov was recalled. When the British occupied Malta, Paul astonished the world by assuming the dignity of the Grandmaster of the Knights of Malta. He laid an embargo on all British imports, to the great detriment of trade conditions in his own Empire.

Ministers accredited to Paul's court never knew if they would be regarded as friends or enemies. The crowning somersault came when Paul decided to approach Napoleon, to whom he wrote: 'I suggest that you and I come together to put an end to all the miseries and disasters now ravaging Europe. . . . I am ready to listen to you. . . . I invite you to join with me in establishing a general peace which will quieten the world.'

One of the immediate consequences of the new policy was the treatment meted out to Louis XVIII—still a lavishly pensioned guest in Paul's dominions. 'The staunch ally of the Bourbons' sent couriers to Mittau to have the King driven out of the castle. It happened in winter; the old gentleman was not allowed any time to have his belongings packed, and his valuables and money were taken from him.

In spite of having concluded a treaty with Turkey, Paul approached the First Consul with the view of having the Porte divided between France and Russia, but the project came to nothing. Then Paul decided that the embargo placed on British imports was not enough punishment for England and the idea of invading India pleased him greatly. Twenty-odd thousands of Don Cossacks were sent across the Urals, Paul writing the following instructions to their Hetman, General Orlov:

'The British are getting ready to attack me. . . . They must there-fore be attacked from the least expected quarter. . . . India is the best objective. . . . It is a four months' march from your head-quarters. . . . All the riches of India will be your reward. . . . You and your men will be covered with glory. . . . I enclose the only map

I could find here. God bless you. Paul.' The letter was followed by another. 'I find that my map goes no farther than Khiva. . . . It will be your business to find the required information. . . . All the mercantile houses in India, which belong to the British, must be taken over as soon as you arrive, and all the natives to be treated kindly and brought over to Russia where they will enjoy a greater independence than they do under the British. . . . I expect you so to arrange matters that the entire trade of India be diverted to Russia. . . . Remember that your business is solely against the British. . . . All along the way you must exert yourself to assure the natives of my friendly disposition towards them. . . .'

The Hetman mustered his forces in February 1801. The spring floods in the country east of the Volga brought the fantastic expedition to a speedy end. Few among those Cossacks saw their native Don again.

India had not been in any danger, but the clumsy gesture could not fail to annoy London. Denmark and Sweden began wondering if a continued friendship with Russia might not bring them into deep peril. By the beginning of 1801 Paul's Empire had hardly a friend left in Europe, and Count Simon Voronzov, still accredited to the Court of St James's, was having a difficult time in trying to explain his master's vagaries to King George's government. In St Petersburg Panin, the Vice Chancellor, dared to make his criticism articulate, was dismissed from office, and exiled into the country. Lord Whitworth, who had been given his passports in 1800, reported that discontent was hardening in Russia. Europe, accustomed to palace revolutions in St Petersburg, expected another outbreak during 1800, and a short sketch of Alexander appeared in a French periodical: 'This young prince astonishes everybody by the purity of his moral principles and his physical beauty, but he lacks boldness and self-assurance. . . . He is far too susceptible to outside opinion. . . .'

By then Paul's friendship could no longer be relied upon by the European comity. It did not greatly matter to the Great Powers what enormities and stupidities he chose to commit in his own Empire, but to have the sovereign of such a country pursue a lunatic's policy outside his own dominions did not promise much for the quieting of European nerves. When 1800 drew to its close, Europe was disappointed not to see a change in the Russian climate.

From Scandinavia to Italy, from Spain to Austria, people began taking an interest in Paul's eldest son and speculating about the future drift of Russian policy. They had scant material to form any theories, but La Harpe and a few others had been receiving most candid letters from Alexander. The consensus of European opinion held that Russia's hopes for the future lay with the young Grand Duke.

Paul, having listened to his spies' reports from London and Berlin, invited his wife's nephew, Prince Eugene of Württemberg, to come to St Petersburg. The boy's arrival and the uncle's attention to him led to a crop of rumours. Some said that the Emperor meant to adopt his nephew. Others held that Eugene would be named Paul's heir in defiance of Paul's own act of succession. But nobody could read the Emperor's mind.

Meanwhile, his suspicion of treason grew daily. Alexander must still deliver his daily reports morning and evening, and his fear of his father was evident to all present. Arakcheev, once again in the Emperor's bad graces, could not shield the Grand Duke from brutalities, and on one occasion Paul sent Koutaissov to him with a message that he should reflect on the fate of Alexis, Peter the Great's son, done to death at his father's orders for his alleged treason.

Paul's suspicions did not stop there. Long since unfaithful to his stupid but loyal and patient wife, he now imagined her to have joined a conspiracy against him. The Empress's frequently observed distress drew Alexander closer to her. Marie had been unkind and unfeeling to Elizabeth, but Marie was his mother and she stood facing the same threat as himself.

If Russia's foreign policy annoyed and angered Europe—with the sole exception of France—Paul's administration was pushing the Empire to the edge of despair. Already in 1799, Victor Kotchubey wrote to Simon Voronzov in London that internal conditions were moving from bad to worse. So deep-rooted was the general uncertainty that it produced an hour of most abominable self-seeking. '*Chacun ne songe qu'à faire ses choux gras....*' No position at court, in the army, or in the civil service, but hung by a cobweb. Imperial favour gained on a Monday was followed by imperial wrath on the following Wednesday. The most trivial details in speech, dress, or manner might incur Paul's instant displeasure. Too much or too little powder on one's hair might mean an immediate order of exile or worse. Officers on duty at the palace always carried money in their pockets in case they were to face the road to Siberia before nightfall. '*L'on se dit*,' wrote Kotchubey, ' "*il faut que demain je me fasse donner quelque chose*",' since Paul, caught in a genial mood, could still be generous, though such moods came more and more rarely.

The Margravine of Baden was frightened by the rumour of personal danger confronting her daughter and Alexander, and Elizabeth must needs admit that her husband was '*trop imprudent . . . c'est que je lui répète sans cesse, mais—entre nous soit dit—ce n'est pas justement son faible que d'écouter les conseils que des gens raisonnables lui donnent . . . il ne fait la plupart du temps et tant qu'il le peut, que d'après sa tête et traite de folie et de poltronnerie ce qu'on lui dit à ce sujet. . . . Mais malgré cela, ne craignez rien pour lui ni pour moi. . . .*' Such was a daughter's hurried assurance to an anxious mother, but it was hardly based on facts. By that time Alexander was the chief suspect in his father's mind. Grand Duke Constantine is supposed to have said that his father had declared war on common sense with the firm resolve never to conclude a truce. Alexander's own 'imprudences' were of a kind which would hardly have deserved the label in a normal environment, but the most innocent remark of his, overheard either by Rostopchin or by Koutaissov, became a darkly coloured hint when reported to Paul.

Already before 1800, many confidential dispatches of diplomats in St Petersburg carried references to the Emperor's 'alarming mental condition'. By 1800, these words were translated as 'madness'. Its evidences were overwhelming. Moods of sullen silence began alternating with outbursts of fury and sadistic cruelty. In the streets, the mere sight of Paul on horseback made people run for shelter. Nobody knew what to expect once his wrath had broken over their heads. Dismissal from service and exile into the country were—relatively speaking—gestures of imperial clemency.

The tension was at its strongest in St Petersburg and the neighbourhood, less so in Moscow and, with the exception of landowners exiled to their estates, there were hardly any signs of unrest in the heart of the country. No earlier dynastic upheaval had involved the masses, and Paul's own case would not create a precedent. In point of fact, had he ever thought of calling upon the peasants, they would have rallied round him in their millions. Many of his *ukazes*, whilst penalizing the nobility and gentry, had brought some easing of the peasants' burden, the ban on Sunday work being one of the measures to better their condition. Nor did the danger come from the army. They showed a surprising loyalty in view of the inhuman discipline enforced by the Emperor, but there again the men in the ranks looked upon him as their defender against the officers' brutality.

The mood among the guards regiments was wholly different. Favoured and continually distinguished by the late Empress, they were despised by Paul, who endorsed Arakcheev's contemptuous remark about the guards' colours being 'the old lady's petticoats'. But there was not a single guards officer capable of starting, let alone leading, a conspiracy.

It fell to a statesman to shape its beginnings.

At that time Nikita Panin was still Vice Chancellor, though he had not much voice in any matters of high policy, all those being determined by the Emperor. Panin saw clearly that no good would result from the rapprochement with Napoleon and that Russia was in no position to threaten, let alone to attack, Great Britain. There was nothing for Panin to decide. There was much to criticize, but in spite of his courageous outspokenness it was not until the end of 1800 that the joint intrigues of Koutaissov and Rostopchin led to his being exiled to his estates at a great distance from the capital. But before it happened, Panin had had many a secret talk with Pahlen, then Governor General of St Petersburg, and the ex-Vice Chancellor left the capital, conscious that those talks would bear their fruit in the near future. He had urged Pahlen that a way should be found to compel the Emperor to abdicate in favour of Alexander and that the first step lay in obtaining the Grand Duke's consent.

Paul, ready to see high treason in an officer's badly polished buttons, did not notice the real peril drawing nearer every day.

For real it certainly was. All the men, including Panin, involved in the matter, must have known they were busily discussing an impossibility. Nobody, having the least knowledge of Paul's character, could imagine him ready to lay down his power. And even were he to do so, where would his future lie? The conspirators talked about a temporary imprisonment in the Fortress, but such a measure would not have answered for long, and to send him into exile to some place like Kholmogory or the Solovetzky Abbey by the shore of the White Sea would assuredly have left a loophole for a counter-conspiracy, its consequences too appalling to contemplate. Once away from the capital, Paul could count on much popular support, and those who planned to dethrone him were only too well aware of it. Exile abroad was out of all question: no European country would have offered him asylum. Therefore, all the discussions about abdication were a polite fiction sustained by the men who had not enough courage to look regicide in the face.

Count Pahlen might be considered one of the very few people Paul seemed to trust—however patchily. Nothing much had been known about the man until in 1798 he replaced Benningsen as Governor General of St Petersburg. His duties were many and complicated, one of his most arduous tasks being to ensure the Emperor's personal safety, but Pahlen soon proved himself both capable and indefatigable. At last the Emperor confided in him his suspicions about the Grand Duke. Pahlen quickly assured him that such could not be the case: if there were any grounds for suspicion in the Grand Duke's behaviour, he, Pahlen, would have discovered it soon enough.

In the autumn of 1800 the Emperor ordered his architects to hasten the completion of St Michael's Castle. That mammoth of a deeply moated fortress was to be guarded day and night by picked sentries chosen from among the most reliable men of the old Gatchina contingent. Within that fastness, so the Emperor told Pahlen, he would feel much more secure than at the Winter Palace. His family were commanded to follow him there, and the prospect gave Alexander and Elizabeth little pleasure.

With Panin exiled to the country and with Arakcheev, whose friendship with Alexander might well have endangered the plan, safely away from the capital, Count Pahlen set to work. It proved a Herculean task to convince Alexander that the country's fate depended on his consent to his father's abdication. Pahlen's most fiery arguments proved useless. The Grand Duke kept saying that he felt himself bound by the oath of fealty to the Emperor. Pahlen tried to counter it by reminding Alexander that Paul had certainly broken his own coronation oath, and the Grand Duke made no answer. Pahlen urged that all personal loyalty should be superseded by one's responsibility to the country. In the end, Alexander gave his conditional consent. Pahlen must promise him that his father's life would be spared. Pahlen promised.

He knew well, and so did Alexander, that if the plan miscarried and if the Emperor were to call on the army, their lives would not be worth a broken groat. He knew well, and so did Alexander, that Paul would never agree to abdicate. But the fiction must needs be maintained.

Pahlen set to work. There were at the time many hundreds of officers dismissed from the service living in penury away from the capital. Pahlen succeeded in catching the Emperor's ear when Paul happened to be in a benevolent mood. Among those to be pardoned Pahlen slipped in the names of the Zubov brothers and General Benningsen. The conspirators began meeting at the house of Madame Zherebzova, sister of the Zubovs. Pahlen being a frequent visitor, no policeman would have dared to watch the house. The guards regiments were 'sounded' one by one. Only the Semenovsky Guards, known for their occasionally embarrassing devotion to the Grand Duke, were thought to be reliable, and Pahlen decided so to contrive matters that men from the regiment would be on duty at the Castle when 'the particular occasion' called for their services.

Meanwhile they had reached 1801, and the Emperor and his family were installed at the Castle. One morning he challenged Pahlen to tell him if it were true that a conspiracy was being formed against the Crown. Pahlen did not waste a second before replying:

'It is perfectly true, sir. A conspiracy does exist, and I have joined the ranks of the conspirators the better to expose them all.'

The Emperor at once asked if his two elder sons were involved. Pahlen replied that they were not, and he could see that Paul did not believe him.

The rest of the day was spent in issuing orders for wholesale arrests. By nightfall, with a draconian curfew imposed on the inhabitants, St Petersburg suggested an entombed city. There was silence in the grand-ducal apartments at the Castle. A few days later the Emperor placed Alexander and Constantine under house arrest. In the evening of 10th March he summoned the colonel commanding the Semenovsky Guards, told him he knew that all his officers and men were revolutionaries, and ordered the regiment to leave the capital at dawn. That night at supper Alexander looked so ill that his father suggested he should see his doctor.

The conspirators were ready. Later the same night they made their way into the Castle, nobody challenging them. Two hussars and a valet on duty outside the Emperor's bedroom were overpowered. Beninngsen and Zubov were the first to enter, and Benningsen announced that Paul was under arrest on orders of the Emperor Alexander and that no harm would come to him if he did not resist. Paul had no thought of resisting. But he asked—'What have I done?', and the question infuriated other conspirators who rushed at him. Candles were overturned. Paul ran behind a table, stumbled and fell. They bore down on him, there followed a hideous scuffle, and in the end he was strangled.

In Paul's bedroom it was not thought necessary to have recourse to fiction. Not a single allusion to abdication was made either by Benningsen or by any of the other six. Pahlen was not among them. He reached St Michael's Castle when all was over.

Several years later, Nicholas I, Alexander's brother and successor, destroyed many valuable family papers. His mother's diary and that of Elizabeth were among them. The loss is irreparable. The events of that night were told and re-told by the regicides and by some contemporaries, but nearly all the extant variants differ one from another. All the records, however, agree on Alexander's pitiful condition and on Elizabeth's heroic calm during those chaotic hours.

Her husband broke down, her mother-in-law leapt from hysterics into fury and insisted that none but herself should succeed her husband, all the others lost their heads. Elizabeth quietened the widow, she gave orders to officers and to servants, she saw to it that the younger Grand Dukes were kept in their rooms, she comforted her sister-in-law, and in between she found time for her husband. In the small hours Rogerson, the physician, on entering a room to receive orders from the young Emperor, found both husband and wife on a sofa in a corner, *'les bras enlacés, leurs fronts appuyés l'un contre l'autre et pleurant tous les deux si amèrement qu'ils ne me virent pas entrer. . . .'* Countess Golovina, however, witnessed a different moment and recorded it in her journal:

'Alexander, pale and shaken, said to his wife between sobs: "I cannot go on with it. I have no strength to reign. Let someone else take my place." Elizabeth begged him to think of the consequences of such a decision, to be energetic, to dedicate himself to the service of his people, to look upon the sovereignty he so hated as a life-long expiation. The Empress would have said much more but Pahlen's tiresome presence restrained her. The man should have left the room as soon as she came in. But he had no manners.'

Elizabeth astonished everybody. '. . . *dans cette nuit de trouble et d'horreur, l'impératrice Elizabeth fut en quelque sorte le seul pouvoir qui, en exérçant une influence intermédiaire accueillie par tous, devint un véritable médiateur . . . entre son époux, sa belle-mère et les conjurés*', said Prince Adam Czartorizky in his memoirs.

But the young Empress's diary alone could have revealed how much she knew of her husband's responsibility for an event—which, whilst freeing Russia from an intolerable yoke, was to cripple many of Alexander's purposes all down the years. Elizabeth's letter to her mother written a fortnight after the murder necessarily avoids the main issue:

'*Ce qui était à craindre depuis longtemps est arrivé. . . .*' Of course, she must have known of her husband's conferences with Pahlen, and she may have guessed that the polite fiction about the abdication could not be maintained at the end. '*La Russie certainement va respirer après une oppression de 4 ans, et, si une mort naturelle avait terminé les jours de l'Empereur, je n'aurais pas éprouvé peut-être ce que j'éprouve à présent, car l'idée d'un crime est affreuse. . . .*'

Elizabeth must have known about her father-in-law's plans to have the whole family imprisoned. She would also have known of Alexander's conditional assent—'provided my father's life be spared. . . .' Yet she was too intelligent not to realize that Alexander could hardly reign with Paul either in prison or in exile.

'*Le Grand Duc Alexandre, Empereur aujourd'hui, était anéanti absolument par la mort de son père, par la manière dont il est mort . . . son âme sensible en restera à jamais déchirée . . . jamais je n'aurais cru qu'il me coûterait des moments assez affreux . . . [il] ne savait pas ce qu'il faisait. . . . Enfin, [il] partit pour le Palais d'Hiver dans l'espoir d'attirer la foule après lui. . . .*' The hope was fulfilled and somewhat lessened the bitterness of that morning.

The idea of serving his country was Alexander's only anchor in those days. '*Il n'y a point d'autre motif qui puisse lui donner de la fermeté. Et il lui en faut, car, grand Dieu, dans quel état a-t-il reçu cet Empire?*'

So many valuable documents have perished that it does not seem

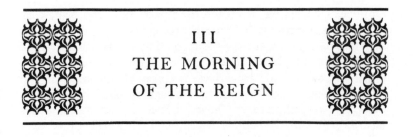

III
THE MORNING
OF THE REIGN

OFFICIALLY, PAUL died of apoplexy, but the fictitious announcement deceived nobody. People knew the truth and, freed of a ghastly yoke, they turned away from the past to lose themselves in the joy of the moment. In St Petersburg, even the weather echoed the national mood: a brilliant sun came out after some weeks of sullen greyness.

Many behaved like children. Clothes of a cut forbidden by Paul were worn the very next day. Crowds strolled along the quays, gathered in front of the Winter Palace, and lingered on the bridges, their movement neither controlled nor questioned by the police. Hostesses began giving parties for the sheer pleasure of not having to ask for official sanction. Tradesmen were happy at the thought of untrammelled imports coming into the country. Nobody had known the exact number of prohibitions issued under Paul. Everybody was certain they would all be removed, and many of them went within the next few days. Men and women of all social colours would have been all too ready to echo Elizabeth's words to her mother: *'je ne puis m'empêcher d'avouer que je respire avec la Russie entière.'*

St Michael's Castle was at once abandoned by the imperial family, who moved back to the Winter Palace where the young Emperor—he was in his twenty-fourth year—must begin learning how to govern his vast inheritance. His training in self-control and his proneness to dissimulation served Alexander's purposes extremely well at every public appearance, the pallor of the beautiful face taking nothing away from the warmth of a smile which seemed to make dust of the distance between the sovereign and his subjects.

Yet the mask, worn with so little apparent effort, could be taken

off in the comparative privacy of the palace walls, and many contemporaries at court would remember the occasional look of despair,
the stumbling gait, and even the tears. The factual entries in the
official court journal speak for themselves: day by day their Majesties
dined and supped by themselves, not even the members of the
Household invited to be present. Through all those first months,
however crowded were the hours, Elizabeth had much of her
husband. For all the sombre background, they had joy of each
other.

With the exception of Count Paul Strogonov, Alexander had no
intimates near him at his accession. Arakcheev was still in the
country, and Arakcheev inevitably meant Gatchina and all the place
had stood for, and Alexander would not recall him until 1803.
Victor Kotchubey was at Dresden, Adam Czartorizky in Italy, Peter
Volkonsky in the country, Novossilzev in England, and La Harpe in
Paris. Kotchubey spoke for them all when he wrote to a friend:

'*Je pars pour la Russie parce que je crois que tous les honnêtes gens
doivent se réunir autour de lui et faire tous leurs efforts pour cicatriser
les plaies infinies portées par son père à la patrie.*' Kotchubey added
a significant postscript in Old Slavonic: 'I know that the person
whose womb carried our friend has great influence, but her rays of
intelligence are few and dim.'

That was true.

The night of Paul's murder, his wife had lost her head, wept and
stormed. Her husband being dead, it followed that she and none
other was the autocrat of All the Russias. It had then fallen to
Pahlen rather than to her sons to make Marie understand that Paul's
Act of 1797 meant that the crown was inalienably Alexander's. Then
the dowager proceeded to clutch at all the rights ceded to her by
Paul, and little by little she found comfort in the thought that she
remained the first lady in the land. The unloved daughter-in-law
must needs walk behind her on all public occasions, and she, Marie,
was still mistress at the Winter Palace and—by her husband's will—
head of the family. Elizabeth cared neither for precedence nor for
the disposal of heirlooms, but she cared for other things, and Marie
did not fail to see where her barbed arrows wounded most. She
began to play on her son's shattered nerves. She easily forgot Paul's
infidelities and cruelties, and mourned for an ideal husband taken
away from her in the full flowering of his years. Hint by hint, the

mother made her son conscious of his debt to her, and Alexander listened to her far more readily than he should have done. Religious feeling played no part in any of it. All came from an exaggerated sense of filial piety.

The destruction of Marie's diary makes it impossible to gauge what she knew or did not know about the conspiracy, but Pahlen's speedy dismissal and exile were due to her influence over Alexander. She hated the man and did not conceal her pleasure at his going, but not all the measures taken by Alexander were approved by Marie, and within the first few months she had a fair example of his obduracy.

Russia's foreign policy must needs be given a shape and a purpose after nearly five years of whims and vagaries. Against much opposition, which included his mother's protests, the young Emperor recalled Nikita Panin—to the pleasure of England and Austria and the discomfiture of France. The Vice Chancellor was welcomed by Alexander with an illuminating remark: '*Hélas, les choses n'ont pas tourné comme nous l'avons cru. . . .*'

Panin had never liked La Harpe, who wrote to Alexander from Paris that peace should be the foundation stone of his reign to enable him to proceed with the important reforms of law and education. Panin had tried to stop La Harpe's return to Russia. In July 1801 the Vice Chancellor wrote to Voronzov in England that 'in spite of the Dowager's protests and mine, the Swiss gentleman has received his passports. I hear from Paris and Berlin that he has some secret commission from the Corsican. . . .' but Panin need not have been anxious: the tie between Alexander and his old tutor would exclude all political involvement for some time to come.

Policy rather than preference made the young Emperor turn to veteran statesmen of Catherine's reign. Trotshinsky was his secretary of state for home affairs. Bekleshov, Alexander Voronzov, Markov and Zavadovsky were all given office. They were old, slightly tired, and marked for little else than an insensate jealousy one of another, but Alexander had no choice at the beginning. The repeal of many laws crippling a subject's personal liberty, the decree that serfs were not to be sold without land—an act which might be regarded as the first tentative step toward emancipation—and several other measures carried out during the first months of the reign led to a volume of sharp criticism among the grey-haired minority, their loyalties wholly committed to the reactionary policy of Catherine's latter years. But Alexander stood firm.

In late spring of 1801 I. Mouraviev-Apostol wrote to Simon Voronzov: '. . . [he] is severe with himself only. . . . From seven in the morning till noon he is absorbed in state business. . . . His only time of leisure is between noon and one o'clock when he dines. . . . Then audiences begin. . . . At five in the afternoon he is back in his study, working, with short intervals, till about eleven or midnight. . . . He is adored by all the young people who have the high honour of coming near him. . . .'

Young men, returning to the capital from abroad or from the country, breathed freely at the high promise of those beginnings. The son of a father who had considered his whim to be the highest law, Alexander delighted, disturbed and angered his subjects by stressing his conviction that autocracy was under the law. A good example of such an approach, gladdening all the liberally minded people in Russia, was the case of Princess Marie Golitzin, who petitioned the Emperor to release her from the debts incurred by her late husband's signature. Such a procedure would run counter to the law, but the lady pinned her hopes on 'the august benevolence'. Alexander replied to the petition by a personal letter:

'If I were to permit myself to break the law, who would consider it their duty to keep it? I cannot stand above the law. . . . I acknowledge no authority to be mine except such as is bestowed by the law, and I am all the more obliged to observe it. . . . Where others might show themselves indulgent, I can be only just.'

Such was Alexander's opinion at the time, and it went far beyond the most liberal clauses of his grandmother's '*Nakaz*'. It was an echo of La Harpe's lessons. Less directly, it affirmed his wife's persuasion that he was to accept sovereignty as a service to his people. But it was hardly a principle to win the approval of the nobility or of the hierarchy.

In September 1801 Alexander and Elizabeth went to Moscow for their crowning. The enthusiasm shown by the old capital was far more than the normal response of crowds to the blinding glitter of a great occasion. A rewardingly personal element entered into the people's acclamations. On every side he was met by signs of genuine affection for his person. The traditional shouts of 'Little Father Tsar' were drowned in 'our little red sun, our *rodimy*,[1] our angel.'

'As gay as a May morning', Moscow found her young Emperor. Men and women milled about the streets and squares, telling one another that there had not been anyone like Tsar Alexander born into the world. The expression on his face, whether serious or happy, became graven in people's memories down many years to come. They wept for pride and joy when deacons and choristers from the Assumption Cathedral told about the moment when Platon, the Metropolitan of Moscow, offered the chalice to the newly crowned Emperor. Once in their lives, at the coronation, the Tsars of Russia had the privilege of administering the Sacrament to themselves. Yet Alexander would not use the privilege. He bowed and murmured that he preferred to take his communion in the manner of any layman. Not a single festivity was arranged for the people but the Emperor would be there—sometimes on horseback, oftener on foot. 'It happened in September,' remembered an eyewitness, 'but you would have thought we were celebrating Easter—such a joy we had of him.'

That was outside—in full view of his people. But there was also the palace in the Kremlin walls, and some of the time passed there had no colour of spring at all. '. . . [*il*] *avait des heures d'anéantisse- ment au point que l'on craignait pour sa raison*,' so said Adam Czartorizky, and his record is not the only one. Alexander's few intimates tried hard to sweeten the bitterness of those moods. '*Je tâchais de la raccomoder avec lui-même, avec la grande tâche qu'il avait devant lui* . . .', said Czartorizky. The efforts made by Alexander's friends certainly helped him. '*Mais le ver rongeur y resta toujours* . . .'

Much in Czartorizky's memoirs, written in the evening of his life, is coloured by prejudices and disillusionments grown in later years, but in 1801, called by the young Emperor to help in the work of reconstruction, conscious and proud of their happy intimacy in the past and confident of the future, Czartorizky would have been in a position to gauge Alexander's mood. He by no means deceived the crowds in Moscow: he was resolved to spend himself in their service.

[1] The word *rodimy* does not easily lend itself to translation. It means someone or some- thing closest to one's heart. It carries the warmth of a complete and joyous dedication to one's beloved.

But '*le ver rongeur*' never ceased to torment him, for all he regarded that service as an expiation for his share in his father's assassination. Even a nature at peace with itself might have found it hard to arrive at an objective view, though a better balanced mind might have admitted the expediency, and it was certainly better for one man to die than for the nation to perish. The contradictions in Alexander allowed of no such simple solution. Later, '*le ver rongeur*' would heighten or lessen the torment in accordance with the Emperor's activity. In 1801 the memory was too stark and immediate.

The common folk had had no share in the horror, and all the festivities were arranged for them. But the nobility were displeased by a departure from tradition. A coronation would invariably be followed by a lavish list of honours, bestowing titles, gifts of money, diamond and emerald snuffboxes and the most coveted largesse of all—numbers of 'souls' from among the Crown peasants. Alexander's list of honours was meagre indeed, and not a single peasant was given away as a mark of imperial benevolence.[1]

When someone spoke to Alexander about the discontent among the landowners, he replied that it would be superfluous to enlarge upon the miseries of serfdom and that he had made a vow not to increase the number of slaves in the Empire. That—together with the recent law prohibiting the sale of serfs without the land—deepened the discontent in the reactionary ranks. La Harpe and the young hotheads, Novossilzev, Strogonov and Kotchubey, were blamed for the Emperor's dangerous proneness to liberal principles.

The obverse of the coronation medal summed up Alexander's intentions at the beginning of the reign. It was engraved with a pillar bearing the word 'law', and the inscription above it ran thus: 'Such is the earnest of universal happiness.'

The young Emperor had vision, fervour, and a sincere desire to govern well, but he had no definite programme in 1801. 'The many wounds of the country', seen by Kotchubey and others, were not hidden from him. Far less clearly could Alexander envisage the remedies except that he knew they must be remedies indeed and not

---

[1] All grants of 'souls' made by the sovereign came from the vast number of the so-called Crown peasants. Technically in bondage to the Emperor, they yet enjoyed a small measure of liberty, which vanished irrevocably once they became the property of private owners.

ephemeral palliatives. The work to be done was Herculean; administration, finance, law, trade, foreign policy, all the several pulses of the national body, cried for reform. The misgovernment of years could not be healed within a few months. All in all, the results of those first deliberations were not as meagre as Alexander's critics contended.

The hotheads were loyal and arduous. They were also impatient. They longed to clutch at the brooms of many reforms and sweep them up and down the country. Barely two months after Alexander's accession, Kotchubey complained that '. . . *rien n'a pris encore une assiette solide. . . . Au désespoir est succédé l'ivresse de la joie. . . . Tout cela est un état violent, et il faut bien de la mesure dans toute la marche du gouvernement . . .*'

It was an unworthy plaint, more so since Kotuchbey himself shared in the '*ivresse*'. Nor did it reflect the day's truth. There could be little 'deliberation' in those first months. The effort to clothe the dry bones of reforming theory with living flesh may not have led to many startling results at the time, but it prepared the ground for further ventures. And even those few results were not as contemptible as was adjudged by some contemporary critics. At the very least, they proved that some respect for the individual as distinct from the state was in existence.

In May 1801 the Emperor convened a private committee of four, Czartorizky, Kotchubey, Strogonov and Novossilzev, charging them to draw up a report on home conditions which would serve as a base for discussions. To learn the state of the country, to map out a landscape of its foreign commitments, to sketch an outline of urgently needed administrative reforms, and, finally, to arrive at a policy which would prepare the way to a constitution 'acceptable to the whole nation', such were the formidable terms of reference given by Alexander to his Private Committee, '*Neglássny Komitét*'.

He and his four friends spoke a common language. They all shared the enthusiasm of youth ready to accept the promise of spring on the witness of winter. They were formed into a committee, but the arid formality of the word was hardly applicable to their meetings. The four dined with the Emperor and Empress on certain appointed days. After coffee, the four friends went into a small room adjoining the private apartments and began the day's business. Later in the evening the Emperor would join them. He proved a good listener, though his own contribution to their debates sometimes puzzled both Czartorizky and Kotchubey who knew him so well. '. . . *l'Empereur ne s'était fait aucun plan. Il frappait pour ainsi dire à toutes les portes,*' grumbled Kotchubey, forgetting that all of them together were knocking at several doors at once.

Those informal meetings point at one of the most exciting moments in the social history of Russia. Not even Catherine the Great during the happiest and most fruitful years of her reign would have a window opened quite so widely. Alexander formed a private '*soviet*'—which in Russian means both 'council' and 'counsel'—and for all its informality, the little committee may well be considered the forerunner of that far greater body engaged in much farther-reaching reforms during the reign of Alexander's nephew in the middle of the century.

The home problems presented the knottiest point of all. By far the greater proportion of Alexander's subjects, having gleaned some immediate benefits after his accession, were satisfied with the existing social forms, their contentment either due to open preference or to blind ignorance. In the forefront of all home reforms stood serfdom and all its accompanying evils. The four were divided in their approach. Strogonov and Czartorizky argued that its retention rather than abolition spelt future dangers for the Empire. Kotchubey and Novossilzev shared that opinion in general, but argued that the approach towards abolition should be made by most cautious inches. In all such discussions, sometimes breaking into fiery arguments, the Emperor seemed to lean towards a vaguely neutral point of view wholly at variance with his real thoughts on the subject. Abolition was patently the most urgent problem of all. In the eyes of the four, for all the difference of their views, it stood for an earnest of an undreamt-of prosperity. 'Our wealth lies in the land,' said Strogonov, 'and the land worked by free men will yield far more abundantly than it does at present.' But it was precisely the question of the land that confused the Emperor.

He found himself between the Scylla of the landed gentry and the Charybdis of the peasants. The landed gentry could hardly be expected to be robbed of their acres. The peasants could not conceivably be freed without the land. Territorial grants made by the Crown would never satisfy such a demand.

The first step in this direction was taken not at the Winter Palace but in a remote province of the Empire. Count Serge Roumiantzev announced his intention to free a large number of his peasants, generous allotments of both arable and pasture being a *sine qua non* of the enfranchisement.

The Emperor welcomed the lead. Yet there was the existing law, and Roumiantzev's plan must first obtain legal sanction. Reactionary ranks began stirring uneasily. There was much opposition, and not till the beginning of 1803 did the Emperor sign the Act whereby landowners were empowered to free their serfs provided certain conditions were fulfilled.

The *ukaze* about '*volnye khlebopaschzy*', i.e. 'free land labourers', led to a storm not only among the hardened reactionaries but even among the ranks of mildly liberal gentry. A re-enactment of 1789 in Russia was prophesied on all sides. Derzhavin, the aging poet, gave full vent to his hatred of 'the Jacobin gang', '*shayka*', the name given by the reactionaries to the members of the Private Committee. Yet the Emperor would not give in. The Act was entered on the statute books. 'Our fathers' heritage is thrown to the dogs', cried a contemporary.

In the long run, the Act had a moral rather than a practical effect. Enfranchisement was hedged about with so many formalities that the majority of landowners had neither the funds, nor the patience, nor even the intelligence to wrestle with them. Yet the mere publication of such a law stirred the imaginations of many. Men like Malinovsky and Kisselev began working at plans for the ultimate abolition. The new leaven, so feared and mistrusted by the majority, entered the national consciousness and richly confirmed the hopes at Alexander's accession.

Decentralization of governmental activity seemed another urgent imperative. There were the Senate and Council of State, the latter created by Catherine the Great to deal with emergencies during her first war against Turkey in 1768. The Senate remained the highest administrative and legislative organ of the Empire. The main qualifications for the rank of senator or state councillor seemed to be an advanced age, great wealth, and the personal esteem of the sovereign. The spade-work was carried out by an enormous staff of secretaries, under-secretaries and clerks of progressively diminishing importance. All the Governors General in the provinces and the large body of the lesser bureaucratic fry were not only answerable to the Senate but precluded from carrying out any measures without its sanction—with the inevitable result of a snail-like progress in all administrative matters.

Alexander was determined to put a stop to it, and in 1802 eight ministries were formed, somewhat recalling the ancient Muscovite '*prikazy*' and Petrine '*collegia*'. State Council and the Senate were thoroughly reformed. The eight ministers formed a committee of their own, with the Emperor at its head, and they were answerable directly to him.

Some of the first ministerial appointments were unfortunate and came as a shock to the liberal-minded. It was obvious that Alexander meant to placate the reactionaries. Derzhavin, whose virulent criticisms of the least liberal breath were known to all, was sent to the Ministry of Justice. Count Alexander Voronzov, having neither natural nor acquired gifts for the office, went to the Foreign Ministry. Zavadovsky, an amiable nonentity, found himself entrusted with the Empire's education. The fatuity of that appointment, however, was happily redeemed by a staff recruited from among men of great promise. Kotchubey, given the Ministry of the Interior, had a brilliant colleague in the person of Michael Speransky. Those two ministries were the most active of all. More was done in the educational field within a bare few years than through the whole of the preceding century. Literature, which had first flourished under Catherine and was later gyved by her and all but strangled during Paul's reign, ceased to be a browbeaten Cinderella. On learning that the conditions of the book trade could not assure any author's livelihood, the Emperor decided to make personal grants out of his own purse. Karamzin and a number of others were enabled to continue their work, the canker of financial troubles no longer harassing them. During 1802 alone nearly two hundred thousand roubles were spent on grants and pensions to the impecunious *literati*.

But Alexander's innate generosity stopped short of all extravagances. The state of the imperial exchequer so appalled him that he created the post of State Comptroller, whose duties were separate from those of the Finance Minister. Economy seemed an urgent need and the Emperor decided to give a personal lead in the matter. The youthful dandy, whose embroidered waistcoats and jewelled shoe buckles used to excite the envious admiration of the court, was gone for ever. By the beginning of 1802 the drive for economy had pruned all the needless expenses of the Emperor's own household and reduced its annual expenditure by some four million roubles. Little by little, in spite of all the protests from the Dowager Empress and the unveiled disgust of society, court life came to be shorn of many splendours. There was no question of any austerity, but the oriental extravagances of the past century grew into memories. Guests at Alexander's banquets were not given buttonholes in gold clasps studded with diamonds, and casual services were no longer rewarded by priceless snuffboxes.

About Christmas 1803, the Private Committee, its preliminary reports finished, was dissolved. Much had been suggested by the four men. A little had been achieved. Those were formative years, and the pulse of reform would continue beating for some time longer until the matter of Napoleon absorbed Alexander to the virtual exclusion of all else.

Already in the spring of 1803, dissatisfied with the progress made by the Ministry of War, the Emperor recalled Arakcheev from his exile at Gruzino in the Novgorod Province. The recall came in a brief personal note: 'Having need of you, I beg you to come to St Petersburg.' On arrival, 'the sergeant-major' of Gatchina was appointed Inspector General of Artillery, a most suitable nomination since Arakcheev was by far the best ballistic expert in the land.

It has often been argued that the results of those first years were far too meagre when weighed against the efforts gone to their making. Such an appraisal is unjust. The moral value of every deliberation was immense. Russia's former policy considered, the new approaches to many problems were examined with a zest which would not be wasted on the generations to come.

Historical conjecture is hardly ever profitable. None the less, it may well be argued that Napoleon's triumph and downfall moulded the history of Russia for the rest of the century. Alexander accepted the sceptre in the spirit of expiation for his share in his father's death. That total dedication to national purposes was abruptly broken by the accident of war. In the end, a ravaged and tired Europe claimed, as the Emperor saw it, his services and what energies still remained to him. It all ended in deep disillusionment. Home development was arrested, liberalism sank into hardened despotism, and the right idea of expiation was engulfed in a sea of neurotic pseudo-mysticism. In 1803, however, all that darkness lay in the future. If it had not been for Napoleon, such a deep night might never have fallen on Russia.

By far the most embarrassing part of Alexander's inheritance was the sorry condition of the imperial foreign policy. At the time of Paul's death, apart from the fantastic approaches made by him to the First Consul and to the Pope, Russia stood in a no-man's-land, Europe having all but despaired of seeing a clear policy emerge from the chaos. Much ground had to be cleared before Russia and Europe could come to some measure of understanding.

Panin was all for a closer rapprochement between Russia and Great Britain. The Emperor did not share his enthusiasm. The embargo on British imports was, however, lifted, and a trade convention signed by Panin and Lord St Helens. It pleased Britain when Alexander did not claim the dignity of the Grand Master of Malta, but there were no really friendly gestures from Russia. It was known that the young Emperor had no particular affection for England, though it is rather a moot point whether he believed in the story about Lord Whitworth's share in the conspiracy against the Emperor Paul.

Panin's recall bode no good for the future of Franco-Russian relations, though Napoleon, relying on secret reports from St Petersburg, hoped for much, relying, as he did, on the lack of harmony between the Emperor and his Vice Chancellor. Soon enough there came hints about Panin's possible dismissal, and Napoleon had no doubt that Russian policy would inevitably change. He even hoped that war might break out between England and Russia, and he sent Durocq to St Petersburg '*pour sonder le terrain*'. Durocq reported that there was nothing for France to hope for and nothing to fear from Russia. '*Le nouvel Empereur est très aimé parcequ'il fait tout ce qu'il peut l'être et qu' à gêne et la tyrannie, sous lesquelles on vivait sous Paul Ier, il a fait succéder une grande liberté.*' At his second audience, Napoleon's emissary hinted about the advantages likely to come to Russia if the late Emperor's friendly attitude were to be given a permanent basis. Alexander's reply was blunt. He desired nothing for himself or his Empire. '*Je ne veux que contribuer à la tranquillité de l'Europe.*' Durocq's conversations with the

Emperor's ministers were hardly more satisfactory. One fact only stood out clearly: Panin's hatred of France in general and of Napoleon in particular. As to the future of Russian policy, little could be affirmed except that the Emperor wished to remain at peace with all the Powers.

The affirmation was correct. All the utterances made by Alexander stressed the fact that he did not want to interfere in any European matters. Panin's gloomy prediction of the danger likely to face Russia if she kept outside the coalition against Napoleon and his repeated arguments in favour of a firm alliance with England irritated Alexander in the extreme. The gulf between the sovereign and his Vice Chancellor widened more and more. Czartorizky's remark that Panin was hateful to Alexander seemed amply justified. Politics apart, Panin's mere presence in the government was a reminder of the events of March 1801. Within a few months he was dismissed to the great pleasure of Napoleon and all the Franco-philes in Russia. Kotchubey stepped into Panin's shoes, and Alexander felt very confident about the appointment since Kotchubey shared his own views about a perfect neutrality.

At a meeting of the Private Committee, the Emperor declared that Russia stood in no need of alliances. 'The Empire wants no further conquests. Her area of victories should be on the home front—on the fields of order, thrift, justice, education, industry and trade.' Commercial treaties must needs be concluded. That apart, Russian interests were best served by a polite indifference to matters beyond her frontiers. At the moment, added Alexander, the horizon was not clouded. There could come no threat from either Turkey or Sweden since both had been weakened by the struggles of the preceding century.

Kotchubey did not win unanimous support. Czartorizky, for one, disapproved of a programme which, according to him, had '*l'incon-vénient de faire tomber dans la nullité le pays qui le suit trop à la lettre*', but this objection was icily received by the Emperor, though Kotchubey's colourless programme would not be followed in every detail. Negotiations with France continued, and 'a treaty of mutual confidence' was signed towards the end of 1801. But, for all the signing of documents, the end of those negotiations had one awkward moment. The tone of the letters written by the First Consul and by Talleyrand greatly displeased Alexander, who read

vulgarity into some of the sentences, and Kotchubey heard him say
to himself: 'Oh what bounders they are!'

The dream of a fruitful neutrality proved a house built of tissue
paper, and it collapsed in a few months.

Early in 1802 enlightened circles in St Petersburg were made
uneasy by the rumour of a projected alliance between Russia,
France and Prussia. A meeting of the Private Committee was
opened in a tautened atmosphere. Novossilzev asked the Emperor if
there were any truth in the rumour. Alexander's reply was most
ambiguous. A treaty with France having already been signed, he did
not see why it should not be framed into an alliance, nor were there
any grounds for the exclusion of Prussia. Novossilzev and Kotchubey were greatly perturbed. Kotchubey remarked that such a
step would inevitably create tension in Europe and possibly harden
the mood in England. Alexander dismissed the objections. He said
he was convinced that such an alliance would prove the surest
means towards putting a check on Napoleon's future intentions.
The members of the Private Committee could not be mistaken in
catching a note of obstinacy in the Emperor's voice, and the discussion died in an awkward pause.

Kotchubey would have been even more upset if he had known of
Alexander's immediate plans. The Emperor had already made all
the arrangements to meet King Frederick William III at Memel in
the following May. By a mere chance, Kotchubey discovered that
'le roi de Prusse avait écrit des lettres particulières à l'Empereur, dont
le ministère ici n'a eu aucune connaissance.' When the news of
Alexander's journey to Prussia became formally public, he told
Kotchubey that the visit to Memel was a purely private affair and
that no political issues would come under discussion. None the less,
Kotchubey and Czartorizky were commanded to accompany the
Emperor to Prussia.

Outwardly, the week spent at Memel had all the appearance of a
private occasion. Emperor and King spent whole days together.
There were reviews, concerts, balls and banquets, and the ladies in
attendance on Queen Louisa were amused to see that Alexander was
'bewitched' by their lovely mistress. But there was also much time
for talk. At the time Napoleon and Talleyrand were distributing
German territories, and Prussia hoped for the Russian approval of
her own acquisitions. The King's private secretary, Lombard,

tentatively approached Kotchubey, who refused to be drawn into any discussion under the pretext of having no instructions from his master.

At the end of the week, a tacit agreement was accomplished. Alexander and Frederick William, having known each other for precisely seven days, parted in such a warm climate of friendship that the chancelleries of Europe faced many a puzzled moment. Some wondered if Alexander's visit could have been arranged at Napoleon's instigation. Others talked quite freely about the magic of '*les beaux yeux*' of Queen Louisa. Alexander's intimates could not understand why within a brief week Prussia had ceased being a country and become a beloved person to Alexander.

The Memel interlude brought no advantages to Russia. They laughed in Paris at the platonic friendship between the Russian Adonis and the Prussian Venus. They did not laugh in London and in Vienna. In St Petersburg, Alexander's ministers all but wrung their hands at the delicately coloured futility for, on Alexander's return to Russia, there was no longer any talk about the projected triple alliance. On the contrary, the Emperor tried to allay his counsellors' anxiety and repeatedly assured them that he was committed to absolute neutrality. None the less, Memel would eventually bear its bitter fruit.

If any among Alexander's contemporaries had guessed at the compulsion behind the visit to Memel, they would hardly have ventured to record their surmises. In 1802 Alexander had not started his excursions into mysticism. But the entire matter of Prussia had gained in importance because of filial piety. Gatchina, 'the little Potsdam of the North', where not a stone but spoke of a dead man's devotion to the Prussian idea, was sacred to that man's son. A mood in which remorse played the major part had driven him to pay homage to, and form a friendship with, the grandson of a man idolized by Paul. Alexander's wife came from Baden, a country which had nothing to say to Prussia. No tie of blood existed between the Romanovs and the Hohenzollerns, but for Alexander there was another link, its call—an imperative. He had possibly expected some easement of conscience to spring from that friendship. We cannot tell.

The following year saw the worsening of the European situation, hostilities between Great Britain and France being re-opened.

Napoleon's perfidy in trampling down the terms of the Treaty of Amiens disturbed Alexander, who wrote to La Harpe that Napoleon seemed '*un des tyrans les plus fameux que l'histoire ait produit.*' By the end of 1803 Alexander's ambassador, Count Markov, left Paris, and d'Oubri became *chargé d'affaires.*

The murder of the Duc d'Enghien was an ominous landmark. De Maistre wrote from St Petersburg in April 1804 that public feeling against the French had risen to a peak. '*Les bonnes Impératrices ont pleuré. Le Grand Duc [Constantine] est furieu, et sa Majesté Impériale n'est pas moins profondément affectée. . . . On ne reçoit plus la légation de France . . .*'

The situation went far beyond a purely social boycott. General Hédouville was asked to leave Russia and a note of indignant protest went to the Russian *chargé d'affaires* in Paris to be delivered to Napoleon. Talleyrand's reply was at once a personal insult and a libel on the British Government.

'*La plainte que [la Russie] élève aujourd'hui conduit à demander si, lorsqu'Angleterre médita l'assassinat de Paul Ier, on eût en connaissance que les auteurs des complots se trouvaient à une lieu des frontières, on n'eût pas été empressé de les faire saisir. . . .*'[1]

The insult would never be forgiven. Alexander's reaction to the French reply was to break off diplomatic relations. A few days later the First Consul was proclaimed Emperor. The title was studiously ignored in the correspondence from the Imperial Chancery. The First Consul became 'General Bonaparte' *tout court.*

The shock of the rupture was followed by yet another '*bouleversement*'. Count Alexander Voronzov resigned from the Foreign Ministry, where he had not particularly distinguished himself. People named Novossilzev or Strogonov as his successor. The Emperor's nomination pulverized everybody: it was Adam Czartorizky.

---

[1] Here Talleyrand made use of a fantastic story about the British complicity in the murder of Paul. The facts were that Madame Zherebzova, née Zubova and sister of Catherine the Great's last lover, offered the use of her house to the conspirators in the autumn of 1800. Olga Zherebzova, a woman of great beauty and immense wealth, had for a time been mistress of Lord Whitworth, the British ambassador in Russia, whose debts she is supposed to have paid more than once. Lord Whitworth was given his passports in May 1800. There is not a shred of evidence that the liaison served for a screen to the conspirators or indeed that the knowledge of the plot had ever reached the British Embassy. But the French residents in St Petersburg and the home-bred Anglophobes did not fail to put two and two together in order to arrive at a total of five.

De Maistre wrote to his master, the King of Sardinia: '[he] will be omnipotent. He is arrogant and double-faced. . . . There is something truly repellent about the man. I gravely doubt that a Pole, born of a family known to have nursed ambitions for the crown, could ever be a good servant to a sovereign of Russia. . . .' Thus spoke a foreigner. His words were to prove prophetic. At the time, however, they would hardly have been heard for the anger of the Russian chorus. They did not care a button for Czartorizky's family ambition. They did care about his being a Pole, and everybody's hand was against him. They did not trouble to hide their feelings in his presence. Even the Empress Elizabeth, usually strictly neutral about government appointments, did not conceal her doubts about Czartorizky's integrity in accepting such a post. Elizabeth no longer spoke to her husband's friend or took any notice of him at public functions. The Dowager Empress was loudly indignant. 'You cannot possibly choose a Pole for such an office,' she is supposed to have said to her son, who replied: 'I have chosen a Pole, Madame.'

'*Des intentions mauvaises*', suspected by Elizabeth and others, were there indeed, and Czartorizky himself would later acknowledge that he accepted the high office for his private reasons. His secret plan was well matured: to make Russia enter the coalition against Napoleon and to labour towards the resurrection of the Kingdom of Poland within the boundaries in existence before the first partition. The plan would have involved the surrender by Prussia and Austria of such Polish lands as went to their share after each of the three partitions. Czartorizky dreamt of a future when the help offered by his countrymen to Alexander in the struggle against Napoleon would assure the only reward acceptable to Polish patriots—the return of their country's sovereignty—and he also dreamt of himself being elected to the throne of a new Poland. It was cynical, to say no more.

One reason behind the Emperor's choice once again points at the curious curve of piety which had driven him to Memel. There were few good deeds done by Paul, but his loathing of the Polish partitions, his generosity to the imprisoned Poles after his accession, his deep regrets that, because of the involvement of Prussia and Austria, he found himself unable to undo the wrong done by his mother, all of it together adds a few touches of light to the otherwise sombre landscape of his reign. The thought of a wantonly dismembered country haunted the son as much as it had haunted the father. In 1804 Alexander had no clear plan of action in his mind. Czartorizky's appointment was but a tentative step towards a road whose signposts were still to be erected, but it pleased every Polish patriot.

The rupture with France was a *fait accompli*. Novossilzev was sent to England on a mission of vaguely defined good will, but the British Government needed more than a declaration of good faith. The mission was virtually fruitless, and the mood in both Russian capitals made it obvious that Alexander's subjects thought the mission to have been a humiliating futility.

Prussia was still bound to France by the terms of her alliance. The Russian rupture with Napoleon disturbed Berlin. Yet, for all the fervent vows exchanged at Memel, King Frederick William did not dare to cause anger in Paris, and Alexander's suggestion that his armies should be given free passage through Silesia on their way to Moravia was met first by a few ambiguous replies and then by a refusal. Czartorizky, well aware of the Emperor's disappointment, assured him that it was all for the best.

The dream of 'absolute neutrality' was shattered for ever. Between November 1804 and April 1805, Russia made alliances with Austria, Sweden and Great Britain, and now stood definitely committed to the struggle. But Prussia still kept hugging the cloak of neutrality. In Czartorizky's opinion, war with Prussia seemed inevitable. Alexander ordered conscription—to the undisguised discontent of the landed gentry. One by one, the commanders received their orders. The total strength of the men under colours was just under two hundred thousand, and their disposition came as a proof that Prussia would have to pay a steep price for her obstinacy. A force of ninety thousand, commanded by Michelson, was sent to the western frontier of Russia, and a smaller contingent, led by Count Peter Tolstoy, left by sea from Kronstadt to threaten Prussia from the north. Fifty thousand men under Kutuzov were to march through Galicia and join the Austrian forces near the Bavarian frontier.

Czartorizky felt triumphant. '*Sa Majesté*' he wrote to Count Razumovsky in Vienna, '*est fermément décidée de commencer la guerre contre la Prusse . . .*' He went on to describe how deeply hated was the Prussian domination in Poland, and assured Razumovsky that '*on y recevra les russes à bras ouverts, les habitants coopéront de*

tous leurs efforts pour aider notre armée contre les Prussiens. . . .
L'armée russe sera nourrie et complétée avec la plus grande facilité et
de nouveaux corps pourront être formés. . . .'
It was all most romantic. Czartorizky knew—none better—that
even the prospect of shattering the Prussian yoke would not make
Warsaw receive the Russians '*à bras ouverts*', nor would Alexander's
forces have been at all happy at the idea of being complemented by
Polish volunteers.

Last-minute plans were being made at the Council table at the
Winter Palace, where Alexander's Foreign Minister himself had to
contend against a bitter and influential enemy, Prince Peter Dolgoruky. A sitting nearly ended in a storm when Dolgoruky remarked:
'By your leave, Prince, a little less of those Polish affairs. You are
still in the service of the Emperor of Russia.'

To the despair of Czartorizky's enemies, Alexander decided to
stay at Pulawy, the country seat of the great Polish family, on his
way to review Kutuzov's army in Moravia. Pulawy received him
royally. Prince Adam's mother 'enchanted' the Emperor. Step by
step, Czartorizky's first plan came to be unfolded, and General
Michelson was to be sent instructions for a march on Warsaw. But
neither Czartorizky nor his mother knew that Prince Dolgoruky had
already gone to Berlin to make the last attempt at dissuading the
King from his policy.

The attempt failed. It fell to Napoleon to administer the first
blow to Czartorizky's dreams. French forces invaded Anspach, and
Frederick William at once dispatched a courier to Pulawy with his
consent to the free passage of the Russian troops. In October
Alexander, greatly heartened by the Prussian's change of mind, left
Pulawy—not for Warsaw but for Berlin, there to use his most adroit
arguments and make his friend join the coalition. Circulars were
sent to all the generals with instructions to destroy any documents containing hostile references to Prussia and her King. The
idyllic days at Pulawy ended in a Potsdam melodrama. The earlier
intimacy between Alexander and Adam Czartorizky gave way to the
ordinary relationship between a sovereign and his minister. Their
easy, confident morning would never return.

In 1801 the Empress Elizabeth was twenty-one. She had then
been married seven years. She had borne and buried a child, and she

could not be sure if she would ever have another. The hurriedly arranged marriage, begun awkwardly enough, had brought her four and a half years of happiness during her father-in-law's reign, when her husband, overworked, frustrated and continually worried, found no assuagement except in her, when they were truly at one, all anxieties and hopes shared together. In those years the child-wife had grown into a woman, and her love for Alexander had entered a permanent harbour. She would neither excuse nor exaggerate his faults. She would never permit herself to measure his feeling for her by careful inches. She had proved to be not only a devoted wife but also a spirited and intelligent helpmeet during the events leading up to his accession. Her timidity and reserve rather warred against the public recognition of her qualities, and her self-effacement would deepen with the years.

In the summer of 1801 Elizabeth's mother, the Margravine of Baden, and her younger sister, Princess Amelia, arrived on a visit which could never have been planned during Paul's reign. The Margravine left. Princess Amelia stayed for good, a source of great comfort to the young Empress. She was lonely enough in that family. Her sister-in-law, Grand Duchess Anna, unable to endure the cruelties and vagaries of her husband, Grand Duke Constantine, returned to Coburg, and Amelia was the only one Elizabeth could cherish. Her husband's sisters remained aloof. The Dowager Empress spent all her time either at Gatchina or at Pavlovsk, and there could never be the least intimacy between her and the young Empress. Elizabeth did not complain. She had her husband.

She followed the Emperor from the Winter Palace to Tsarskoe Selo. She accompanied him on some of his excursions into the country, and for a short while it seemed as though the halcyon era begun on Paul's accession in 1796 would continue. All seemed in perfect accord between the husband and wife. Elizabeth rigorously abstained from all interference in state matters, but she welcomed the formation of the Private Committee and she warmly responded to the Emperor's enthusiasm for reforms. She endorsed all the economies in the household and herself suggested that her own Civil List should be cut down to about one-tenth of the customary amount.

She shared Alexander's dislike of all pomp and ceremonial. Compared with the preceding century, the Russian court was simplicity itself, etiquette whittled down to the minimum. None but intimates were received during the week. *La grande tenue*, which bored Alexander and intimidated Elizabeth, was observed only on Sundays and on great feasts. The austere appointments of the private apartments were a cause for caustic comment at Gatchina where the Empress Marie clung to the accustomed splendour with the zest of a young woman.

Yet barely within a year of Paul's death vague talk began floating in St Petersburg. Now one woman's name, now another, always mentioned in studied whispers, began to be coupled with that of the Emperor. It is impossible to say if any of it came to Elizabeth's knowledge at so early a stage. Her first '*cri du coeur*', sent to her mother at Baden, carried a date in 1803. Yet it is hardly conceivable that she had not guessed. In her maturity she must have learned that difficult truth about her husband, that there were '*plusieurs Alexandres*' and that one of them was a man whose sensual appetite was exercised with very little restraint. To that Alexander a woman's body was a drawer in a chest which he might shut or open at his will.

About 1802 the Saxon Minister reported to Dresden that it was rather difficult to determine whether the young Empress had any influence over her husband. 'She seems to have made it a rule never to interfere in any affairs. Yet it is far from easy to arrive at any conclusions: she appears so little in society and is known to very few.'

Elizabeth's greatest fault lay in her forbearance. Delicate from birth, an easy victim to fatigue, excruciating headaches and severe colds, she kept falling in with every plan of the Emperor, whose restlessness began to appear soon enough. In November 1801 Elizabeth wrote to her mother on her return to St Petersburg after one of those breathlessly arranged excursions into the interior. '*Nous sommes arrivés ici samedi soir après un rude voyage—ainsi n'en suis-je pas remise encore. . . . L'Empereur voulait absolument arriver le cinquième jour de sorte que nous n'avons fait que nous reposer quelques heures sur des chaises ou par terre, les lits n'arrivant pas avant le matin. . . .*'

Alexander went on those excursions because they pleased him and also because he was genuinely anxious to become acquainted with the country and the people. But purely social occasions infuriated him. During the 1803 Carnival Elizabeth had a most difficult time in persuading him that his presence was essential at some of the balls in the capital—'[il] *a un accès de paresse terrible pour le monde*', she wrote to her mother. When her arguments proved successful, Elizabeth had to contend with a wearying aftermath—'. . . *il faut entendre tout le lendemain des lamentations d'y avoir été. . . .*' In the spring of 1803 the Archduke Palatine of Hungary was coming for a visit. Alexander had no deep affection for his brother-in-law, but the Dowager Empress greatly looked forward to his arrival. Elizabeth supposed that the coming of the guest would somewhat '*rompre la vie monotone que nous menons quoique je ne crois pas que l'Empereur se mette fort en frais pour l'amuser . . .*'

It is odd to hear Elizabeth speak of monotony, since she had no hunger for the social whirl, and few were the ballrooms in St Petersburg which saw her. She was satisfied with little enough—provided she had Alexander.

It was precisely in 1803 that vague rumours retreated to give place to an ugly fact. Marie Naryshkina, born Princess Czervertinska, a beautiful Pole, with a courtesan's cunning and a harlot's outlook, had Alexander in her web and openly boasted of her victory. She was the wife of Leo Naryshkin, a man holding a court rank, an amiable nonentity, who provided a very convenient screen for her amusements. Society learned the news and was not particularly shocked. Elizabeth realized that except for her sister, Princess Amelia, and her ladies, she stood alone. She could expect no support from her mother-in-law, who had curried favour with her husband's mistresses.

The winter proved hard for the young Empress. In April 1803 she wrote to her mother: '*Je vous dirai en gros . . . que tout est comme cet hiver . . . qu'il faut bien de la patience . . . non pour persévérer dans mon opinion, qui est désormais inchangeable, mais pour supporter avec une certaine indifférence bien des choses qui me munéraient si je ne travaillais sans cesse mir es nicht zu Herzen zu nehmen. . . . Je me dis sans cesse qu'on est dans ce monde, non pas pour jouir, mais pour supporter, cependant je ne puis m'empêcher alors de trouver un peu injuste que je doive supporter seule la peine d'une chose dont la faute n'est certainement pas à moi seule. . . .*'

Elizabeth loved her husband with a heroic love. Neither questioning nor probing, she loved him not for what he was or what he was not, not for what he did or did not, but solely because he was and because his true signature, its virtues and vices so closely interwoven, was engraved upon her heart. Alexander was a man of great stature, but he was not great enough to merit such devotion, and Elizabeth unhappily never paused to reflect that the few years of their happiness had been built upon no normal foundation.

It was a public humiliation for her. Naryshkina had the entrée and was brazen enough to use it. At a court ball the young Empress steeled herself to inquire after the woman's health. Naryshkina's insolence was incredible. '*Elle repondit: "je crois que je suis grosse." Elle savait très bien que j'ignorais pas de quelle façon pouvait être sa grossesse . . .*' The Empress schooled herself to move away without a word of comment or a trace of anger. But the words, '*je ne sais ce que tout cela deviendra, et comme cela finira . . .*' point at a step taken towards despair.

Elizabeth knew Alexander was dedicated to a life of service. She knew that he won hearts wherever he went. She had lived long enough in Russia to realize that however indulgently society might regard the affair, the very nationality of the mistress spelt a danger to the Emperor's popularity. Had he continued his brief liaison with the feather-brained Countess Bobrinska, Elizabeth's humiliation would have been as sharp—but a Bobrinska would have been less harmful. A Pole was hateful in the eyes of the Russians.

Naryshkina continued to appear at court so long as her condition permitted. The Dowager Empress shrugged her shoulders at her daughter-in-law's reserve and dignity. Marie would have hastened to offer sympathy, blended with curiosity, if ever a rumour of a scene between husband and wife had reached her. But there were no scenes for an outsider to hear about.

Elizabeth, having lost her infant daughter and having all but given up the hope of having another child, must be the witness of her husband's anxiety over Naryshkina's labour, his relief when it was over, his joy at having a child. His behaviour beyond all excuse, Alexander should have become a stranger to her. But he did not. Elizabeth still regarded him as her husband, the man whom she hoped to see ascending a pinnacle one day. Nor, in so doing, did she think that she was sharing him with his mistress. No other woman might have of Alexander what she had, and what she had of him was left unused until he returned to her.

God alone knew, she confessed to her mother in a letter which might have been written in blood rather than ink, what she wanted most in this world. No plea based on religious principles would have answered the purpose. To the Emperor, religion meant little more than a sequence of boring observances to which he, being an anointed Tsar, must necessarily conform. Her own faith informed by a tranquillity which barred the way to all extravagant piety, Elizabeth could only pray that some such faith might one day be his. In her moments of leisure she allowed herself to weave a fantasy where Alexander once again came, love in his heart and in his look. *'Quand j'y pense, quand je bâtis sur cette chimère, ma première idée est celle du plaisir extrême que j'aurais à vous l'annoncer. . . .'*

In the summer of 1804 the Emperor desired her presence at the annual manoeuvres held at Krasnoe Selo in the neighbourhood of Tsarskoe. There, strangely enough, a little comfort came to the Empress. *'. . . avec son goût pour le militaire, [l'empereur] est dans son centre et quand je le vois content et de bonne humeur, cela me gagne bien vite . . .'* But the manoeuvres were over; Naryshkina came to her villa at Peterhof, and soon enough the world heard of her second pregnancy. *'Il y a mesure de patience qui surpasse les forces humaines . . .'* Elizabeth held herself aloof. On the rare occasions when Alexander came to see her, he confessed himself unable to understand the attitude she had taken. More than that: he mocked at her prudery. . . . *'l'Empereur est le premier à tourner en ridicule une conduite sage . . . il tient à ce sujet des propos réellement révoltants dans la bouche de celui qui doit veiller à l'ordre, aux moeurs, sans lesquels il n'y a point d'ordre . . .'* Her faithfulness to him forbade her to make light of the affair, to follow in her mother-in-law's steps and to shower favours and gifts on Naryshkina. *'Voilà ce qu'on ne peut pas comprendre et ce qui cause des reproches.'*

It could hardly fail to do so: Elizabeth's behaviour was a rebuke. She was scandalized by the servility of the hierarchy, none among whom had the courage to tell the Emperor that his treatment of the Empress was an insult to his office and his Christian profession.

Elizabeth could only wait. The head and front of all her anxieties, kept rigidly apart from the personal grief, lay in her constant fear lest the infatuation were to cripple the duty he owed to the state. She clearly saw the mistake of having Czartorizky sent to the Foreign Ministry. She could not quite gauge the sudden outburst of romantic friendship with the King of Prussia. She foresaw the coming of the gigantic struggle with Napoleon, and she dared not reflect upon its outcome.

She must wait in comparative solitude. In the winter, she no longer went to the Winter Palace. During the Emperor's frequent absences, she had a refuge of her own—a small palace on Kamenny Island where she would retire with Princess Amelia and her ladies-in-waiting. The Empress spent her days in sewing for the poor, writing letters, reading and praying. Her migraines grew more and more frequent. She still looked very beautiful, but those who knew her best could not but notice how rarely she smiled. '*Je suis extrêmement "noire" depuis quelques jours*', she once admitted to the Margravine and sometimes whole weeks would pass before the Empress put pen to paper again. Before Christmas 1804 she shed her reticence:

'*Il y a bien longtemps que je n'ai pu vous parler à coeur ouvert . . .*' In spite of the long interval, Elizabeth could not mention any change in her environment. The Emperor was away, but even if he were not, she could hardly expect him to come to Kamenny Island. '*Je ne sais si Amelie vous a écrit un événement qui m'a bien frappée . . .*' It was the death of Naryshkina's child, which did not greatly affect the mother but came as a staggering grief to Alexander.

'*. . . je plaignis l'Empereur de fond de mon coeur . . . la part que je prenait à sa peine me valut presque de la tendresse de sa part, mais pendant une quinzaine de jours seulement . . .*' It was a unique situation that the wife should have been the one person to comfort her husband after the death of his mistress's child. But that wife was Elizabeth.

The Margravine felt the time was come for her to help. A journey to Russia being out of the question, she suggested that she should put the case into a letter. She would not however write it unless she received her daughter's consent. Elizabeth withheld it. Not even her mother must be allowed to fight her battles for her and moreover '*je doute qu'une telle lettre aît de l'effet.*'

At the end of 1805 Naryshkina was absent for some time, and people of good will hoped that she would not return. They were later mistaken. None the less, at the beginning of 1806 Alexander and Elizabeth were reconciled. In November she bore her second and last child, Elizabeth, called Lizanka in the family. The care for the baby comforted the mother when the reconciliation came to an end.

Alexander's dichotomy comes into striking evidence in his liaison with a woman who satisfied his body as it pleased her, who deceived him and flaunted their relationship in a manner so vulgar as to belie her own exalted origin. It has sometimes been said that Elizabeth might have brought about her rival's downfall if she had been more energetic, more cunning, and far less pliant. But those who argued in this way forgot that the Empress did not consider Naryshkina as a rival. She was a woman her husband chose to sleep with. She was not the woman who lived for the Emperor, suffered with him, shared the burden of his undying remorse, and believed in his future as firmly as she believed in God. That belonged wholly to Elizabeth. If it did not lessen her grief, it certainly sustained her hope.

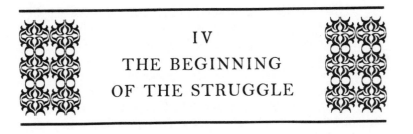

IV
THE BEGINNING
OF THE STRUGGLE

PUBLIC OPINION in Russia, however inarticulate its press, was certainly puzzled by Alexander's foreign policy. The negative results of Novossilzev's mission to England still rankled; the growing intimacy with Prussia promised little advantage, and alliances with Austria and Sweden increased the general anxiety. Hopes had been fixed on the improvement of home conditions. Now it looked as though the Empire were being sucked into the whirlpool of European commitments. The older generation, accustomed to Catherine's campaigns of conquest, were bewildered by the unaccustomed approach. The others were frank in their denunciations of any war. Britain, they argued, was Napoleon's chief enemy. Where did Russia's business lie? They put all their grievances together and blamed the Foreign Minister for a policy so patently running counter to the Emperor's earlier plans and so unpromising for the future of Russia.

Czartorizky himself, his secret hopes crushed, asked to be relieved from office, but Alexander refused to let him go. Even more: he insisted on Czartorizky accompanying him to Berlin in October 1805. There, King Frederick William at last allowed himself to be persuaded that Prussia's entry into the coalition promised well for Prussia's health. At the tomb of Frederick the Great, Emperor and King embraced each other and swore an oath of eternal friendship, Queen Louisa's gratitude bringing tears to Alexander's eyes. He would have liked to linger in that romantic atmosphere, but he had to hurry away from Berlin on receiving the news of Napoleon's victory at Ulm.

At Olmütz in Moravia Alexander met his new ally, the Emperor Francis I of Austria. The Russian headquarters were at Branau in the neighbourhood, and Kutuzov's men had no stomach for the war.

The services of the commissariat limped badly and the supplies promised by the Austrians were always coming the very next day. The men were often hungry, their boots were past cobbling, and their uniforms were in tatters. Many soldiers, having followed Suvorov into Italy, remembered the 'Austrian tricks' and looked upon Alexander's new allies as old enemies. There were some cases of desertion and much marauding. The Emperor's arrival certainly heartened the men but hardly to the degree of making them go into battle like heroes.

Conditions were even less promising at the headquarters. Kutuzov had led the army from Russia, but officially supreme command was not his, nor did the Emperor assume it himself. The Russian generals, particularly Miloradovich and Bagration, felt that they were paying for their Tsar's courtesy to the Austrians in very hard coin. Francis I was anxious to promote General Wehrother, a painstaking strategist on paper, who had about as much imagination as his own horse. With a map spread on the table and the army statistics learned by heart, Wehrother worked at a disposition for a major attack on Napoleon's forces already in occupation of Vienna.

Kutuzov's position was virtually untenable. He went as far as he could to insist that his men were in need of rest and sound equipment before they were fit for action. He pointed out that the scouts' reports were contradictory and that very little was known about the numerical superiority of the French and still less of Napoleon's intentions. But the Emperor Francis was determined to avenge Mack's defeat at Ulm and Alexander was equally determined to follow the Austrian lead. Many years later he would say, remembering the blunders of Austerlitz: 'I was young, I lacked experience. Kutuzov kept telling me that our plans were no good. He should have been more obstinate.'

An unimportant affair at Wishau turned the scales very slightly in the Allies' favour. To the Austrians' pleasure, out of all proportion to the gain, an attempt was made to open negotiations with Napoleon, and Peter Dolgoruky was sent to the French headquarters where Napoleon dubbed him '*un fréluquet impertinent*'. There could be no negotiations and on his return to Olmütz Dolgoruky reported his impression that the French forces were not as large as had been supposed and that their morale was rather low. The two Emperors at once met in a private session. Wehrother completed his disposition and it was read at an urgently summoned council of war. The reading took over an hour. Kutuzov fell asleep to Wehrother's voice droning on: '*Die erste Kolonne marschiert, die zweite Kolonne marschiert, die dritte Kolonne marschiert* . . .' None of the Russian commanders could follow the interminable German periods. No translations of the paper were made in time, and divisional commanders had received their marching orders before seeing the disposition.

The first mistake of the day happened during a movement of the Austrian cavalry. Headquarters having decided that the centre was sited at too great a distance from the right flank, the cavalry were ordered to move to the right flank to give better support to the centre. In so doing they barred the way to the advancing infantry. Within a bare half hour before the battle, Austrian and Russian commanders began accusing one another about the lack of synchronization.

The battle, begun at nine in the morning, was finished within two hours, the shortest and bloodiest engagement experienced by the Russians. It ended in a complete rout of the Allies. Kutuzov was wounded at the beginning and narrowly escaped a fatal shot before the end. Both Emperors had to flee for their lives. In the general confusion of horses and of men, the officers in attendance on Alexander were cut off from him. The Russians ran, flinging away muskets and ammunition. It was panic at its worst, and rumours ran that Kutuzov was either killed or taken prisoner and that the Emperor was fatally wounded.

There were some few fine moments that morning when men stopped thinking of themselves, their weariness and their peril, when two young standard bearers, wounded unto death, waited for their comrades to run up and take the colours out of their dying hands, or when the flower of the Russian cavalry galloped into the heart of the French ranks to cut off their envelopment of the Russian infantry, and out of fifteen hundred horsemen only eighteen returned. Yet even those fine moments were not enough to redeem the day doomed before it dawned. The regiments who turned and fled by no means shamed their oath. They were flung into a battle which should never have been fought and they could not be blamed if they did not understand what had not been understood by their commanding officers.

Bülow called Austerlitz '*eine sonderbare Begebenheit*'. The Allies adopted a plan against an enemy they could not see, they imagined him to occupy a position which was not his, and not in vain did Napoleon boast that out of some thirty battles Austerlitz was the easiest and most decisive victory he had won.

An uneasy truce was arranged between France and Russia, but Austria was plunged into more bitter waters by the Treaty of Preissburg. In Berlin, King Frederick William turned away from all the vows of eternal friendship with Alexander and sent a representative to Schönbrunn there to sign a treaty with his ally's enemy. The thirty pieces of silver came to be paid by the cession of Hanover which, belonging to Great Britain, was not for Napoleon to cede.

Alexander's youth was ended on the field of Austerlitz. The battle over, he was seen seated under an apple tree, his face buried in both hands. French cannon balls and bullets had indeed spared him. Not so the actuality of war. The whorls of crimson-grey dust stirred by the feet of running men, the acrid smell of gunpowder and the iron smell of blood, the shrieks of wounded horses and the groans of dying men, the chaos of a retreat when men forgot all things except the urge not to let their breath be stilled for ever, the recognition that experienced and loyal soldiers had it in them to turn into wild beasts—all of it was learned by Alexander that day. His tears were genuine enough. The carnage, the resultant rout, the bestial fear—all must needs be laid at his door. The apple tree witnessed a sincere enough outburst of compunction.

A little later someone brought a horse to him. Alexander rode to the nearest village where fever gripped him in the night. His doctor asked an orderly for a little red wine. None was to be had, and a messenger was sent to the headquarters of the Emperor Francis, whose steward refused the request since those who could sanction it were asleep and he dared not disturb them. The doctor got a few apples, squeezed their juice into a cup, and thus refreshed his patient. The story reached Russia in time and played its part in shaping the Russian conviction that Austerlitz was the consequence of Austrian perfidy, ineptitude and selfishness.

That day brought a rude awakening to Alexander. He had drawn his country into the coalition against France and made an alliance with Prussia—without reckoning the military potential of either friend or enemy. He had made friends with Austria, forgetting the harsh lessons of Suvorov's Italian campaign. He had declared that peace was his goal and tranquillity his banner. Austerlitz had taught him how heavy was the responsibility of a declared intention, and what he had learned would always remain with him.

The Emperor returned to Russia. He reached St Petersburg at dead of night, and wildly cheering crowds welcomed him. By morning, the Winter Palace Square teemed with men and women who had kept an all-night vigil. Alexander came out to them. Countess Strogonova remembered that '*on s'est jeté pour lui baiser les mains, les pieds, et même son habit.*' The nation was at his feet. The general feeling was that Kutuzov would have won the day had it not been for the Austrians. The disaster being firmly laid at the Austrian door, Russia began fêting the sovereign and his commanders. The vaster reaches of the struggle were still remote from the national consciousness, and many people were only too ready to interpret the truce in terms of peace.

Yet Alexander's family thought differently. From Gatchina the Dowager Empress sent a letter of ironic criticism. Grand Duke Constantine, back from the campaign, delivered himself of an unprintable verdict on the conduct of foreign affairs and the state of the army. Alexander's favourite sister, Catherine, his junior by some eleven years, endorsed their mother's judgment, and Marie followed her first letter by another urging Czartorizky's instant dismissal. She attributed the disaster to his policy. '*Vous vous rappelez de ma douleur profonde à sa nomination au ministère . . . à vous de juger . . . s'il est de l'intérêt de votre service de le laisser lutter contre des sentiments assez prononcés . . . ou s'il est plus utile de lui demander la retraite qu'il vous a demandée . . .*'[1]

---

[1] Grand-Duke Nicholas (*The Empress Elizabeth*, vol. I, p. 42) quotes from Czartorizky's memoirs a paragraph affording ample proof that suspicions against him were well founded. '. . . *les russes m'ont toujours soupçonné de vouloir faire pencher la politique de la Russie vers un lien intime avec Napoléon; cela était bien loin de ma pensée, car il m'était évident que toute entente entre les deux Empires ne pouvait manquer d'être contre les intérêts de la Pologne. . . . L'idée de son rétablissement se trouvait implicitement comprise dans l'ésprit même de mon travail et dans la tendance que je voulais donner à la politique russe.*' Such is the admission of Alexander's Foreign Minister. Cynicism could hardly reach further. Yet, in justice to Czartorizky, it should be remembered that his enthusiasm for the restoration of the Polish sovereignty had been sustained and encouraged by none other than Alexander himself in the early years of their friendship.

By the end of 1805 there seemed little for Czartorizky to do. He was universally hated and distrusted. He was surrounded by men who despised his nationality, hated his policy, and doubted his morality. Malice coupled his name with that of the young Empress, than which nothing could have been more preposterous.

Czartorizky had worked for a rapprochement with Great Britain and for a more fruitful alliance with Austria. England and Russia were indeed joined by the terms of a treaty, but Alexander seems to have inherited his father's mistrust of the British and, contrary to his Foreign Minister, the Emperor felt that England had taken her stand against Napoleon out of self-interest rather than from concern for Europe. The campaign of 1805 had proved Austria to have an odd idea of mutual obligations. There remained Prussia with its vacillating King and its Niobe of a Queen, and Alexander's solicitude for Berlin barred the way to any discussion, let alone action, about Poland. Czartorizky gradually came to the conviction that his country's *status quo* satisfied the Emperor. The Prince asked to be relieved from the burdens of an office where all liberty of action was denied him, and once again Alexander refused to let him go. The other ministers no longer troubled to conceal their antipathy. 'He is a man with but one idea in his head, and that idea is the crown of Poland,' they said of Czartorizky, and still the Emperor would not consent to let him go.

Alexander's absence had left Elizabeth '*désolée*' as she wrote to her mother in the autumn of 1805, '*à cause de la tendre amitié qu'il m'a témoignée ces derniers temps.*' She added that she had great hopes for better things in the future. She reconciled herself to wait at the small palace on Kamenny Island.

Alexander's return, however, shrivelled all the hopes she had cherished. He conformed to appearances and duly called upon her. Elizabeth moved to the Winter Palace and was present at the banquet given in honour of an imagined triumph over Napoleon. But Naryshkina was ready with her revenge for the attentions paid by the Emperor to the Empress earlier in the year. It was not enough for the mistress to make scenes in her own house. She threw away what little discretion she had, and '*l'affaire Naryshkin*' became the property of herring-women, rag-and-bone merchants and bakers in the capital. Unsavoury details seeped from one market place to another, and they helped to lessen the ardour felt for the Emperor's person—not out of condemnation, still less out of sympathy for an Empress they barely knew, but because the mistress belonged to a race hated by every Russian. 'Na-yazikié miod, pod yazikóm liod'— 'Honey on the tongue and ice under the tongue'—was the national idea about the Poles, formed during the centuries of struggle.

A diplomat in St Petersburg asserted that since the Emperor's return, '*la Naryshkine affiche son crédit et en obtient des preuves les plus marquantes, aussi tout ce qui brigue les honneurs de la cour est à ses genoux. . . . Cette galanterie qui afflige et tourmente l'impératrice . . . ne contribue pas moins que les étourderies si funestes d'Austerlitz, à diminuer la considération de l'Empereur, l'amour des russes, et cette éspèce de culte qu'on lui rendait généralement. . . .*'

The judgment is somewhat exaggerated. '*Les étourderies funestes*' of Austerlitz meant nothing to the nation at large, and the matter of Napoleon was still too remote to touch the Russian pulse. But the retention of an unwanted Foreign Minister was ascribed to the influence of the Emperor's mistress, and the sentimental abandon over Prussia was judged unworthy of Catherine's grandson.

So much had been hoped for in 1801, and something had indeed been achieved in the first five years, but the country was longing for the peace promised by Alexander. A war with Persia begun in 1804 seemed unnecessary. A new dispute with Turkey, which led to the Russian occupation of Moldavia and Wallachia, added to the burdens of taxation, and the novel involvement in European problems was taken to be a dangerous deviation from a course full of such brilliant hopes in 1801.

Alexander's waning popularity received yet another shock when in July 1806 King Frederick William decided to offer his friendship to Napoleon. The new alignment had no precedent in history: Prussia became an ally of France against Russia and remained an ally of Russia against France. All of it was explained by the expediency created in a difficult moment, but discontent in Russia turned to indignation, and Czartorizky was accused of currying favour with the French. He was at last allowed to resign, and Alexander chose Baron Budberg to succeed him. The Baron, according to Count Rostopchin, might have had just enough intelligence to manage the foreign policy of the Republic of San Marino. This amiable and painfully honest nonentity was now expected to hold his own against men like Fox, Talleyrand, Metternich and Hardenberg.

The Dowager Empress looked with deepening anxiety on her son's friendship with Prussia. She reminded him that his grand-father's worship at the Potsdam shrine had cost him his throne and his life, and she went on: '. . . *l'attachment de votre père pour cette même cour [Berlin] lui a été bien funeste, et le vôtre . . l'a été suffisam-ment jusqu'à ce moment.* . . .' But the letter led to nothing except an ambiguous answer about loyalty to one's friends. For all the crippled pledges, Alexander still believed in Frederick William and main-tained that the breaking of a single promise did not justify an ulti-mate rupture.

At the end of the summer of 1806 the King of Prussia had Harden-berg replaced by Haugwitz, whose *leit motif* was the aggrandizement of Prussia. Soon the idea of a North German Union appeared in the diplomatic sky. It was interpreted by all the German states as a step towards Prussian predominance. The Princes appealed to Alexander and the free cities turned to Napoleon for support. Before either Alexander or Napoleon could arrive at a decision, Frederick William brought matters to a crisis by sending an ultimatum to Paris. He demanded an immediate withdrawal of all French troops from Prussia and a negative answer to the appeal made by the free cities. The King, assuring himself of Alexander's support, imagined that he could bluff Napoleon with impunity. Napoleon at once called his bluff. The Prussian armies were routed at Iena and Auerstädt, within a week the Kingdom of Prussia was shattered, and at the end of October Napoleon entered Berlin, the King and his family fleeing to the eastern borders of Prussia.

Of all the Russian ministers, Budberg alone considered that it was essential to go to Prussia's aid, and for once the nonentity showed an amazing sagacity. The uneasy truce which had followed Austerlitz was torn like a piece of worn silk. The threat to Russia's western provinces became markedly less distant, and Prussia was her nearest neighbour.

Yet there were delays. The army held in battlefield readiness since 1805 still lacked a supreme commander. Arakcheev could hardly have been chosen. Kutuzov should have been, but his lack of sympathy for Prussia and even more the Emperor's dislike of him decided against the only prudent nomination. There were two elderly generals, Field Marshals Kamensky and Prozorovsky, their fame won in Catherine's Turkish campaigns. Both had long since retired. Prozorovsky was nearly blind, and Kamensky suffered from so many ailments that he could not remember their number. One of them prevented him from riding. There were also men like Bagration, Miloradovich, Barclay, Benningsen and Bukhshoevden. Bagration's heroic stand at Austerlitz had fully proved his quality, but the Emperor chose to call on Kamensky. The ailing old gentleman succeeded in reaching the headquarters, took to his bed, and gave up the command within seven days, having created enough chaos to last for seven months. Benningsen was then given the command hungrily desired by Bukhshoevden. In Paris, they laughed at the cartoon on '*la marche précipitée de l'armée russe volant au secours des Prussiens*', with Frederick William, the crown falling off his head, flying through the air, hands outstretched—'*Venez, venez à mon secours,*' and Benningsen riding a crab, followed by the Russian army mounted on tortoises.

But there was no laughter in St Petersburg. Nobody wanted that war, and all would have endorsed the Empress Marie's anger. '*Il est certain,*' she wrote to her son, '*que vous avez repris les armes pour aider et finalement pour sauver la Prusse, mais il n'en est pas moins vrai non plus que, par cette série de circonstances, nous avons vu nos frontières menacées et que vous avez été obligé à demander à votre nation des secours considérables et inconnus jusqu'à ce moment dans les annales de la Russie. Il faut donc que dans votre marche politique, vous persuadiez la nation que vous n'agissez que pour sa gloire et son repos, et que l'influence prussienne n'existe pas . . .*'

The Empress Marie was wrong. All personal considerations apart, there was every reason for the Russian support of Prussia at the moment. No peace having been made with France, it was imperative for Russia to be on the defensive. Napoleon penetrated into Prussian Poland and made a solemn promise at Posen to take the Poles under his protection. He was also inciting the Turks to attack Russia's southern provinces.

Not 1812 but 1806 saw the first effort to rouse the national consciousness to the immediacy of a peril outside the gates. Over 600,000 recruits were mustered, and the Holy Synod published an extraordinary proclamation meant to stir up the masses.[1] The proclamation, ordered to be read aloud in every parish church of the

[1] Full text in Schilder, op. cit., II, 156.

Empire, spoke of Napoleon as 'the chief enemy of mankind, who worships idols and whores. . . . He has summoned the Synagogue and has established the Sanhedrin in Paris. . . . Now he is contemplating the reunion of all the Jews in the world . . . to use them for the destruction of God's church. . . . There is yet an even more dreadful crime, surpassing all the others in wickedness, to be laid at his door: he intends to proclaim himself as the Messiah. . . .'

This extraordinary invective should be interpreted in the light of the Russian mentality. Judaism, to a Russian peasant, stood for the greatest crime known to a Christian: the betrayal of Christ. The entire race was condemned for all time in the person of Judas. A nation had to be moved to anger against an enemy whose armies devoured distances with the rapidity of a starveling given a loaf, and the surest means of achieving the purpose lay in linking Napoleon with the ancient enemy of all Christian folk, a Jew and the Devil being bedfellows in the peasant mind.

The proclamation being read, the peasants understood that a conflict had started, with Satan as the chief antagonist, but in their opinion the anointed Tsar could wrestle with all the devils in the world and not be bested by them. Therefore, it was legitimate to grumble at the sudden and speedy recruitment. In the country, landowners complained about the sacrifices demanded of them, and the drawing rooms of both capitals echoed to the repetition of 'nous avons tort de faire la guerre pour le roi de Prusse.' Briefly, the war was most unpopular.

In February 1807 Benningsen met Napoleon at Preussisch-Eylau. It was no battle but a shambles, costing twenty-six thousand Russian lives, but Benningsen's lines remained unbroken, even in retreat, which should not have been necessary, his forces being superior to the French, and which enabled Napoleon to boast of a victory he had not really won.

In April Hardenberg, recalled by King Frederick William, and Budberg hammered out the terms of a new treaty between Prussia and Russia. They also drew up a draft of a convention. They planned to end the Union of the Rhine and to found a constitutional federation of German states under the joint leadership of Prussia and Austria. Territorial gains were promised to Britain and to Austria if they signed the Bartenstein Convention. Russia asked nothing for herself. Austria hesitated. Canning decided that such a step would lead to the eventual supremacy of Prussia. In the end, there were no signatories to the Bartenstein Convention.

None the less, the document did not speak in accents of romantic diplomacy. Its moral value lay in the fact that, though 1806 could be considered the most brilliant twelvemonth for Napoleon, though Prussia was crushed and Russia counted but a single uncertain victory to her credit against 'the world's enemy', yet there still remained room for constructive thought and for discussions of a future unmapped by Napoleon's will. In that sense, at least, the Bartenstein Convention, unsigned and rapidly forgotten, was not altogether Dead Sea fruit.

The Emperor showered honours on Benningsen after Preussisch-Eylau, but every officer and private in the Russian army considered the battle to be but another defeat. Grand Duke Constantine's outburst at the end of the retreat was echoed by many: '*il valait mieux que l'Empereur ordonne que chaque soldat charge son fusil et se tue lui-même. . . .*'

Both Benningsen and Bukhshoevden, for once in accord, suggested a respite, but Alexander knew there was no time. On a day in June 1807, at Friedland, Napoleon gained a decisive triumph. The Russians had to fall back to the east bank of the Niemen, Königsberg fell, and the whole of Prussia was in the hands of the French.

Benningsen's men were tired and their morale did not stand very high—which could explain the defeat of fifty thousand Russians at the hands of an enemy whose strength was about half of theirs. Benningsen, having been too hopeful, gave way to despair, but the Emperor did not reproach him. Prince Lobanov-Rostovsky was sent to Napoleon at Tauroggen to open truce negotiations. From Olita, Benningsen's headquarters, Prince Kourakine wrote sadly to the Dowager Empress at Gatchina: '*Jamais notre situation n'a été plus critique. . . . En faisant la paix, si on peut y parvenir encore convenablement, il ne peut être question par malheur d'autre chose que de la faire la moins onéreuse que possible . . .*' Kourakine said nothing about the instructions given by the Emperor to Prince Lobanov-Rostovsky. He may not have known about them.

Those instructions were in the nature of a somersault. Prince Lobanov-Rostovsky was to assure Napoleon of Alexander's sincere desire that 'the closest alliance between us might atone for the disasters of the past. I am convinced that such an alliance alone can guarantee happiness and tranquillity to Europe.'[1]

Those words were written a fortnight after Friedland. An alliance from which Alexander would have recoiled in 1805 became a necessity of the hour in 1807.

The change could hardly have been brought about by the reverses of the two brief campaigns. Neither Austerlitz nor Friedland had exhausted the Russian war potential. The instructions given to Lobanov-Rostovsky meant a departure from the policy adopted by all the Russian statesmen in the preceding century. Again, the change in Alexander's attitude can hardly be explained by a desire to smoothe down the discontent in Russia by the conclusion of a speedy peace. Neither Budberg nor any of his ministers could have advised the Emperor on such a course of action. It was a gigantic private gamble of his own—to gain a little breathing space, *'reculer pour mieux sauter,'* with nobody, not even himself, foreseeing the time or the nature of the future leap.

As will be seen later, Tilsit did not afford any real proofs of Alexander's change of heart. He came to that meeting, calmly determined to stave off the approaching menace to his own frontiers, to help in so far as it was possible his dispossessed ally of Prussia, to take his own measure of Napoleon, and then, a little time gained, to return to Russia where matters of great importance were awaiting him.

The first words exchanged at the meeting appeared to draw the two men together. 'I hate the British no less than you do and I am ready to assist you in any undertaking against them,' said Alexander, and Napoleon replied: 'If such be the case, then everything can be settled between us.'

Once again we are faced by a palpable contradiction. There is Alexander's desire to see 'a quietened Europe' and his readiness to join Napoleon in the extension of the struggle against his enemy in chief. With all his dislike of Britain, Alexander could never have thought that its total destruction would contribute to the European peace. But to Alexander, words were like chessmen, each move to be made with the utmost deliberation. He spoke to convince Napoleon. The words used were no more and no less than paving stones for

[1] cf. Schilder, op. cit., II, p. 179 and p. 292.

the negotiations. Their purport would indeed be embodied into the clauses of the secret treaty. Their immediate purpose was to throw a pontoon bridge across a gulf, and there Alexander succeeded.

The behaviour of some among Alexander's subjects might have caused embarrassment. At Tilsit the French were ready enough to be polite to the Russians, but the officer commanding one of the most famous Guards regiments, Count Michael Voronzov, pretended to be ill and would not cross the Niemen. It was necessary to issue an order of the day admonishing the men 'to be civil to the French' and to remember Napoleon's imperial title. They were strictly forbidden to use the name 'Bonaparte'. But the regimental chaplains still had their copies of the Synod proclamation where the Emperor of the French was designated as the servant of Satan and the worshipper of whores and idols. Much pleasure was felt by the Russians on seeing King Frederick William, whom they considered to be the author of their misfortunes, treated rudely by Napoleon.

It is true that Alexander exclaimed, the first meeting over, '*Que ne l'ai je vu plus tôt! Le voile est déchiré et le temps des erreurs est passé,*' but the words were spoken for the benefit of several eyewitnesses and Alexander's private letters written from Tilsit carry much more conviction. He had indeed been curious to meet Napoleon, but it was inevitable that to a man of Alexander's antecedents and upbringing much would have appeared unpleasing in someone shaped by fortune rather than by inheritance. The Emperor wrote to his sister, Grand Duchess Catherine: '*Dieu nous a sauvés . . . nous sortons de la lutte avec une sorte de lustre. Mais que dites-vous de tous ces événements? Moi, passer mes journées avec Bonaparte, être des heures entières en tête-à-tête avec lui. . . .*' The little word '*moi*', written in italics, colours the whole letter, and the Emperor may well have written it with his mouth curved in disgust. He used even greater candour when writing to his mother:

'*Heureusement que Bonaparte avec tout son génie, a une côté vulnérable. C'est sa vanité, et je me suis décidé à faire le sacrifice de mon amour propre pour le salut de l'Empire.*' This was a reply to Marie's letters against a war fought to save the chattels of the King of Prussia. Alexander had gauged his opponent unerringly, and that was an advantage his countrymen did not see at the time. He freely recognized Napoleon's genius as a commander—but '*le métier militaire*' was not enough to assure a permanent global victory, and '*c'est le seul métier connu par Bonaparte.*'

For all the grave matters involved, there lingers a touch of Ruritanian operetta about those days in Tilsit. The sumptuously appointed raft in the middle of the Niemen, the glitter of gold uniforms and gay plumage in the grey streets of a little town, its history begun and ended in those June days of 1807, drums beating and banners flying, meals served on gold plate, grandiloquent speeches, even the tearful dignity of Queen Louisa—all this formed a theatrical setting. None of it could quite erase the newness of Napoleon's imperial title and make the Russians forget that the name of Bonaparte had not yet earned a dynastic significance. The acquired could not reach the level of the inherited.

Napoleon mistook Alexander's charm for simplicity. A Hohenzollern and a Habsburg having been crushed, it might well be the future turn of a Romanov if such a contingency should arise. For the moment, Napoleon did not see it. His vanity was deeply satisfied by all the elaborate courtesies paid by Alexander, and Napoleon could not have believed that in the Russian's mind the idea of the ever-increasing power of France was already irreconcilable with the safety of his own Empire. There was no insincerity in what he said to his Prussian allies: 'At last we do gain time. Napoleon may yet ride to his fall. I am your friend and I mean to prove it some day.'

In 1810 Bonaparte would complain to Prince Kourakine: '*Pourquoi l'Empereur Alexandre a-t-il rejeté à Tilsit le premier plan que je lui ai proposé?*,' which was no more and no less than a division of the world between them. During those long *tête-à-tête* meetings, the discussion touched at all the points of the compass, and some of the topics almost suggest that Napoleon's need of Alexander was greater than Alexander's of him. The idea that it was time to finish with Turkey, the urge to occupy Finland so as to ensure safe coverage from the possible Swedish threat in the future, the offer of Jerome Bonaparte's hand to Grand Duchess Catherine, all these and more were tempting titbits spread out by Napoleon the deeper to establish an alliance he needed.

Early in July 1807 '*le traité de paix et d'amitié*' was drafted. Budberg had no part in it, Napoleon objecting to his German origins, nor was a Prussian representative invited to take part in the preliminaries. Princes Lobanov-Rostovsky and Kourakine met Talleyrand.

King Frederick William had part of his dominions restored to him, but he lost all the lands on the left bank of the Elbe as well as his Polish possessions, and had to pay an indemnity of forty-one million thalers. Mindful of the promise he had given at Posen, Napoleon succeeded in creating a new Duchy of Warsaw, its crown to be given to the King of Saxony. Danzig was declared a free city, and the kingdom of Westphalia, carved out of Prussia, was given to Jerome Bonaparte. On Alexander's insistence, the Dukes of Coburg, Mecklenburg and Oldenburg were given back their territorial possessions. Bialostock Region went to Russia, and the Emperor pledged himself to conclude a truce with Turkey and to withdraw his forces from Moldavia and Wallachia. The most difficult clause of all embodied Russia's adherence to the Continental blockade. '*Le Traité de Paix et d'Amitié*' was duly published. Another document, kept secret, set out the terms of an alliance between Russia and France against Great Britain.

When the clauses are examined one by one, it becomes rather difficult to understand Alexander's assertion that '*nous sortons de la lutte avec une sorte de lustre.*' The latter would come later, but in 1807 there was not much evidence of it. Bialostock Region was not needed by Russia and its cession would soon enough shape its own difficulties. The creation of an artificial duchy in the heart of Poland did not satisfy the Poles and led to a host of complications. The truce with Turkey was made at another's dictation. The necessity to join the blockade and even more so the secret alliance against England were thick with dangers likely to cripple Russia's economy, to mention but one of the risks.

Tilsit was no more than a very uncomfortable cross-roads, but it gave Alexander some breathing space, and the hours spent with Napoleon would serve the Russian purposes in the years to come.

But Alexander's subjects did not think so. The Emperor returned in July. There were no excited crowds to welcome him. The peace manifesto was published and the nation answered by a sullen silence. In August Napoleon sent General Savary to represent him in St Petersburg, and the unfortunate man found himself ostracized on every side. The Emperor kept inviting him to dinner in the hope that some members of the imperial family and others might follow the example and ask Savary to break bread at their table. But the Dowager Empress closed her doors and Grand Duke Constantine was supposed to have said that he would rather see a convict seated at his table than a hanger-on of Bonaparte's. In September 1807 the Guards returned to St Petersburg and disembarked at Vassily Island. A gloomy crowd watched them leave the troop ships. Nobody waved a hand or sent up a cheer. Tilsit stood for a humiliation the Russians found hard to swallow.

The Swedish Minister, Count Stedingk, reported to his King that the discontent against the Emperor was growing most alarmingly. The merchants were quick to assess the disastrous consequences of adhering to the blockade. The landed gentry still grumbled about the last recruitment and fulminated against the taxes. The immediacy of danger from a French attack was scornfully discounted on all sides. According to Stedingk, those standing closest to the Emperor were almost in despair at his swiftly ebbing popularity. 'Les propos que l'on entend de toute part sont effrayants . . . dans les sociétiés particulières et même dans les assemblées publiques on s'entretient souvent d'un changement de règne . . .'

It might be argued that Stedingk lived in St Petersburg and gathered all his knowledge from there and that St Petersburg was but one city in a vast Empire. Be it remembered that opinion as such existed nowhere else in Russia. The national barometer rose and fell according to the rhythm dictated by the northern capital. In the hundred years preceding Alexander's accession it was always St Petersburg—and not Moscow—that created a climate most favourable for conspiracies and palace revolutions, and the skies went particularly dark towards the end of 1807. The imperial family consisted of Alexander, the two Empresses, three Grand Dukes, two of whom were aged eleven and nine respectively, and the Emperor's sisters, one of whom, Catherine, newly married to Prince George of Oldenburg, was named in some drawing rooms as a likely successor to her brother. Failing her, no other Romanov would have won the allegiance of the Guards.

The Emperor was well aware of the discontent. In his memoirs Savary quotes some words of Alexander to prove it, and it should be remembered that Napoleon's emissary, debarred from shaping any social links, would hardly have arrived at an independent judgment of the situation. The Emperor was determined to make his family and the people see Tilsit as he saw it.[1]

'*Je pousserai la Russie vers la France tant que je pourrai. Ne voyez pas l'intention dans quelques misérables dont je ne me sers point et qui sont trop lâches pour entreprendre quelque chose. J'aime mes parents beaucoup, mais je règne et je veux que l'on ait pour moi des égards. Vous voyez . . . que j'ai bien de la confiance en vous, puisque je vous entretiens de l'intérieur de ma famille . . .*'—a startling admission for Alexander to make, but a true one: the centre of the discontent was at Gatchina where the Dowager Empress had convinced herself of a doom soon to fall on her son's Empire. The Empress Elizabeth, now living in a virtually unbroken retirement, was herself taken aback by the Tilsit interlude; but she kept faith in her husband, even though she wondered and wanted to know, as she wrote to her mother, '*quelle est la magie dont il se sert pour métamorphoser les opinions si subitement et à tel point,*' but such a question might be asked in private only, and Elizabeth was justified in deploring the behaviour of her mother-in-law who, the first to start the discontent, saw to it that the ripples spread more and more widely. '*Elle a réussi à ressembler à un chef de fronde. Tous les mécontentements qui sont en très grand nombre se rallient autour d'elle. . . . Il y a des moments où ce bon Empereur me parait trahi et vendu par sa propre famille.*'

Nor was Alexander any more fortunate in the circle of his old intimates. The friendship between him and Adam Czartorizky was shaken for good. Paul Strogonov was sent by him to London, and Novossilzev, too, had gone abroad. Kotchubey alone remained.

Budberg's sojourn at the Foreign Ministry was a brief one, and gossip insisted that Alexander dismissed him to please Napoleon. The successor was Count Nicholas Roumiantzev, hated for his Franco-mania and despised for his poor intelligence. The unexpected appointment of Arakcheev to the War Ministry caused waves of consternation throughout the entire army.

---

[1] cf. Schilder, op. cit., II, 299.

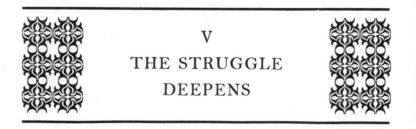

V
THE STRUGGLE
DEEPENS

IN THE seventh year of his reign, Tilsit having assured him at least some semblance of tranquillity, the Emperor once again became absorbed in home problems. The Private Committee had been dissolved in 1803, but the projects discussed in a small room at the Winter Palace had not been altogether sterile. Something had been achieved. Much more remained to be done—chiefly in the field of judicature.

During the five years between Tilsit and the thunders of 1812, two men were to exercise their influence on the course of Russian home policies, establish themselves in their sovereign's confidence, and influence him by the ideas they had to offer. With Speransky, whose sun was to set so abruptly and tragically within five years, it seemed as though the morning of the reign were about to return. For all the mistakes he made, the man deserved well of his country. A genius in his own field, his services should have become a happy permanence. Arakcheev's activities little by little began foretelling the midnight of Alexander's reign. Appointed Minister of War to deal with the limited problem of reorganizing Russia's military strength, rudely shaken after the two campaigns, Arakcheev became an odious permanency. Alexander's decree that Arakcheev's orders were to be considered as binding as his own spread deep gloom not only among the army but also in civilian circles. A sadistic bully and a coward, Arakcheev had withdrawn from the front line at Austerlitz on the plea that the sight of a battlefield was too much for his 'sensibilities'. The latter, however, in no way prevented him from weaving a web of callousness and brutality from his armchair at the War Ministry.

The two men, having nothing in common between them, might be said to represent the entire Russian Government at the time.

Arakcheev hated Speransky, who committed the mistake of answering the odium by his contempt for 'the Gatchina sergeant-major'. Arakcheev envisaged the life of the Empire under the conditions of a vast military camp. Speransky's vision of a reformed, constitutionally healthy Russia carried him nearly a century beyond his generation. It looked as though the deep-rooted duality in the Emperor was satisfied by having those two men in his service at one and the same time.

Michael Speransky, a priest's son, was born in 1772 in a village in the Vladimir Province. The Russian clergy forming a more or less hereditary caste, he was sent to Kiev Seminary. So great and obvious was Speransky's promise that at the age of eighteen he was teaching mathematics at the Theological Academy in St Petersburg. About 1793 a happy chance brought him to the notice of Prince Kourakine, who persuaded the Empress Catherine to have Speransky released from the obligation to take orders given by him on entering the Seminary. Speransky became Kourakine's secretary. His brilliant ability to go to the heart of a complicated administrative problem, his titanic capacity for work, his zeal in filling up the lacunae left by the Seminary education, his modesty, occasionally brushed by servility, all served Speransky in good stead. At the accession of Alexander, the might-have-been cleric of twenty-nine was spoken of as a coming man in the highest circles. In 1803 Kotchubey had him join the Ministry of the Interior, and soon enough Speransky became his chief's right hand.

Married to an Englishwoman, living most modestly in a small flat, Speransky considered each promotion in terms of incentive to harder and still harder work. He would have been welcomed in every important drawing room, but he had no leisure for society. He should have allowed himself some time to study the social currents and cross-currents of the day, to gauge the drift of the inevitable opposition to his work and, finally, to protect himself against Arakcheev's malice by according him a certain measure of confidence. Speransky did none of those things. He devoted what free time he had to studying history, philosophy and political economy. Obliged to appear more and more frequently at the Winter Palace, he never succeeded in becoming a courtier, never interested himself in any factions or rivalries. His single-mindedness was phenomenal for those days.

Speransky's crowning opportunity came in 1805 when, during an illness of Kotchubey's, it fell to him to present the Ministry reports to Alexander. Kotchubey having acquainted the young man with some of the bold projects initiated by the Private Committee, Speransky's imagination, brilliantly supported by his extensive studies, saw nothing fantastic in the grandiose sweep of radical reforms. His attitude carried a contagion the Emperor could not escape. By 1806 Speransky, now Minister of Justice, was indispensable. Alexander's benevolence increased after Tilsit, when, among the general discontent and criticism, Speransky showed himself an admirer of Napoleon and a defender of the treaty. It pleased the Emperor to listen to a minister with enough vision to look towards the future, confidence rather than despondency informing his words.

Napoleon's empire, according to Speransky, was certainly a reaction following the excesses of the revolution, but it could not be regarded as an absolute return to the ancient pattern. 'His conquest of Germany,' Speransky said to the Sovereign, 'has dealt a death-blow to feudalism, and may yet be taken as the beginning of a movement towards the liberty of German states,' an opinion which would hardly have been endorsed by Hardenberg or Metternich, but whose boldness appealed to Alexander, who said to Prince Alexander Golitzin that Speransky would prove one of the most valued collaborators.

In 1807 Speransky was invited to submit a detailed draft of administrative and judiciary reforms. The following year he accompanied the Emperor to Erfurt, was greatly impressed by Napoleon, and had many conversations with Talleyrand. Apart from this brief interruption, Speransky was engrossed in the task committed to him. A commission for the revision of laws was appointed, two French experts being invited to act as corresponding members. The existing Ministries were radically reformed and their number slightly augmented. Little by little, all the administrative branches came under Speransky's scrutiny.

In 1809 he presented his great 'Plan', the *opus* being commanded and carried out in absolute secrecy. The text would not be published for several decades. There is no record left to tell us of the Emperor's personal reaction to the document. The basic ideas expressed by Speransky were in harmony with all that had been hoped for in

1801. The document remains as a heroic feat of a man whose service to the Tsar and the country remains to this day his defence and his acquittal.

From the very first pages Speransky stressed the fact that absolute power in the hands of one man warred against the development and well-being of the state.

'Already during the reign of Tsar Alexis[1] there existed a feeling that absolute power should be limited. . . . Peter the Great had no clear intention of giving absolute freedom to Russia . . . none the less, the way was prepared by giving opportunities to commerce and education. The foundations laid by Peter the Great were so firm that on accession of the Empress Anna[2] in 1730, the senators knew themselves to be in the right when demanding political recognition from her. . . . The attempt was premature and a court intrigue wrecked it. . . . Means can be found to make the basic laws of the state inviolable for all, not excluding the person of the Monarch. . . . No government should be recognized unless the will of the whole nation accords the recognition. . . . The despotic form of government can be permissible only during the infancy of a society. . . . The power of the government should be counterbalanced by the power of the people . . . a government should have no other authority than that entrusted to it by the nation. . . . All property should be heritable. . . . All public offices should be subject to election. . . . Today, there are two estates in Russia: slaves of the crown and slaves of the landowners, and the former are free only in relation to the latter. . . . In reality, nobody is free with the exception of vagrants. . . . All national energies are being atrophied by the interrelationship of the two estates. . . . Landowners expect complete submission from peasantry. The latter expect the like submission of landowners to the crown. . . . In such a way, Russia is wasting her strength in a fruitless struggle. . . . A great state should have a Crassus as well as a Julius Caesar. . . . Abolition of serfdom will be a very difficult task, but the public conscience should be made to acknowledge—without much delay—that serfdom is a condition warring against common sense, to say the least, and that its evil should be uprooted.'

[1] Alexis, the second ruler of the Romanov dynasty (1645-1661) and father of Peter the Great.

[2] Niece of Peter the Great, widow of the Duke of Courland; succeeded Peter's grandson, Peter II.

Speransky went on to suggest the Council of State should be the unifying Government organ, that Ministries should concern themselves solely with administrative matters, and that the Senate should be the highest juridical body in the Empire. He also thought that a Duma should be founded 'as a legislative assembly, its members elected from over the Empire', and that no new law should be passed without a majority vote of the Duma.

The paper was a draft. The country knew nothing of it. It went into the Emperor's private archives. It was a startlingly new departure, but it had many defects. Speransky was born in the country, but the conditions of the countryside were not well known to him. He did not allow enough scope for the transitional period between autocracy and national representation. Yet, all the defects notwithstanding, the sweep of Speransky's ideas is breath-taking. When, in 1810, Finland was annexed to Russia and Alexander granted it autonomy, Speransky went with him for the opening of the first Diet at Borgo. The instrument of the constitution was the work of his hands and it proved a triumph.

There were not to be many more of them. In 1809 Speransky, then at the very height of his power, succeeded in passing two comparatively unimportant laws which led to grave consequences. The first decreed that men holding a court rank and exempt from any duties to the state were now compelled to serve either in the army or in the administration. That provoked the first storm against Speransky. The other law made promotion in the civil service dependent on the length of service and on academic qualifications, and men who had not been to a university had to undergo examinations. The bureaucratic ant-hill was roused to fury. Was it necessary to construe Horace and Virgil and to read Montesquieu to ascend another rung of the ministerial ladder, the civil servants asked one another. At the War Ministry, Arakcheev heard of the murmurs and they pleased him.

In August 1809 the Emperor's carriage was overturned on the way to Peterhof. His left leg badly hurt, he had to keep to his room for nearly a month. In St Petersburg they heard that Speransky alone had daily access to the Sovereign and that sometimes their private sessions lasted for hours. Speransky's enemies began making plans for his downfall. Those must needs be very secret: Alexander's approval lay on every measure carried by the man. And more:

Alexander's confidence in him grew day by day, and Speransky's activities soon spread over every branch of the administration. Every breath of change, welcomed by an eager minority, sent the majority into a panic. The speech made by the Emperor at the first meeting of the reformed Council of State made history: the tone of absolute power and authority was wholly absent from it, and the speech was Speransky's handiwork.

All the social circles were disturbed by the ever-increasing benevolence Alexander showed to 'the upstart'. Speransky's enemies were many. To the forefront stood the Dowager Empress, who distrusted him for his leanings towards France. Grand Duchess Catherine was jealous of his influence over her brother. Grand Duke Constantine called him 'a Jacobin'. Arakcheev's feelings were a mixture of jealousy, envy and hatred. Many others took their stand against Speransky because of his obscure origins.

Often enough the man played into his enemies' hands. He led a solitary life, absorbed in work which could be discussed with none except the Emperor. Those hermit habits were interpreted as a proof that Speransky was engaged in a conspiracy. His position dizzily high, he accepted no bribes, asked for no favours, and lived within his salary. What irked most was Speransky's implacable refusal to be turned into the gateway leading to imperial favours. That, according to those who wished him ill, proved him at once greedy and selfish.

Alexander heard much of it and remained impassive. Early in 1811, when he stayed with the Oldenburgs at Tver, his sister Catherine gave him a manuscript of Karamzin's—'A Note on the Ancient and Modern Russia'. The Grand Duchess knew well in what esteem her brother held the historian, and she had engaged his services in an attempt to overthrow 'the dangerous reformer'.

Karamzin's 'Note' struck a lugubrious key from the very beginning. 'What is the good of reforms if they lead to the anger and bewilderment of the most enlightened minds in the country?' And he went on to argue that the grandeur and might of Russia rested on autocracy alone and that the faintest breath of liberalism was harmful to the nation's health. Taken as a whole, the 'Note' was a fulsome panegyric of the past. One of its wilder claims—'In Moscow and Novgorod paper, gunpowder and printing were known and used immediately after their discovery'—prompted a later historian to make the caustic comment: 'For example, books were printed in Russia a full century after the discovery of printing and nobody knew much about the use of gunpowder until the days of Peter the Great.'[1]

Needless to say, Karamzin was a fervent supporter of serfdom, and he considered national representation to be wholly alien to the Russian way of life.

If Grand Duchess Catherine had hoped that the historian's arguments would prompt Alexander to action, she was disappointed. He made no comment at all.

All through 1811 the political horizon was darkening. As will be seen, the inevitability of the gigantic struggle drew closer and closer. Speransky's reforms, and his attempts at further changes, had created a climate of venom against him. Now his undisguised preference for France, his respect for Napoleon, his correspondence with Talleyrand—and admittedly his own indiscretions, such as sharp, ironical remarks at the expense of many, not excluding the Emperor—all these were now seen by his enemies as so many potential weapons. Arakcheev and others began hinting to Alexander that Speransky had put himself between the throne and the nation. There were other accusations. All of them, however exaggerated and absurd, served to swell the tension until Count Armfeldt said to the Emperor:

'Sir, whether guilty or not, Speransky must be sacrificed. We are being drawn close to a great danger. It is necessary to bring the throne and the people together, and nothing except Speransky's removal will achieve it.'

At the beginning of March 1812 Speransky was relieved of his office and that very night sent into exile at Nijny-Novgorod under heavy police escort. The very next day Prince Alexander Golitzin found the Emperor in deep distress. 'Would it not hurt you if someone cut off your right hand?' he said to Golitzin. 'Last night they made me part with Speransky and he was my right hand.'

Contemporary records leave no doubt that Speransky's fall was acclaimed as the first real victory over the French.[2]

The reasons for his dismissal ended by creating a legend. In

[1] Pypin, op. cit., p. 217.

[2] cf. Schilder, op. cit., III, 366. Schilder quotes from Runich's unpublished memoirs: 'Speransky was ambitious enough to become a Cromwell, a Washington and a Mirabeau rolled into one.'

reality, there was no mystery about it. It came at a moment of grave danger and of paralysing uncertainty about the outcome. The national mood was tautened to the extreme. Armfeldt was right in urging Alexander to accept the necessity of a scapegoat, and Speransky had to be that scapegoat. He was no traitor, but the country had to be given a proof that no highly placed public servant could afford to have even a rumour of treason linked with his name.

We know of Alexander's distress. We cannot tell if his conscience really troubled him. It should have done. The very manner of Speransky's dismissal was but another proof that no trust should be placed in princely favour. He should have been relieved of his office with the honours his work and his integrity demanded.

Speransky should have been born a century later. In his own day he had no collaborators whose quality was comparable to his own genius. He worked alone, wholly relying on his Sovereign's support and understanding. Had he had men like Witte and Stolypin to share his own daring and to confirm his policy, Speransky would have forestalled 1905 by a series of reforms falling like rain upon the national desert. His energies devoted to one end, namely, the union of the crown with the country by means of a fully implemented national representation, Speransky might well have prevented the shipwreck of the dynasty in 1917.

The spirit of the Tilsit treaty had a short lease of life. Its letter, rather lamely observed by both signatories, came to mean nothing some time before 1812. It did not take Alexander long to realize that Napoleon expected Russia's foreign policy to fall under the tutelage of France. The affairs of the Duchy of Warsaw, ruled by the King of Saxony, an obsequious nominee of Napoleon's, became a monopoly of the French. The Russian policy towards Turkey fared no better, and the costly war with Sweden added to the general humiliation. Its ultimate territorial gain, the annexation of Finland, made the Russians uncomfortably conscious of having identified themselves with 'the enemy of mankind'.

The *casus belli* in this instance added no laurels to Russian diplomacy. King Gustav IV not only refused to ally himself with Russia against Britain but returned the insignia of St Andrew's order to Alexander because it was not fitting for a king of Sweden to share decorations with Bonaparte. French agents in St Petersburg exploited the situation to the utmost and Alexander allowed himself to be persuaded that the Swedish sovereignty in Finland constituted a perpetual threat to the northern provinces of his Empire. In February 1808 an army commanded by Benningsen crossed the frontier. Within a few months the whole of Finland was overrun, but Benningsen's spectacular triumphs won no applause in Russia. 'The conquest of Finland came about at Napoleon's dictation'; such was the sullen verdict when at the end of 1809 not only the Finnish mainland but the Aland Islands were joined to Alexander's Empire. The status of autonomy granted to Finland was interpreted by many of the Emperor's subjects as a bargain with an uneasy conscience and an effort to conceal an aggressor's action under the cloak of liberalism.

1808 was a year of many griefs for Alexander. Napoleon's invasion of the Iberian Peninsula could not but shake the Emperor's faith in the promises of a peace to assure Europe's tranquillity for ever. The tautening mood of his own people was another disturbing factor. The earlier fulminations of the Holy Synod against Napoleon had little by little penetrated the national consciousness. Tilsit and its complications could not be understood by the masses except that they imagined their Tsar baptizing the infidel in the waters of the Niemen. The fable, however, struck no permanent roots. Crippled survivors of Austerlitz and Friedland capped all their stories by the refrain that Bonaparte's men were devils incarnate, and the enlightened urban minority held the same opinion under a less fanciful dress.

In the imperial family, the mistrust of the French superseded all else. The Empress Elizabeth alone did not permit herself to disapprove openly.

In May 1808 the infant Grand Duchess Elizabeth, her mother's 'Lizanka', died. The parents' sorrow silenced all those who imagined husband and wife to be approaching the point of final rupture. Wylie, Alexander's physician, tried to comfort him by saying that he and the Empress were still young and that more children might yet be born to them. But the Emperor would not be comforted. 'No, no, my friend,' he said to Wylie, 'it seems that God does not want me to have children.'

Alexander was thirty at the time. He hardly spared himself at work. His family's criticisms of his policy did not seem to interfere with his affection for them. From Tsarskoe he would go to Pavlovsk every day to see his mother. His manner still drew and enchanted all who came near him—and that in the teeth of his waning popularity. At the time probably none except his wife knew much of the moods which came to him whenever the skies grew dark, when fatalism gripped him and the iron fangs of remorse bit deep. People remarked on his passion for travel. Elizabeth knew the reason for this restlessness which would grow with the years.

Count Roumiantzev kept finding cogent reasons for every decision made by Napoleon, but in the summer of 1808 the Emperor wondered if the assurances given at Tilsit were little more than spent breath. There was the Turkish problem, which had then appeared so cynically simple: to rub Turkey's name off the European map—such had been Napoleon's thought at Tilsit. It was a design that had been familiar to the Romanov mind since the days of Peter the Great, and Bonaparte had played on that chord adroitly enough. Now he suggested that Moldavia and Wallachia could be ceded to Russia if Silesia were given to France, but Alexander angrily repudiated the idea and, during a somewhat awkward audience given to Caulaincourt, the Emperor said bluntly that he had the right to expect some concrete proof of Napoleon's goodwill.

Poland marked the thorniest point of divergence. The formation of the Duchy of Warsaw had stirred much unease among the Russians. That clause of the Tilsit treaty might well be called the heel of Achilles so far as the Franco-Russian alliance was concerned. The Duchy had been considered a temporary arrangement. Now Bonaparte declared that he would not object to the restoration of the Kingdom of Poland so long as its government remained under the aegis of France, provoking Alexander to a spirited answer: '*Le monde n'est pas assez grand pour que nous puissions nous arranger sur les affaires de ce pays.*' It was bad enough to have the Duchy of Warsaw ruled by a nominee of Napoleon's. To have the whole country turned into a kingdom for the purpose of serving French interests was unthinkable from the Russian point of view.

In August 1808 the Emperor confided to his family that he had arranged to meet Napoleon again at Erfurt. Elizabeth begged him not to go. Grand Duke Constantine wondered if the cession of the entire Empire to Napoleon might not simplify the future. The Dowager Empress urged that such a meeting ran counter to the imperial dignity and to the interests of the nation. But Alexander's obstinacy won the day and, to the disgust of many, including Arakcheev, Speransky was told to accompany the Emperor.

The meeting at Erfurt did not open favourably. On Alexander's arrival, Talleyrand waited on him, and Talleyrand's first words were a curious prediction of 1814:

'*Sire, que venez-vous faire ici? C'est à vous de sauver l'Europe et vous n'y parviendrez pas qu'en tenant tête à Napoléon. Le peuple français est civilisé, son souverain ne l'est pas; le souverain de la Russie est civilisé, son peuple ne l'est pas. C'est donc au souverain de la Russie d'être l'allié du peuple français.*'

Such words would never have been spoken if it had not been for the French reverses in Spain. Alexander understood it but too well. They repelled him. But they also fired his imagination and could not but colour the conversations he had with Napoleon, who was heard to complain that the Emperor of Russia was '*entêté. . . . faisant le sourd lorsqu'il ne veut pas entendre. . . .*' In a sense not immediately apparent, Erfurt atoned for Austerlitz and Friedland. Napoleon's hat thrown so angrily on the floor and the ugly loosening of his temper suggested something of an admission of a power he could neither define nor combat. Alexander's icily calm words that he would leave Erfurt at once unless Napoleon chose to behave reasonably brought Bonaparte to his senses, and Alexander could write to his family that he meant to do everything to convince France of his own sincerity. 'We shall watch his fall—if such be God's will— quite calmly . . .' and Alexander used even stronger terms when writing to his sister Catherine: '*Bonaparte prétend que je ne suis qu'un sot. Rira mieux qui rit le dernier, et moi, je mets mon espoir en Dieu.*'

Chateaubriand was there, and hardly a clearer picture of Erfurt exists than the one given by him[1] of Napoleon reporting his conversations with Alexander to his marshals and one of them explaining: '*Nous allons faire avaler un verre d'opium au Czar, et, pendant qu'il dormira, nous irons nous occuper d'ailleurs.*' Bonaparte laughed at Alexander and called him '*un niais*' and '*un grec du Bas Empire*', and strutted about with a conqueror's air.

The fruits of the second and last meeting between the two enemies were negligible. They exchanged pledges neither meant to observe,

[1] Chateaubriand, *Memoires d'outre Tombe*, ed. 1952, Vol. III, p. 156.

Napoleon promising to recognize the annexation of Moldavia and Wallachia and Alexander assuring him that he could count on Russian help in a war against Austria. Documents were signed. Members of reigning houses invited to Erfurt dined and rode together. Talleyrand, Speransky and other statesmen spent hours in discussion. But a sombre curtain had already fallen on the supposed alliance. The exchange of courtesies at parting could hardly have been more hollow than the exchange of promises. When in the following spring Napoleon's forces marched into Austria, no Russian help was given. The troops were there. Of action there was none. '*Cette alliance finira par être honteuse,*' Napoleon said angrily, and he did not know that he was using the wrong tense. The alliance was finished.

Whilst statesmen all over Europe were studying maps and trying to surmise where the French hammer would fall next, an incident in St Petersburg all but brought about a major family catastrophe at the Winter Palace. At the end of 1810 De Maistre wrote to King Victor Emmanuel that the estrangement between the Emperor and his wife '*se perfectionne au point que je ne vois pas trop d'espérance pour un rapprochement si désirable . . .*' Those words were not occasioned by casually overheard gossip, and the expression '*si désirable*' is most telling. For all her retirement, Elizabeth was no cipher in the national life. Her unrivalled dignity in the face of much provocation, her unfailing generosity to those in distress, her steadfast refusal to join any factions, all had made her loved and honoured. Her in-laws might indeed despise her. Not so those whose opinion stood for much.

At Derpt, Parrott, Rector of the University, who had the privilege of Alexander's friendship, had heard enough to write one of the most candid letters a subject could have written to his sovereign.[1]

The Emperor, said Parrott, no longer stood where he had once stood, and no sovereign could afford to lose his people's respect and affection. '*Vous êtes tombé dans une frivolité qui ne vous est naturelle. . . . Vous avez pleuré vos enfants . . . c'était alors le moment de revenir à vous-même. . . . Rentrez dans l'état de nature; attachez-vous à la seule personne digne de tout votre attachement. . . . Renoncez aux autres liaisons . . . que votre coeur doit condamner . . .*'

[1] Grand Duke Nicholas, op. cit., Vol. II, 232.

Had all this been concerned with a rumour, Elizabeth's dignity and good sense would have made her ignore it. But what happened in 1810 was a rude fact. A suite of apartments was being hurriedly prepared at the Winter Palace—for a lady. Some of the extant letters say baldly enough '*pour Madame Naryshkine ou une autre maîtresse . . .*' Was it for Naryshkina? Was there another? Many names were bandied about in the drawing rooms of the capital. The fact about the suite came to the knowledge of the Empress's ladies who, after taking counsel, decided that their best course was to tell their mistress's sister, Princess Amelia. The latter did not hesitate to take it to the Empress, whose reaction could never have been imagined by any of her intimates. Elizabeth told Amelia that she could not endure to stay under the same roof with any mistress and that she would return to Baden.

A situation of that kind demanded advice from members of the family. But the Empress knew the futility of such an approach. Her in-laws, beginning with the Dowager Empress, would have been about as helpful as a group of marionettes. Nor could Elizabeth contemplate any discussion with her husband. Neither love nor loyalty—and she had given many proofs of both all through the years—would have made her shed her pride. She knew that nothing at the palace was ever done without Alexander's orders, and the command about that suite was a challenge to her. She accepted it, made her decision, and meant to abide by it. Princess Amelia, herself horrified by her brother-in-law's conduct, nevertheless tried to dissuade her sister by every argument she could use, but Elizabeth kept saying that she had nothing to add to what she had said. She would leave Russia for ever and accord her husband full liberty for the future.

Amelia remembered the departure of Grand Duchess Anna and all the resulting repercussions among the European courts, but Anna was not the wife of an Emperor, nor could Alexander be compared with his brother Constantine.

'Compared with that sot and bully?' cried the Empress. 'Certainly not! I shall remain devoted to the Emperor all my life.'

Amelia, baffled and desperate, wrote to Baden. The Margravine replied in haste: '*Amélie pense comme moi sur la résolution funeste que vous avez prise, et à la laquelle, j'espère, vous renoncerez. Vous avez raison de ne pas souffrir un manque d'égard pareil . . .*' and she insisted that Elizabeth should do her duty and exercise her right in making '*des représentations et cela hautement* . . . *Vous le devez même à votre honneur et à la place que vous occupez* . . .' Here the Margravine put in a sentence of bitter complaint about her sons-in-law: '*Il n'y a que Louis qui est le seul honnête homme parmi ce nombre.*[1] . . . *Je frémis de l'idée de ce que cette démarche pourrait occasionner. . . . Ce pas vous ferait perdre dans un instant une reputation acquise depuis des anneés à si juste titre* . . . *quels regrets et remords vous vous prépareriez en étant la cause d'un bouleversement dans l'Empire* . . . *je redoute* [*ce projet*] *comme le plus grand malheur. . . . Renoncez-y pour l'amour de Dieu* . . .'

The Empress Elizabeth's journal, destroyed by her brother-in-law, would have thrown much light across those difficult months. We can tell nothing about the '*représentations*' she must have made to Alexander, but no mistress of his was ever installed at the Winter Palace, and in May 1811 the Margravine could thank her daughter for having given up the idea of an open and irrevocable rupture.

The episode smote at Elizabeth and all but snapped her moorings. She rescinded her decision—without in the least excusing or condoning Alexander's behaviour—and she turned back to her earlier faith in a cleaner and happier future. She stayed on, satisfied that even the grossest physical betrayal had not enough iron in it to kill her love.

The years between Erfurt and 1812 went in a maze of complicated diplomatic moves, alignments and realignments of policy, unpleasant surprises and half-screened suspicions. Under the cloak of meaningless courtesy the French in St Petersburg and the Russians in Paris were assuring their hosts that Tilsit was built upon the rock of imperial honour not to be shaken by anything however apparently untoward. But the pretended friendship was a thinly woven tissue, and few were the people either in France or in Russia who doubted the ultimate outcome.

At Erfurt, acting at Napoleon's orders, Talleyrand suggested that Grand Duchess Catherine might make a suitable Empress of France. There was no definite reply from the Russians, but soon

[1] The Margravine's sons-in-law were Alexander; Gustav IV, King of Sweden; the King of Bavaria; the Grand Duke of Hesse-Darmstadt; and the Duke of Brunswick. The 'Louis' referred to in the letter was the King of Bavaria.

after his return to Russia, Alexander had his favourite sister engaged to Prince George of Oldenburg, and to sharpen the arrogant moment the King and Queen of Prussia were invited to the wedding. Napoleon answered the slight in his own fashion. Eighteen months later he formally asked for the hand of Grand Duchess Anna, Alexander's youngest sister. The request led to a family storm, and Bonaparte's insistence on as speedy an answer as possible deepened the anger. Before a carefully worded refusal reached Paris, however, Europe heard of Napoleon's betrothal to Marie Louise, and the Russian anger at the gratuitous insult was dismissed by the French as a puerility.

Russia would never have spared the least important of her Grand Duchesses, but it was intolerable that a Romanov refusal should have been annulled by cheap and vulgar trickery. Napoleon's remark to Prince Kourakine that the Austrian marriage had no political bearing should have been dismissed for the nonsense it was. It served to deepen the gulf. 'Bonaparte need not imagine that I send fools to represent me in Paris or anywhere else,' said Alexander.

All the actions of Napoleon at the time from the invasion of the Netherlands to the seizure of the Duchy of Oldenburg were now explained by him as 'inevitabilities ordered by circumstances', and it was natural for Alexander to feel anxious lest some French interference in Poland should be interpreted in the same way. So he resumed his correspondence with Czartorizky and established points of contact with Prince Ogynski, member of a leading Polish family. Napoleon, hearing of it, complained that some conspiracy was being formed to change the Duchy of Warsaw into the Kingdom of Poland under the Russian aegis. He also complained about the leakages in the Continental blockade. In his turn, Alexander kept asking that the French troops in Prussia should retreat beyond the Oder.

In the autumn of 1811 the Emperor recalled from Paris the most promising young diplomat of the day, Nesselrode, a brilliant pupil of Speransky's. Nesselrode left France, Talleyrand's parting advice written down in cipher in his diary: Russia was to '*se rendre forte et encore plus forte afin de sortir par une négotiation de cet état de tension qui n'est utile qu'à la France.*'

But by then Alexander's last illusion had gone and Talleyrand's message was like a crowbar used on an open door. Preparations for a defensive campaign had already been going on for some time. However unpleasant Arakcheev's activities would be in the future, he certainly did not spare himself in preparing the armies of Russia for the gigantic task which awaited them. The entire machinery of the army commissariat was thoroughly overhauled. Obsolete guns were scrapped. Many regulations were jettisoned. The training of recruits was divorced from the punctilio of the parade ground. The munition works at Tula and Alexandrovsk were allowed to break the law of the Church by disregarding some of the major feasts of the year. It was a case of guns against observance, and the guns won. An experienced gunner, Arakcheev transformed the Russian artillery within two years. In 1810 he left the War Ministry to devote himself wholly to the task of reorganization. His successor at the Ministry was Barclay, whose administrative gifts could not have been more happily used.

Yet, strange though it was in a country whose population ran into millions, the numerical discrepancy between the Russian and French forces gave food for anxiety in St Petersburg. Only about two hundred thousand could be put into the field. Alexander's agents in France reported that the military strength of Napoleon stood at over half a million.

There was no regular conscription in Russia. All depended on recruitment at irregular periods. The two earlier campaigns having taken a heavy toll, the landowners asserted that a further call on their serfs would inevitably interfere with field labour. The landowners had something of a case, though all such considerations were swept overboard both by the Government and the landed gentry, to say nothing of the peasantry, in 1812.

That campaign used to be seen in terms of a gigantic clash between two men foremost in Europe, who, on Alexander's own admission, 'could not reign together in the world'. The idea, given a poetic form by Lermontov in his *Two Giants* (written in 1832), was shared by many historians.

> *In his helmet of pure gold,*
> *Did the Russian giant rise,*
> *Waiting for another*
> *From a far and alien land.*
> *Over the hills and through the valleys*
> *Rang the story of his fame,*

And to test each other's prowess
Was their common wish.
Martial thunders rumbling, crashing,
Came the hero three weeks old,
Insolent, he raised a hand
To unhelm the enemy.
With a smile a doom foretelling
Did the Russian answer him,
Shook his head and glanced but briefly.
And the upstart cried and fell,
And he fell into the ocean
On an unregarded rock . . .

Such a view, however permissible in poetry, carried simplification to an absurdity. 1812, when observed in a large perspective, was the second attempt made by the West to oust Russia from the comity of European nations. Chateaubriand's impression of the real issue behind the Erfurt meeting was based on a profound historical truth. This second attempt was far bloodier and more decisive than the first, though it lasted six months instead of several years. Charles XII, however invincible until the Poltava rout, was no Napoleon, and Peter the Great ruled a country but barely stirred out of its Muscovite slumbers. Yet there is a parallel between the Great Northern War and 1812. Had Charles XII been left a conqueror, it is open to question whether Russia would have been able to enter the European comity in the eighteenth century. A defeat of such proportions would hardly have enabled even a Catherine the Great to pursue her policy of aggrandizement.

Had Napoleon's plan not miscarried, there would have been nothing to prevent Alexander's Russia sharing the fate of Prussia. In brutal truth, Russia had not a friend in Europe. The hurriedly contrived alliances with Great Britain and Sweden could not have saved her from Napoleon's yoke and all its consequences. Neither Prussia nor Austria were in a condition to come to her aid even if they wished to do so, and it is fairly evident that neither had the desire. All the immense, as yet barely tapped natural wealth of Russia would have fallen to France, thus enabling her to enlarge her own war effort on an undreamt-of scale.

In Russia, 1812 meant thousands of different things to millions of people. Lofty purposes and heroic sacrifices were intermingled with petty regrets for looted silver and shabby hopes that small debts contracted in July would be forgotten by the following December. Many people lost their heads, beat their children and serfs, ran away, and blamed all the generals in turn. They virtually deified the Emperor's person for his firm refusal to surrender and they cursed Rostopchin for his glib promises of an easy triumph. Wealthy merchants emptied their storehouses and market women wept over a purloined sack of turnips. Saintly beggars prophesied the Second Coming of Christ or the Hour of the Antichrist. Boys awoke to premature manhood, and gently nurtured women learned the use of pike and musket. Some praised Kutuzov. Others cursed him. And all through the six months of that briefest, bloodiest campaign, the Emperor, now acclaimed as Alexander the Blessed, all his ambiguities discarded like winter clothing at the coming of spring, never once allowed himself to sway from the stony way of uncompromising resolve. He made a most brilliant use of a great moment, but he was not its creator.

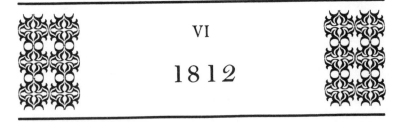

VI

1812

1811 HAD gone by, and French agents in Russia began finding more and more material for their reports. Arakcheev's activities were intensified. Armfeldt from Finland, Stein and Pfuel from Prussia, all three implacable enemies of France, were frequently received by the Emperor. Barclay was still at the War Ministry, and there were many conjectures as to which of the three generals would receive the supreme command when the hour came: Barclay, Benningsen, or Bagration. Kutuzov's name was not mentioned. He was away in the south, and people at court and elsewhere took care not to speak of him in Alexander's presence.

Barclay's undoubted ability, to call it by no finer name, was, however slightly, shaded by his alien origin. The same could be said of Benningsen, though it was argued that he had merited high promotion by his successes in Finland. Bagration, senior in rank to the other two, suggested the most likely candidate. It was said on all sides that Austerlitz would never have been lost if he had been at the head.

But, in spite of all the fruitful administrative efforts made by Arakcheev and Barclay, in spite of the high-pitched activity of ordnance works at Tula and Alexandrovsk, even in spite of the frequent discussions between the Emperor and Pfuel, a fanatical armchair strategist from Potsdam, there was no plan of action because nobody could read Napoleon's mind. Some were certain that he would interfere with Poland to the utter detriment of Russian interests. Others said they were sure that he would make an alliance with Turkey and attack Russia from the south. A minority wondered if the *casus belli* would be contrived by some fresh and intolerable demand on either Prussia or Austria. But nobody, not even the Emperor, imagined that Russia would be invaded.

The military preparations went apace, but the pulse of the

country beat to a rhythm unconcerned with any alarms. Shishkov, who had stepped into Speransky's shoes, was working at his notes for the codification of laws. Karamzin was busy at his researches. Kisselev and Malinovsky were gathering data for their reports on emancipation. Alexis Olenin was appointed head of the first public library in the Empire, an enormous building on the Nevsky Prospect, at once enriched by Alexander through the gift of his grandmother's priceless collections which included the libraries of Voltaire and Diderot. Educational reforms continued, and the Imperial Lyceum was opened at Tsarskoe Selo and it had 'many pupils of promise', among them a twelve-year-old, curly-headed Alexander Pushkin, who idolized Derzhavin and was known to dabble in versification during school hours.

The New Year was opened with the traditional '*sortie*' at the Winter Palace. Diplomats tried to gauge the Emperor's mood and were rather baffled by his apparent serenity. The smile and the courtesy extended to everybody present, including Napoleon's ambassador. A certain lassitude in manner could well be attributed to a slight indisposition at Christmas. There was also some talk about the increased frequency of the Emperor's visits to the Alexander Abbey at the end of Nevsky Prospect.

It has sometimes been argued that Alexander's absorption in religion did not begin until after 1814 when the English Quakers, Lutheran pastors, Madame Krüdener, Mademoiselle Tatarinova and Archimandrite Photius, to say nothing of lesser stars in the pseudo-mystic firmament, began attracting his attention. There is ample evidence to prove that 'the change' in the Emperor had started much earlier.

There had always been strict conformity to observance, but La Harpe could never have turned his pupil into a fervent son of the Orthodox Church. Samborsky's teaching was not likely to fill the existent lacunae, still less to make Alexander take to exaggerated piety. Conformity to church rules was very much of a lacquer; it had been demanded of Alexander since his childhood days, and later it answered a certain coldly formal streak in his personality. In church he appeared before his Deity much as he appeared at a review. Pious conventions never engaged the purposes of his soul. The change came slowly. To judge by a letter[1] written to Koshelev at the

---

[1] Full text of the letter in Grand Duke Nicholas, *The Emperor Alexander I*, II, 6.

end of January 1812, the process was in curious accord with Alexander's changing views on morality.

He had gone to the western provinces to examine certain lines of fortifications. He was by then deeply convinced that the coming year would bring possibly the greatest challenge in his life. He assured Koshelev of his ardent faith which was gaining strength every day, and which made him acquainted with a joy wholly unknown in the past. And the Emperor added rather startlingly:

'. . . ne croyez pas que [ma foi] date de ces derniers jours: il y a plusieurs années déjà que je cherchais cette voie. . . . Adressez vos prières à l'Etre Suprême pour qu'il me donne les facultés nécessaires pour achever ma tâche publique en rendant ma patrie heureuse, mais non dans le sens vulgaire: c'est à avancer le vrai règne de Jésus-Christ que je place toute ma gloire . . .'

To be asked to believe that Alexander's religious awareness went back to 'plusieurs années' is surely impossible. Barely a year before, his wife had reached the most bitter decision any woman could take: to leave him because of a contemplated injury no wife could have endured, and that incident was by no means an isolated episode in the sad chronicle of Alexander's married life. And yet his account of his soul's condition and his future aims is genuine enough. The momentous demands of the year would prove his rock-like faith in Providence, the steadfastness of his hope in the outcome of the struggle, and the sincerity of his wish to achieve lasting peace not only for his Empire but for the whole of Europe.

1812 threw as much light on Alexander's dichotomy as did the Congress era. No mistress was allowed to make her home under the palace roof, but the reconciliation between husband and wife had not led to the return of any affection on his part. Naryshkina and others would be given up, in time, but on the very night of Napoleon's intrusion into Russia Alexander was present at a ball given by his equerries in his honour, and 'the person most likely to please the Emperor was invited to be hostess'. Tolstoy does not mention the name. It was not Madame Naryshkina.

It is tempting to ask if Alexander was the greatest actor not only of his generation but of the whole century. For a man to claim as his ultimate purpose the establishment of Christ's Kingdom on earth postulates a singleness of mind, a perfect fusion between the outward and the inner within the heart and in the thought. That the dream was no more than a dream is self-evident, but even to have dreamt it must have meant an uplifting of the spirit and a ruthless spring-cleaning of all the dusty corners in the soul.

No solution seems to answer. Neither an actor nor a hypocrite could have so carried the year's burden as to turn it into his people's greatest triumph. In the end we are left with the sense of being able to do no more than study separately each feature of 'the crowned sphynx', a man who had the strength of will to rise to the heights and who yet had moods which made him sink into the abyss. That is not to say that Alexander's virtues cloaked his vices, or that the latter made dust of the former. It is merely to say that he, who puzzled friend and enemy alike, had a personality so halved that its very halvedness all but reached perfection.

To the ill-disguised irritation of all his commanders, the Emperor now singled out a certain Colonel Pfuel, whose rather flickering star would hover at the council table for a few months. A colonel in the Prussian army, Pfuel had come to Russia soon after the Austerlitz débâcle. His manner anything but amiable and his vanity enormous, Pfuel modelled his strategic theories on the examples left by Philip of Macedonia, Alexander the Great, Julius Caesar and Hannibal. He insisted that Frederick the Great owed his military glory to his profound knowledge of ancient exploits. Pfuel's six years in Russia had taught him little enough about his adopted country. He spent all his time over dusty tomes and no less antiquated maps. He learned neither the language nor the terrain of the country, but he had the habit of speaking with a certain sour authority, and Alexander's proneness to admire meticulous detail was well answered by a man capable of discussing the progress of the Seven Years' War in a manner which all but suggested an eye-witness.

When invited by the Emperor to submit a plan of campaign, Pfuel rightly thought that, since Napoleon's forces would pre-sumably be coming from the west, a check should be offered in the east. He toiled for a long time over a complicated diagram of a fortified camp on the left bank of the Drissa, a tributary of the Dvina. Such a camp would, according to Pfuel's theory, inevitably check the French advance. He proposed that the camp should be manned by one corps and that the other should make an adroit detour and thus be in a position to attack the enemy from the rear.

Every paragraph of his plan was couched in complicated verbiage, but Pfuel insisted that the whole draft was simplicity itself and absolutely foolproof.

It could never be that. The maps studied by Pfuel certainly gave him an idea of distances, but even his visits to the banks of the Drissa had taught him nothing about the colour and the shape of the terrain. He brought all his papers to Alexander and engulfed the Emperor in an avalanche of allusions to a strategy which might have answered on the mainland of Greece or in Gaul, or even in Silesia in 1758, but not in the west of Russia in 1812. Yet Alexander was impressed. Thousands of men were sent to the banks of the Drissa to start on the fortifications.

Yet the disposition of the available forces was not entrusted to Pfuel. It was worked out by Arakcheev, Barclay and others. The First Western Corps under Barclay's command, one hundred and twenty thousand strong, had its headquarters at Wilno to the south-west of the Drissa. The Second Western Corps, given to Bagration and numbering less than forty thousand, was stationed at Wilkowissy midway between the Niemen and the Bug. General Tormassov, in command of forty-six thousand, had his headquarters at Lutzk south-east of Wilno.

Such was the total strength Russia could then put into the field against Napoleon's forces, their number still unknown to the Russians.

Barclay was vaguely supposed to be in authority. In reality, there was no unity of command. People named Benningsen as the most likely commander-in-chief, but he had not even been given a corps. There was no harmony between Barclay, Bagration and Tormassov. Kutuzov was still in the south arranging a truce with Turkey. Nobody remembered him except by making ironical remarks about his bulk, his appetite, and his tremendous capacity for sleep.

In April 1812 Napoleon left for Saxony. Contradictory information about his strength and his intentions had already begun seeping into Russia. Here and there ran uneasy whispers that the alliance made with Great Britain and Sweden had angered the French. But such voices were few and they troubled nobody in Russia. The

Emperor left his capital for Wilno, having told the French Ambassador that he remained '*ami et allié le plus fidèle*' of Bonaparte. The words were palpably false. What was true, though Napoleon would never admit it, was that Alexander did not desire war. All the preparations, however extensive, were purely precautionary. There was no recruitment ordered throughout the Empire. The three commanders near Wilno were told to remain in their places.

Wilno received Alexander in a spirit of idolatry. Polish magnates and their wives vied with one another in devising entertainments and festivities, each more splendid than the preceding one, and the humbler inhabitants of Wilno endorsed the feeling of their lords. It was enough for the Emperor to appear at the end of a deserted street for it to seethe with cheering crowds within a few instants. Women did not spare their richest shawls and threw them under the hoofs of his mount. Children tossed bunches of spring flowers on the cobbles. Church bells pealed. Not a window but had flags and gaily coloured carpets hanging from it. The Poles' welcome sprang from the conviction that the Emperor of Russia was alone able to restore their ancient regal dignity, and Alexander's graciousness certainly confirmed their hopes.

Handsome and elegant, his beautiful mouth folded into a smile, he had the air of a man whose favour and friendliness excluded nobody, and the first impression was soon confirmed by pleasant facts—however trivial. Alexander took notice of street boys, of crippled beggars in church porches, of elderly peasant women bent under the loads they were carrying to the market. As to the drawing rooms of Wilno, the Emperor could not enter them without capturing everybody on the instant. His charm carried a fragrance which inebriated and never cloyed, and painted the day's horizon in bright and hopeful colours. Countess Tiessenhausen wrote in her memoirs that . . . 'the Emperor's good looks meant less than his kindness and charm which captivated everybody . . .'[1]

Numbers of society men and women left St Petersburg not to miss the delights of that *partie de plaisir* at Wilno. Not a manor for miles in the neighbourhood but was ready to offer lavish hospitality. Life became a whirl of banquets, balls and garden parties. Barclay's men were reviewed in heightened splendour, and so was Bagration's corps. Within a few days Wilno became St Petersburg in little.

[1] cf. Schilder, op. cit., III, 76.

People spent their time in dancing, drinking, gambling, and forming gossamer liaisons with *les belles Polonaises*. Jewish and Polish *filles de joie* were reaping an incredible harvest, and so were the innkeepers.

Couriers kept arriving from the north, and everybody knew that the Emperor spent his mornings hard at work with his secretaries, but everybody remembered that the Empire must be governed whether its sovereign was in St Petersburg, at Wilno, or at Odessa. Nobody mentioned the fortifications along the left bank of the Drissa. The news of the Bukharest Treaty, marking the end of the war with Turkey, was received almost indifferently. The gain of Bessarabia seemed a poor enough recompense for the retention of Moldavia and Wallachia by the Turks, and people found keen pleasure in blaming Kutuzov because they never forgot the Emperor's dislike of him. The Bukharest Treaty was not a matter to engage their attention for long. There were all the pleasures offered by the hospitable Poles.

On 25th June Alexander's aides-de-camps were giving him a great ball at Zakret, Benningsen's country seat in the neighbourhood of Wilno. In the middle of a dance General Balashev was seen entering the ballroom. He approached the Emperor who turned and went out on the terrace, the general following him. A few minutes later Alexander, his face pale but his manner perfectly composed, asked the hostess to excuse him because urgent business demanded his return to Wilno. He left so unobtrusively that few among the guests remarked his going.

Balashev came to tell him that Napoleon had crossed the Niemen.

They continued dancing at Zakret, but a number of generals returned to Wilno for an urgently summoned council of war. All were excited. A few seemed scared. The Emperor was coldly angry when he vowed that he would not lay down his arms until the very last enemy soldier was gone from Russian soil. Pfuel's plan was loudly criticized, but nobody had anything else to suggest.

Napoleon could hardly have chosen a better moment to strike. Utter lack of cohesion among the Russian commanders had been in evidence during armchair discussions when war had been little more than a probability in some undefined future. Now, with the French marching across Russian soil, such an atmosphere spelt disaster for the moment and a likely doom further ahead.

When the news of the French invasion reached Europe, the

general opinion maintained that the very first battle lost by the Russians would point the way to the final French victory. Diplomatic circles thought that not a single man in Alexander's service could hold a candle to Talleyrand. Military experts supposed that they would see the re-enactment of Austerlitz on a gigantic scale, the defeat followed by the inevitable extinction of Russia as a Great Power. All agreed that the Emperor Alexander's kindliness was really due to weakness. 'On losing the very first battle,' said Gneisenau, 'the Emperor of Russia is likely to cede all his territories along the Dvina and the Dnieper and after a second defeat St Petersburg and Moscow are certain to be surrendered to the French.' The Russians being unprepared, the war would certainly end before winter. *La Grande Armée* would enjoy a good rest in a country famous for its plenty.

That night in June Alexander was closeted with Shishkov and Prince Peter Volkonsky. At dawn General Balashev was summoned to the Emperor's study and given a letter for Bonaparte, the finest, strongest and most dignified letter ever written by a Romanov.

'*Monsieur mon frère, j'ai appris hier que malgré la loyauté avec laquelle j'ai maintenu engagements envers votre Majesté, ses troupes ont franchi les frontières de la Russie, et je reçois à l'instant de Petersbourg une note par laquelle le Comte Lauriston, pour cause de cette aggression, annonce que votre Majesté s'est considérée comme en état de guerre avec moi dès le moment où le prince Kourakine a fait la demande de ses passeports. . . . En effet cet ambassadeur n'y a jamais été autorisé . . . et aussitôt que j'en fus informé, je lui ait fait connaître combien je le désapprouvais en lui donnant l'ordre de rester à sa poste. Si votre Majesté n'est pas intentionné de verser le sang de nos peuples pour un malentendu de ce genre et qu'elle consente à retirer ses troupes du territoire russe, je regarderai ce qui s'est passé comme non a venu et un accomodement entre nous sera possible. Dans le cas contraire, votre Majesté, je me verrai forcé de repousser une attaque que rien n'a provoqué de ma part. Il dépend encore de votre Majesté d'éviter les calamités d'une nouvelle guerre.*'

Kourakine's clumsiness and Lauriston's feeble note seemed almost irrelevant at the moment except in so far as they enabled Alexander to leave the door ajar.

Balashev found Napoleon at Rykonti by the Niemen. The

Russian's mission was unsuccessful. Napoleon lost his temper and accused Alexander of starting hostilities by his alliances with England and Sweden. He boasted of his own superiority and threatened to have Prussia wiped off the face of Europe if the Russians dared set her against France.

'And let your sovereign give sanctuary to all his German kin.'

At dinner, Napoleon, having asked about the churches in Moscow, remarked that such piety could not be seen anywhere else. Balashev permitted himself to say that he understood Spain to have an even greater number of churches. To shatter the awkward pause, Marshal Ney asked which was the best road leading to Moscow, and Balashev again acquitted himself neatly:

'Is it not said that all roads lead to Rome? In Russia we think that all roads lead to Moscow—including the one of Poltava taken by Charles XII.'

But Balashev's mission brought no results. Napoleon refused to retreat, and the general returned to Drissa, the letter he had brought marking the end of Alexander's correspondence with Bonaparte.

The Emperor's headquarters were now at Drissa, Wilno being taken by the French. Pfuel's little star glimmered no longer: the famous fortifications were pronounced to be well-nigh useless. Meanwhile the French advanced beyond Wilno and cut in a wedge between Bagration's corps at Wilkowissy and Barclay's, now at Drissa. There followed some lightning-swift skirmishes with the French, but Barclay, now definitely invested with the supreme command, avoided a major clash. Pfuel's plan was finally abandoned, a wit remarking that the author of such an absurdity deserved either the madhouse or the gallows.

Barclay still hoped that Bagration would join him. A retreat was ordered from the bank of the Drissa. The Commander-in-Chief's position was no easy one: the Emperor's presence at the headquarters meant that every order given by Barclay must be given imperial approval before being published. There were many muddles and delays. The French were still advancing, but nobody imagined that the enemy could penetrate into the heart of Russia. Officers and men grumbled at the retreat orders, but Barclay had no alternative. The chances of Bagration joining him were getting smaller every day.

At that time, Arakcheev, Balashev and Shishkov composed a very difficult letter to Alexander. They were daring enough to suggest that he should leave the army and return to the north. As head of the state, he was answerable to none, but for him to assume the leadership of his armies meant shouldering the responsibility for the possible reverses. Supreme command could only be given to a subject whom the sovereign could dismiss in case of necessity. The Emperor had indeed appointed Barclay, but Barclay had no real liberty of action so long as the Emperor remained among his troops. Further, the Russian forces were greatly inferior to the French and a great many thousands of men were taken off their normal duties to safeguard the Emperor's person against all possible hazards in the vicinity of the enemy.

To say that Alexander's vanity was wounded is to leave much unsaid. He had always longed to lead his armies. Yet Austerlitz had taught him that the training received on parade ground was no training for a battlefield and he had never known any other. He told the three signatories of the letter that they were right.

The Emperor's arrival in Moscow in July was one of the finest things accomplished by him. He had left Barclay retreating to Witebsk, all the attempts of Bagration to join him having ended in failure. Barclay's men had no thoughts of mutiny, but they retreated, their mood sour with disappointment and shame.

Alexander came to Moscow determined to make his people see the firmness of his purpose and the steadfastness of his faith, and he succeeded most brilliantly. The old city met him with an even greater enthusiasm than had been shown at his coronation. Nobility and gentry, rich merchants and small shopkeepers, artisans and factory hands in their thousands, all were eager to prove to their Tsar that they were at one with him in the determination not to surrender. In Moscow, the fateful moment was accepted in a spirit of naked realism. They did not waste their time in asking questions about the cause of the war. It had happened. The French had crashed in. The business must be dealt with, and it needed all the national sinews. They were determined to grapple with it and they were conscious that they must be united with one another and with the Tsar to win the blessing of God.

Alexander inspired them superbly, linking their faith and resolve to his own. Grave, he yet had the air of a man to whom hope was his daily bread. Imperial in his bearing, he was most happily approachable. Certain of God's help, he did not make his few speeches in the accents of a braggart. At church services, some of which were held under the smiling summer skies, the Emperor's calm and recollection were contagious. Having acknowledged himself unable to lead his armies into battle, he certainly proved that he could lead the entire nation. If the end of the matter were to be a Thermopylae, they wished for no finer memorial.

Those days in Moscow turned the war into an intensely national business. Never before did Alexander find himself so close to his people who now named him 'The Blessed'. They repeated the words of his great vow until they knew them by heart. They did not curse the French with any particular vehemence—they were so busily blessing their sovereign.

When the Emperor's carriage took the road to Tver and the north, Prince Peter Volkonsky heard him say that defeat was unthinkable with people of such courage.

'These days in Moscow,' wrote a Kaluga landowner, Dimitry Poltoratzky, to his wife in the country, 'have been like a spring dawn. No sacrifices can be great enough for such a sovereign,' and, along with thousands of others, Poltoratzky formed a battalion of his serfs to join the forces. Merchants did not count the gold they gave and the poor gave their coppers.

On arrival in St Petersburg, Alexander drove to the little palace on Kamenny Island. Husband and wife met at a grateful distance from all court ceremonial. There he came and there he stayed—though the heightened moments of Moscow soon grew somewhat pale in the memory, and one of the Empress's ladies-in-waiting once heard him complain about his uselessness.

In general, with one exception, the morale was anything but exemplary in the imperial family. For all her bravado and her exhortations that her brother should not yield an inch to 'the Corsican monster', Grand Duchess Catherine did not feel she was safe at Tver and escaped to Yaroslavl, followed by a great train of her valuables and other possessions. The Dowager Empress was still at Gatchina, but she had started making preparations for going to Kazan accompanied by her three younger children. Grand Duke Constantine spent his leisure in writing gloomy letters to the north, describing all the quarrels among the commanders and the thickening discontent among the ranks.

The one exception was the Empress Elizabeth. She stayed where she was, but she stepped out of her retirement, founded a society for the care of war orphans, took an active interest in everything designed to ease the lot of the wounded and the crippled, and all secretly devoted ninety per cent of her Civil List to war charities.

Meanwhile the retreat continued. Witebsk was surrendered, the inhabitants themselves setting fire to it. At a short distance outside Smolensk Barclay and Bagration met at last. Barclay's position was growing more and more difficult. There was not even a semblance of accord at his headquarters, and councils of war began sullenly and ended stormily. All the other generals distrusted Barclay, and the Grand Duke went the length of writing to his brother that he and others suspected treason in Barclay's retreating tactics. Yet what choice was there for him? Several thousands of his men were on the sick list. Bagration's corps had suffered many casualties. The total manpower under Barclay was scarcely one hundred and forty thousand, and the entire *Grande Armée*, its strength estimated at something like half a million, kept advancing towards him. Barclay had no hopes of Tormassov's corps reaching him.

The grumbling grew, and Grand Duke Constantine had something of a case when he asked whether Barclay had the intention to surrender the whole Empire. 'The men are longing to come to grips with the enemy and he will not even consider offering battle. Will our retreat take us to the shores of the White Sea?' Benningsen did little but confirm the Grand Duke's complaint. Bagration wrote to Arakcheev that he felt he could not serve under Barclay much longer. Barclay's man kept misleading him about the French position and strength. 'And now he has decided—much too late—to defend Smolensk by attacking the French, and we shall lose.'

Smolensk fell. The French entered the smouldering ruin of a city. From a village some distance away from the surrendered city, Bagration sent another appeal to Arakcheev. 'We dare not think of a truce, but the whole army is cursing Barclay. How much longer?'

Bagration's was not the only voice. From other parts of the country came loud expressions of the national will, Moscow being well to the fore. 'We want Kutuzov to lead the army—'. On 17th August Kutuzov was invested with the supreme command in accordance with the nation's desire and against Alexander's will.

Kutuzov left the capital at once for the front line now many miles north of the abandoned Smolensk. Alexander said to an intimate:

'*Le public a voulu sa nomination. Je l'ai nommé. Quant à moi, je m'en lave les mains.*'

In 1812 Kutuzov was sixty-seven. His father had served under Peter the Great, a circumstance which greatly endeared Kutuzov to the men. He had been trained in the hard school of Catherine's 'eagles', Golitzin, Potemkin, Roumiantzev and Suvorov, himself to become the last surviving eagle, his brilliant promise having been proved in the Turkish wars. Now his immense bulk made it difficult for him to ride long distances and he travelled about in a small open carriage. He loved good food and wine, women, sleep and other comforts of the flesh, but the sybaritic streak did not interfere with Kutuzov's capacity for enduring cold, hunger, dirt and any other hardship falling to the lot of his men. His strategic genius came out in his orders, always brief, many of them baffling and even angering lesser men under him. Kutuzov had no use for the strategic niceties of people like Wehrother and Pfuel, and technical verbiage so bored him that he had been known to fall asleep in the middle of a council of war.

The army loved him for his language, the spurts of rough affection, for the prodigious memory which enabled him to recognize faces and names of comrades in long-since finished campaigns, for his care of their lives which he would never risk in a futile battle. Above all, Kutuzov was loved for that indefinable something linking him to the men he led, something far beyond loyalty and personal affection. A born leader, never wasting his breath on flamboyant speeches to the ranks, never seeking danger or turning away from it when once it faced him, the old man embodied an ideal the men recognized even though they were unable to give it a name. Under him they were safe without the least regard for the ultimate issue. They knew him to be one of themselves, bone of their bone and flesh of their flesh. There was no gulf between the Field Marshal and the rawest recruit.

Kutuzov was known to mock at the word 'patriotism', to him little more than a sound made by mannered men eager to draw attention to the inaccessible heights. Nor did he ever refer to 'Holy Russia', though he loved all her sanctuaries with a son's devotion. He would have made an ironical and possibly rude reply on being told that he was Russia in that summer of 1812.

He well knew the Emperor's dislike of him. He had heard enough about intrigues against him. Now he accepted the supreme command without any loud phrases, astonishment, or hesitation, aware, though, that he would be maligned and criticized all along the difficult way. He brushed it all aside and, vested with new authority and the princely rank reluctantly bestowed by the Emperor, Kutuzov hurried to join the army.

Barclay's retreating tactics had angered the nation. On reaching the headquarters Kutuzov was not afraid to issue his first order—which ordained further retreat. On 5th September a halt was made in the fields surrounding the peaceful villages of Shevardino, Gorky, Semenovskoe and Borodino, all of them lying within one hundred and twelve versts from Moscow, just off the main Kaluga road. The halt was meant to be something of a check to the advancing *Grande Armée*. Kutuzov's position was strictly defensive. He accepted the battle offered by the French without the least show of enthusiasm.

The forces met at dawn of September 7th. By sunset, over one hundred thousand dead lay in those fields. The Russians lost fifty-eight thousand men and seven hundred were taken prisoner. Borodino cost Napoleon fifty thousand, among whom were forty-seven of his best generals. The most grievous Russian loss was that of Bagration.

The battle came to be idealized by poet and novelist. In brutal reality, it was a day of appalling carnage. Each side claimed the victory, but the day ended in a stalemate, and Kutuzov's forces, however shattered, retreated in perfect order. Yet the first news of Borodino reached the north so coloured that church bells broke into peals and St Petersburg wondered why Napoleon had not been taken prisoner. When further reports came in, gloom cloaked the capital.

Nobody could guess that a beginning had been made—a beginning which would lead to Paris, to Elba and to St Helena. They were still in 1812. Kutuzov had not checked the ominous advance. Napoleon was known to be making for Moscow. What was the Field Marshal doing, they asked in St Petersburg.

He made a brief halt at the village of Fili and called a council of war. Few of the generals had much to say. But Benningsen and one or two others were most voluble. They insisted that the forces should be reorganized with all urgency and a real check made to the *Grande Armée*. They claimed that the war would be lost once Moscow fell to the enemy, who would then make for Tver and the north. Kutuzov listened to it all, his eyes closed, and some of them indignantly thought he was asleep. When Benningsen came to the end of his passionate peroration, Kutuzov rose and brought the council to a close.

'*Je vois que c'est moi qui payerai les pots cassés. J'ordonne la retraite*,' and within a week his army passed through Moscow, then turned abruptly south-east, making for the Riazan road, and Kutuzov wrote to the Emperor: 'I venture to say to your Majesty that the coming of the enemy to Moscow will not mean the subjugation of the Empire.'

Kutuzov's decision to strike south-east after passing through Moscow was one only a genius could make. In so doing, 'the old fox', as Napoleon called him, went to earth, and for more than a fortnight the French would not know where the Russian army lay. Kutuzov, having brought his weary men into a country untouched by the invader's ravages, ordered a halt and slept for twenty-four hours.

Rostopchin, the city Governor, reported the surrender of Moscow to the Emperor, a surrender made without a single attempt to defend the old capital and against the opinion of all the other commanders. The news shook St Petersburg. Nobody as yet knew the reason behind the Field Marshal's decision, but the wounding fact remained and made them think of him as coward and traitor. Men who had never smelt gunpowder in their lives discussed Kutuzov's strategy and said it was as full of mistakes as a sieve of holes. He had never made a single effort to advance or to recapture Smolensk. He had merely followed in Barclay's steps and the result was the loss of Moscow, probably the loss of the war. Kutuzov's note to the Emperor having been delayed through the stupidity of a courier, Rostopchin's sorrowful letter, heavily charged with self-righteousness, was the only source they had. Anger and shame gripped the capital.

The masses were angry, but it was left to the Emperor's family to start discussions about a truce. The Dowager Empress implored her son to start negotiations at once so as to save something out of the disaster. Grand Duke Constantine, Arakcheev and Roumiantzev at the Foreign Ministry joined the truce party. But the masses remained staunch. Neither in St Petersburg nor elsewhere did any crowds assemble to shout for a conciliatory hand to be stretched out towards the enemy. The Empress Elizabeth's letter written to her mother some weeks before the battle of Borodino proved to be prophetic:

'*Plus Napoléon s'avancera, moins il doit croire une paix possible. C'est le sentiment unanime de toute la nation. . . . C'est sur quoi Napoléon ne comptait pas, il s'est trompé en ceci comme en bien des choses . . .*'

And now she would not join her voice to those of her in-laws. Her husband was right in refusing all such suggestions.

Alexander stayed on at the palace on Kamenny Island. The news of Moscow all but stunned him for a time, but it left his firmness unbroken. When a messenger from Kutuzov's headquarters reached St Petersburg, the Emperor said to him: '*Napoléon ou moi—nous ne pouvons plus régner ensemble. J'ai appris à le connaître et il ne me trompera plus.*' He was angry with the Field Marshal even though Colonel Michaud explained that the choice had been between the army and the old capital and Kutuzov had thought it wiser to surrender Moscow than to sacrifice the men. There were tears in Alexander's eyes when he said that even with Moscow fallen and in flames, he would not dream of any surrender. A few days later he wrote to Bernadotte:

'The loss of Moscow gives me a chance to prove to Europe how strong is my determination to continue the war. All other wounds are as nothing compared with that hurt. More than ever before my people and I stand together . . . determined to perish under the ruins rather than make peace with the Attila of our days . . .' The Emperor went on to mention Napoleon's letter disclaiming his responsibility for the fire of Moscow, a letter left unanswered by Alexander. '*Elle ne contient que des fanfarronades.*'

'My people and I stand together,' so the Emperor wrote and believed, and it was true. They were with him to a man in not wishing to conclude a shameful peace. But they began longing for action. As one week slipped into another, St Petersburg felt uneasy.

The French were still in Moscow. It was October, and the dry golden days succeeded one another without any news from the Field Marshal. Would he allow the French to move northwards? Tension gathered up. People met here and there, and they began clamouring for action. On the occasion of a Te Deum at the Kazan Cathedral, Elizabeth must persuade her husband to use a closed carriage instead of a horse, and he agreed reluctantly. They were met by a sombre silent crowd. 'I shall never forget that day,' wrote Mademoiselle Sturdza in her memoirs. 'There was not a single cheer as we mounted the steps to the cathedral. . . . I happened to glance at the Emperor and I understood what he must have been going through . . .'

It was a bitterness created by the dearth of news from the south. The people had not lost '*ces réserves de vertus nationales, à étonner le monde*,' as Madame de Staël, then in St Petersburg, expressed it, and Alexander still had the right to say that his people and he stood together. He shared their anger and their impatience.

Little by little the clamour quietened, and Paul Strogonov could write to his wife in the country that '*l'occupation de Moscou est affreuse, néanmoins s'il est possible de considérer cette calamité du point de vue militaire abstrait, on en tirera de consolantes conclusions . . . [Napoléon] a cru fermément . . . que Moscou était le but final, que de là il partirait agrandi pour subjuguer les parties de l'Europe qui lui résistaient encore . . . [mais] personne ne lui parle de paix et nous anéantissons Moscou au moment où nous ne pouvons plus la défendre. . . . Il n'est guère habitué à des pareilles receptions dans les autres capitales de l'Europe; même celle d'Espagne a été plus aimable . . .*' and the secretary of the Empress Elizabeth, Longuinov, echoed his mistress's opinion that the Russian case came to be strengthened by the surrender of Moscow.

No foreigner could understand all Moscow meant to a Russian. It was far more than a name and a symbol of the past; more than the sound of bells, the white walls of the Kremlin, the smell of stale incense in its sixteen hundred churches, the bird market in Trubnaya Square, the little timbered houses huddling along the banks of the Moskva. It stood for a truth indispensable in the life of any healthy nation: unity, its pulses sustained by a vision. It was so in the thirteenth century in the very teeth of the Tartar invasion, and two hundred years later when one of its princes shook off the Tartar for ever, and still later, in 1613, when it put an end to a troubled time by choosing a youth from an ancient family to be the Tsar. A century later, the youth's grandson, Peter the Great, established another capital on the banks of the Neva, but Moscow retained the supreme privilege of having the Sovereign anointed within its walls because Moscow was Russia, no matter how many windows were opened to the west, and Alexander knew it by virtue of a rare intuition. In 1812 the ancient city proved the same truth once again, and did not shrink from the flames to fight the way back to its unity. The loss of Moscow should have been a wound unto death. But it proved a Good Friday which extended for five weeks until the national Easter morning broke upon the city. Therein lay the seeds of Napoleon's ruin: he did not understand a people who would not surrender even with the enemy within their gates.

In spite of all the losses at Borodino, *la Grande Armée* entered Moscow in all its terrifying martial panoply. The French found the city deserted, but its wealth was theirs for the taking. Moscow spared nothing from the bolts of rare brocade to its sacred vessels studded with fabled jewels. So *la Grande Armée* entered Moscow— never to leave its gates again.

Precisely five weeks later a vast horde of undisciplined marauders left Moscow, all but drunken at the thought of the great wealth they were taking home. They straggled out of the gates unaware that the city had worked its worst on them. Moscow was like a she-bear lying in her lair, tranquilly conscious of her strength. The she-bear used her strength without mercy.

Meanwhile Kutuzov, wholly unconcerned with anyone's impatience or anger, waited for the result on which he had staked everything. Being elderly and rather tired, he did not exhaust himself still more by futile fretting. His men, as he knew, were recovering from all the recent stresses and agonies. Kutuzov read French novels, wrote witty letters to Madame de Staël and to his daughters, enjoyed his meals, and slept a lot. Rostopchin cursed him for an old fool, and ironical remarks were made by quite a few officers at the headquarters, but General Knorring checked them soon enough.

'You say the Field Marshal sleeps eighteen hours out of twenty-four? Let's thank God for it. He needed rest more than any of us and every day of inactivity is another nail in the French coffin. You say he has a mistress with him? Well, old Roumiantzev used to have four of them following him on all his campaigns and none of them interfered with the job he had to do.'

Nor did Kutuzov exert himself greatly when he heard of Napoleon leaving Moscow. He made a sign of the Cross, thanked God for the country's deliverance, and went to sleep again. Later there were battles of minor importance, and partisans harried the remnants of *la Grande Armée* right down to the frontier, but Kutuzov said '*tout cela se fondera sans moi*,' and he had the right to say it.

By the end of November 1812 a few thousand Frenchmen and nine guns crossed the Niemen, and Russia was purged of the enemy leaven. A few days before Christmas Alexander reached Wilno where Kutuzov met him. Great honours were paid to the Field Marshal, but the Emperor's retinue could not help noticing a certain chilliness in his manner towards the old man. With the crisis overcome, Alexander once again resented advice. He was resolved to continue the war. Kutuzov said that the ranks were sadly thinned by epidemics. 'Why pursue a vanquished and vanished enemy, Sir?' he asked the Emperor. 'Our men need a good rest. Your Majesty's vow has been kept—not a single enemy is left in your dominions. Let the British finish Napoleon.'

But Alexander replied rather coldly that Napoleon had not ravaged London. A few days later he wrote to General Saltykov in St Petersburg: 'Thank God that everything is going well here. It is a little difficult to get rid of the Field Marshal, but it is absolutely necessary to do so.'

The Emperor was determined to have the peace terms arranged in Paris.

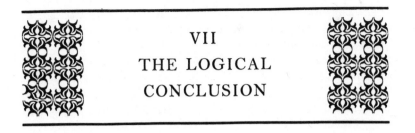

VII
THE LOGICAL
CONCLUSION

By the end of 1812 vast reaches of Russia stood ravaged by the passing of the enemy. The harvest was wholly destroyed in at least six provinces. Moscow, Smolensk, Witebsk, to say nothing of innumerable lesser towns, villages and hamlets, were little more than huddles of charred ruins. *La Grande Armée* had melted away, its strength devoured by debauchery and disease almost as much as by hunger and frost. The Empire was delivered of Napoleon, but the deliverance had not been purchased in a cheap market. The nation had all but spent itself to save its truth from the enemy. People were weary almost beyond weariness. Epidemics broke out. The treasury was depleted. Te Deums for the momentous triumph were all but outnumbered by requiems for the fallen. The Emperor's vow, however, had been fulfilled to the letter.

The home landscape so heavily scarred, it did not seem unreasonable that many people expected the march of the armies to be brought to a halt and hoped for a respite so as to evoke order out of chaos and—in more immediate terms—to see the taxes lightened and the burnt houses rebuilt.

Such were the wishes of the masses. Such also was the opinion of those who stood closest to the Emperor: Shishkov, Arakcheev, Rostopchin, Roumiantzev, to cite but a few. Arakcheev was uncertain about the commissariat. Roumiantzev and his colleagues in the Government felt that it was time to return to many activities broken off by the war. All those people certainly had a case, and later many historians blamed Alexander for not having listened to the voices of prudence.[1]

---

[1] Prof. G. E. Afanasiev in *Napoleon and Alexander*, 1912, p. 5 said that 'Catherine the Great concerned herself solely with national interests. . . . The same cannot be said of some of her successors. Alexander I was far more influenced by the drifts in European

The Emperor's determination to continue the struggle was said to be the result of foreign influence, and Stein was named then and later as the chief instigator.[1]

Foreign influence was very much there, but it did not go all the way. Stein's famous note in which he invited Alexander 'to be the liberator of Europe' must certainly have flattered the Emperor's vanity and strengthened his resolve to redeem the promise given to King Frederick William. But the whole issue was immeasurably greater than the freeing of Prussia and Alexander knew it.

Whatever his earlier and later mistakes, the Emperor then stood on a height never before or after attained by a Romanov. He gave prudent answers to counsels of prudence—even when disallowing their purport. He declared himself unable to reign together with Napoleon, but that, however personally expressed, had nothing narrowly subjective about it. The peace treaty must be arranged in Paris not in order to heal one sovereign's wounds but for the greater good of the whole of Europe. The latter, as Alexander knew, would never know peace until the throne of France was vacated by Bonaparte.

All of it is true. Yet it is also true that there is a proudly national meaning in the campaign of 1813-14. Far from severing himself from Russian interests, Alexander was now jealous of them with a heightened jealousy. Napoleon's attempt to enslave Russia had failed, but the attempt had been made not only to add to the French laurels but also with a purpose of closing all the western windows of Russia. Another titanic effort was now needed to prove that Russia had earned her right—and that not merely by virtue of conquest— to a voice and a seat at the European council table.

Alexander's decision was unpopular, but he had no false ideas about Napoleon and knew that the man's genius could devise ways of recuperation undreamt of by lesser men.

The 1813-14 campaign can hardly be seen in any other light.

---

politics than by Russian needs and advantages.' Grand Duke Nicholas (*The Emperor Alexander I*, Vol. I, p. 128) expressed himself even more strongly: '. . . thus in December 1812 began the liberation of Prussia from the French yoke, a process wholly at variance with Russian interests.'

[1] It is true that the three most prominent foreigners in Alexander's service, Czartorizky, Stein and Capo d'Istria, were chiefly concerned about the future welfare of their own countries, i.e. Poland, Prussia and Greece. Of those three Stein alone achieved his purposes.

Even though the Russian forces played no part at Waterloo, it is a moot point whether Waterloo would have been possible without Leipzig.

To say that the Emperor reached his decision lightheartedly would be fatuous. In the letters written about that time to members of his family and others, the dreamer does indeed cede place to the man of action, but the change did not come about without anguish. He did not minimize the dangers facing him. Napoleon was still Emperor, the mere magic of his name still moved the people of France, and his powers of rapid recuperation were well-nigh fabulous—as the Russians were to experience soon enough. Alexander was able to count on Britain's financial support, but gold alone could not ensure a success. Who were his immediate allies? A prostrate and ravaged Prussia, her King without a gosling's courage, and an equally ravaged Austria, whose loyalty could be compared with a weathervane. They would indeed acclaim Alexander as the saviour of Europe in 1814, but at Christmas 1812 he knew that the task he had shouldered was criticized on all sides and that those who could see its advantages were very few. He knew too that his armies were tired and hungry, ill-shod and tattered, that a multitude of urgent tasks awaited him at home and, finally, that if he were to fail, he would lose not only his people's devotion but the future of the dynasty together with that of the Empire.

It is customary to judge a man's action by its success or otherwise, but common standards are of small use in this case. Had Alexander failed and Napoleon's gyves gripped Europe once again, the Emperor of Russia would still be remembered—not as an Agamemnon, perhaps, but as an Epaminondas, his virtue given a lasting recognition by all men of good will and clear vision.[1]

Early in January 1813, with Kutuzov in somewhat reluctant command, the Russian army crossed the Niemen. Its numbers were gravely depleted and reinforcements were not expected until March. Kutuzov had asked for a rest. Now that his men were marching

[1] Twice in the present century Germany might have done worse than remember the words of one of her great soldiers, Gneisenau, who in 1833 wrote to a Russian friend: (cf. Schilder, op. cit., III, p. 381) 'If after Napoleon's withdrawal from Russia, the Emperor Alexander had not continued the war, if he had made peace with the invader, Prussia would still be under France and Austria would not have dared to raise her banner against Napoleon . . . [who] might still be alive today. God only knows in what manner he would have avenged the disasters fallen upon him in Russia. Our present independence is wholly due to your help and your friendship.'

again, he kept asking for provisions, boots and ammunition. Sometimes he got them. More often he did not. And they were marching through a country, its very bones laid bare by constant requisition, much marauding and a succession of thin harvests. To add to all the other hardships, the war to liberate Europe was started at a time when neither Prussia nor Austria would commit themselves to an open rupture with France. Not until March 1813 did King Frederick William decide that it was safe for him to join Alexander.

Meanwhile Napoleon had recruited an immense force again. Much to Alexander's annoyance, Kutuzov refused to hurry even after the Prussian army had joined with the Russians. The Emperor, mindful of the old man's great services, tried to rein in his impatience and even continued to show favour to the Field Marshal. The Oder crossed, the local population sent a laurel wreath to Alexander who at once forwarded it to Kutuzov with a flattering enough note: 'all the laurels belong to you,' but 'the old fox', duly grateful, still refused to hurry his pace. The Prussians, thinking solely of themselves, blamed Kutuzov for ineptitude. He took no notice of their taunts. Worn out and ailing, he knew his life's work was done. He reached Silesia in April and there at Bunzlau he died. Russia went into deep mourning. The Emperor, duly recollected at all the requiems, was relieved.

The old man's wise counsels never to be heard again, the Allies surged forward, their numbers reinforced by the Austrians under Schwarzenberg. On 24th April they entered Dresden where the enraptured population met them with cheers and flowers, its King having prudently run away to Bohemia, so frightened was he lest his servility to Napoleon were to bear its Nemesis. The Allies' triumph lasted barely ten days. At Lützen Napoleon dealt them such a blow that Dresden must be left in a hurry. The general morale could not benefit by the panic of the King of Prussia and his plaintive cries: 'God in heaven, does this mean that I must return to Memel?'

The Lützen débâcle shook Vienna, and Metternich began considering a quiet withdrawal when his envoy at the Allied headquarters, Lebzeltern, succeeded in persuading him that everything was not yet lost. '. . . si notre coopération manquait [à l'Empereur Alexandre], il en serait découragé, et il ne serait nullement surprenant qu'il abandonnât les puissances à elles-même, convaincu surtout qu'il a fait assez pour fixer l'opinion publique en sa faveur.'

Dresden was indeed a Pyrrhic victory for Napoleon. In August 1813 he suffered a defeat at Kulm where Marshal Vandamme was taken prisoner. Bonaparte asked for a two months' truce, and it was accorded.

There would have been little harmony at the Allied headquarters where Wittgenstein, Schwarzenberg and Barclay took little trouble to conceal their dislike and mistrust of one another, if it had not been for Alexander—now the virtual Commander-in-Chief. At Kulm he had been under fire, his imperturbable air spurring whole regiments to heroic action. At the council table, he spoke and was obeyed. His singleness of purpose underlined every order he gave. 'Our goal is Paris' he had said at the beginning, and the intention held firm against all the reverses and uncertainties of the hour. No victory, however brilliant, on German soil would be accepted by Alexander as the achievement of the aim.

On 16th October 1813 began the three days' battle of Leipzig, into which Napoleon flung all his strength. In the afternoon of the first day a sudden flank movement of the French cavalry led to the Allies' hurried retreat. King Frederick William and the Emperor Francis considered the day lost. It was to prove Alexander's most brilliant moment. Leaving his two august allies to commiserate with each other, the Emperor galloped towards his Cossack regiments, commanded them to check the French advance, and ordered Barclay to call out all the available artillery reserves. The Cossacks' whirlwind attack routed the French cavalry, and the next day Napoleon sent one of his marshals to the Allied camp. He would agree to cede the Duchy of Warsaw, to evacuate the Hanseatic cities, to recognize the independence of the Union of the Rhine, the Netherlands, Spain and the Italian states, and to ask for nothing except that the French colonies then in British hands were returned to France. The offer was left unanswered. On 18th October began the last day of the battle, Alexander once again among his troops and often enough in danger. At midday of the 19th he rode into Leipzig, whilst the shattered French forces were fleeing towards the Rhine.

The Allies reached Frankfurt, and by November not a French soldier was left in the German states. The Emperor Francis, counselled by Metternich, considered that the entire matter was settled with the liberation of Germany. 'There still remain France and the rest of Europe,' answered Alexander with a firmness which took Metternich aback. Napoleon, the Emperor pointed out, was on his way to Paris, he would arise like a phoenix out of the ashes of defeat and inflict further disasters upon the world. 'In such a case,' went on Alexander, 'I might not be able to hurry to your rescue. Peace must be signed in Paris—with him dethroned.'

Stein recorded his impressions in his diary: 'The Emperor Alexander does everything in a brilliant and beneficent fashion. He is wholly dedicated to the needs of the hour, no self-sacrifice seems too great for him. . . . He is truly inspired. . . . Let nothing mean or sordid hamper his actions and prevent Europe from enjoying the happiness offered by Providence . . .'[1]

Alexander was indeed inspired. In the words addressed to the hesitant Francis and the pusillanimous Frederick William, he outlined the rest of the task: '. . . *rendre à chaque nation la pleine et entière jouissance de ses droits et de ses institutions; les placer toutes et nous placer nous-mêmes sous le sauve-garde d'une alliance générale, et les préserver de l'ambition des conquérants. Telles sont nos bases. La Providence nous a mis sur la route qui mène droit au but. Nous en avons parcouru une partie. Celle qui nous reste à faire est hérissée de grands obstacles. Il faut les applanir.*'

Blücher and Gneisenau upheld Alexander. The King of Prussia had not much to say. The Emperor Francis was uncertain. Yet in the end Alexander won his way, and the winter campaign was decided upon. In early January 1814 Alexander wrote to La Harpe: '. . . *laissez-moi vous dire que, si à côté de l'ocuvre de la Providence quelque pérséverance et énergie que j'ai eu l'occasion de déployer depuis deux ans ont été utiles à la cause de l'independance de l'Europe, c'est à vous et à vos instructions que je le dois . . . le désir d'être digne de vos soins, de mériter votre estime m'a soutenu. . . .*'

Those were indeed Alexander's finest hours. Inspired by success, undaunted by defeat, calmly assured of God's help in the undertaking, Alexander stepped out of his century to become an early crusader. He meant to act chivalrously by all the nations in Europe, including the French, but the Austrian wiles ended by dropping some poison into his cup. Austria presented an ultimatum to Switzerland: she was either to join the Allies or else to accord free passage to their forces. Either condition violated her neutrality.

[1] cf. Pypin, op. cit., 41.

Alexander argued against it long and arduously, but all the commanders, including Blücher, were in favour of the Austrian idea, and the Emperor wrote sorrowfully to the north: '*Metternich s'est conduit détestablement dans la question suisse. . . . Il s'est compromis lui-même, son Empereur et moi avec. . . . Si vous êtes dans le cas de parler à des Suisses, dites hautement que je suis complétement contre la violation de leur territoire. . . .*'

The second stage of the campaign was started on 13th January 1814 with the Allied forces crossing the Rhine.

Alexander's ultimate aim seemed nearer and nearer. But many obstacles remained. In the first place, diplomacy was making most disturbing inroads. Alexander's government had concluded an alliance with England, and British gold was of incalculable value to the Allies, but, on meeting Alexander for the first time, Castlereagh felt unsure of him. England was determined to end the Napoleonic era as speedily as possible, but the way even then envisaged by the Emperor said nothing to the British. They had had trouble with Alexander's grandmother and father. What guarantee was there that the Emperor would not follow in his predecessors' steps? He kept repeating that he had no territorial ambitions. Could he be trusted? Castlereagh reported to Lord Liverpool that in his opinion nothing seemed to foretell so much danger for the future as the Emperor's chivalrous attitude to all. 'In what concerns Paris, [his] personal inclinations are at variance with all military and political considerations. It looks as though the Emperor of Russia were seeking an opportunity to enter Paris at the head of his glorious army for the sole purpose of having his magnanimity compared with the ravages committed by the French in his own capital.'[1]

Nothing could have been more unjust. Duplicity was not alien to Alexander's nature, but in 1814 his chivalry stood above all suspicion and his integrity did not carry a single blemish. He had no intention of making for Paris there to play a conqueror's part. From the moment his armies had crossed the Rhine, he kept saying that he had no quarrel with the French people and every action of his confirmed the words, yet in a sense he did owe Paris to his people and to his Allies. Alexander's faults could indeed be understood by Castlereagh. Not so his virtues.

[1] cf. Grand Duke Nicholas, *The Emperor Alexander I*, Vol. I, 149.

The Allied forces were now in France and to the French they were enemies. The magic of Napoleon's name remained evocative. He had mustered fresh resources, and he fought like a lion. Four defeats were inflicted on Blücher's corps alone. After their victory at Champeaubert, the French morale hardened. Prussia took to wavering again, though both Gneisenau and Blücher shared Alexander's resolve to carry on.

The Allies met at Bar-sur-Aube for an urgent council of war. It proved a tumult. Britain and Austria, with Prussia a timid third, were in favour of a truce. Alexander had but one answer to give them: 'I shall not make peace until Napoleon is dethroned,' and they set their faces towards Paris on 25th March. That very day Schwarzenberg met the French at Fére-Champenoise. The Russian cavalry were in time to make Marmon and Mortier retreat towards Paris. It was the last battle in Alexander's life. For some moments he found himself all but surrounded by an enemy column. '*La présence de l'Empereur,*' wrote an eye-witness, '*électrisa la cavalerie à un tel point que rien ne put l'arrêter.*'

In less than a week armistice terms were being signed at an inn, '*Le Petit Jardinier*', near the gate of St Denis. The municipal authorities waited on Alexander at Bondy, and through them he sent his message to the people of Paris. '*Dites donc . . . aux Parisiens que je n'entre pas dans leurs murs en ennemi, et qu'il ne tient qu'à eux de m'avoir pour ami, mais dites aussi qu j'ai un ennemi unique en France, et qu'avec celui-là je suis irréconciliable.*'

Alexander's voice was heard alone in those days. The Emperor Francis would join him later and make no weighty utterances. The Kings of Bavaria and Prussia kept prudently silent. After the triumphant entry on 31st March, with the population cheering themselves hoarse as Alexander rode past them, 'a conqueror seeking no other honour than the happiness of the conquered,' he wrote to his friend, Prince Alexander Golitzin: '. . . the entry into Paris was magnificent. . . . The crowds' joyous voices were everywhere. But my soul was experiencing a wholly different joy . . . [My soul] was almost dissolved in gratitude to God. . . . I was hungry for solitude so that I could pour out my heart before Him.'

More will be said later about the inward change in Alexander. His letters at the time seem like so many mirrors reflecting a purity of purpose and a singleness of mind which amazed all who met him and captivated the finest minds in Europe even more than his greatly lauded charm. Alexander had had eighteen months of war, and its hideous reality, from which at Austerlitz he had fled weeping, became an evil not to escape but to conquer. Now his faith was confirmed and his hope fulfilled. Thus the entry into Paris brought back the most solemn moment of his coronation when, chrism on his brow, he had believed himself to be accepted of God. Now not the sacred oil but the hand of God rested on him. The spring skies smiled upon the enthusiasm of Paris and the gaiety of her streets and squares, and Alexander himself appeared as a denizen from the gardens of spring. The conclusion of his labours—the gathering of the nations into a hall of abiding concord—now seemed inevitable and easy. Tranced by a vision, its beauty having saved his hopes from the grave, Alexander had no doubts that others would see the splendour as clearly as he did. It would be no matter of self-stained politics. It was all simple and also terrible: the will of God for the world at that particular hour.

Within a few days Napoleon abdicated. The throne of France could not remain vacant for long, and it was Alexander's business to see it occupied again. Longing for solitude, he must needs spend his days in lengthy, frequently acrimonious discussions, and he steeled himself to accept all the discords as part of the ordained pattern. 'Here I am,' he wrote to Russia in April 1814, 'once again plunged into the muddy waters of politics, but this is God's will for the moment.'

He did not know France and the needs of her people, and he kept his mind open about the most likely candidates for the crown always so long as the French were allowed full liberty of choice. So far as he was concerned, he confessed himself ready to approve of a republican régime if such were the will of France.

Because the recall of the Bourbons answered Talleyrand's interests, he mustered together as many royalists as possible, and their decision was represented to Alexander and his allies as being in accordance with the wishes of the whole nation. If the Emperor had any misgivings about the choice, he left them unrecorded. On 29th April Louis XVIII, having left England with many tearful asseverations of his gratitude, reached Compiègne. Returned to his homeland after more than twenty years of exile, the King-elect learned that not only the people of Paris but millions of others were thanking God—not for the restoration of a Bourbon to his ancestral throne but for their deliverance by an alien hand.

Alexander had by then spent a month in Paris. His popularity showed no signs of growing stale. Stories of the Emperor's generosity, tolerance, kindness and courtesy were winged from street to street, repeated by great ladies in their drawing rooms and by tattered flower sellers at draughty street corners. The Parisians were quick to appreciate that Alexander, having dethroned Napoleon and sent him to Elba, paid constant attention to Josephine and her daughter, Queen Hortense. '*On voyait que tout émanait de lui, que tout roulait sur lui . . . le roi de Prusse passait inaperçu,*' said a contemporary, and the sour demeanour of the Austrian Emperor made the Parisians shrug in contempt. The Emperor Francis and King Frederick William, for all their plumage and the gilt embroidery on their tunics, were unremarked pygmies. The shabby chronicle of their behaviour during the war made the Parisians turn away from them as though they were part of a fishmonger's rather tired stock. They were in Paris only because the Russian Emperor's valour and constancy had made it possible for them to get there, thought the Parisians, and lavished all their homage on Alexander.

Madame de Staël having come to Paris, the Emperor was her frequent visitor, and a German diarist recorded an incident which became known all over Paris.[1]

'One evening they were discussing slavery in America in Madame de Staël's salon, and someone ventured to remark that it also existed in Russia. The Emperor Alexander flushed but replied calmly: "You are right. I do know that serfdom is an evil. God willing, I mean it to come to an end during my reign." Sounds of approbation came from all over the vast drawing room. The Emperor had spoken loudly, and his words were soon repeated all over Paris.'

King Louis XVIII had heard many such stories. He regarded Alexander as a self-invited guest in France, sovereign of a country habitually inimical to England, and Louis XVIII's intention was to curry favour with the British. In a fulsome letter to the Prince Regent, Louis made it plain that he considered his restoration to be wholly due to the British efforts on his behalf. It was a toady's letter unworthy of the great name borne by the writer, who conveniently

---

[1] cf. Schilder, op. cit., III, p. 216 and Pypin, p. 287.

forgot the days when England would have none of him and when Russia harboured him and treated him royally.

He now behaved in the manner of a petty grocer disappointed with the week's takings. Alexander came to Compiègne. Louis remained seated and gestured his guest to a chair. He made petty complaints about some details of etiquette ignored at his arrival, and the poor quality of wax candles at Compiègne. He asked anxiously about the gold plate and the gobelins at the Louvre. When dinner was announced, he sprang out of the chair and hurried out of the room, leaving Alexander to follow behind. At table, he loudly ordered the stewards to serve him first. On return to Paris Alexander said to Nesselrode: 'You would have thought that *he* had restored the throne to *me*. We are supposed to be barbarians from the savage north, but we have better ideas about treating our guests. Let the French keep him if they want him. In my opinion, the Bourbons are past praying for. They have learned nothing from their misfortunes.'

The Parisians shared Alexander's verdict. Before long they coined a biting story: '*Les anglais ont nourri un cochon; les français l'ont achété pour dix-huit louis, mais il ne vaut pas un napoléon.*'

In June 1814 the Emperor left Paris for a visit to England. The people of Paris shouted a fervent '*au revoir*', but the parting between Alexander and King Louis was an awkward formality, and the Emperor left, his mind full of misgivings about the future of the French throne.

It has often been said that the rather unfortunate impression created by Alexander's visit in England was due to the foolish and tactless behaviour of Grand Duchess Catherine, who, having preceded her brother to London, curried favour with the Whigs, made unpleasant jokes about the Regent's figure and appetite, and was rude to Lady Hertford. The Grand Duchess, whose behaviour shocked Whig and Tory alike, may well have tried to convince Alexander that the best way to win popularity was to pay attention to the Princess of Wales and to cultivate the friendship of the Opposition. Yet it seemed more likely that Alexander's mind had been prejudiced before his arrival. The exchange of views he had had with Castlereagh and Cathcart would certainly have deepened the traditional dislike felt by the Romanovs towards 'the prosperous, cunning and perfidious Albion'. The very first words addressed by Alexander to Napoleon at Tilsit, 'I hate the British as much as you do', were no mere figure of speech.

Now he was coming not as 'a rude barbarian from the land of the Scythians' but as 'the Agamemnon of our days', laurels on his head and echoes of great triumphs in his wake. There had been sharp misunderstandings with British representatives. There had been insults from a king Alexander had restored to his throne and who was deeply influenced by British opinion. All of it together was unlikely to make the Emperor look forward to a visit so urgently advised by his counsellors.

His reception at Dover greatly surprised Alexander by its robust spontaneity, which sprang from the pleasure of seeing the hero of the year, the conqueror of the most dreaded enemy, come to England. The vociferous crowds in London should have assured the Emperor of a welcome equal to that he had had in Germany and in France. Such things considered, Alexander's behaviour in England is difficult to understand. His breeding did not allow him to be as grossly brutish as Louis XVIII had been. None the less, he behaved badly.

Expected at St James's Palace, he went to the Pulteney Hotel there to join the Grand Duchess. The immense crowds in the streets prevented the Regent from paying a call at the hotel, and Alexander went to Carlton House for the first and last conversation with the Prince. Neither liked the other and neither seems to have made much effort to conceal the dislike. Whilst Alexander's ambassador and Nesselrode were having discussions with Lord Liverpool and Castlereagh, the Emperor delighted in accepting the hospitality of the Duke of Devonshire, Lord Grey and other notabilities of the Opposition. He went to many of their functions where the Prince of Wales did not appear and once he was late at a dinner given by the Regent, his excuse being that he had been detained at Lord Grey's.

The masses were pleased with him. So was Oxford. So were the Quakers. Jane Austen wrote to her sister Cassandra, then on a visit to London: 'Take care of yourself, and do not be trampled to death in running after the Emperor. The report in Alton yesterday was that they would certainly travel this road either to or from Portsmouth. I long to know what this bow of the Prince's will produce.'

It produced nothing at all from the political point of view.

Nesselrode would write later that '*ce séjour ne passa pas sans quelques désagréments. [L'Empereur] ne sympathisait pas avec le Prince régent [et] quitta l'Angleterre peu satisfait de son séjour, mais rapportant cependant une haute idée de la prospérité et de la grandeur de ce pays . . .*'

After an absence of eighteen months, Alexander returned to St Petersburg on 24th July 1814. At his express orders there was no official welcome. In fact none but his family and the court knew about the date of his return. He stopped for a few minutes' private prayer at the Kazan Cathedral on his way to the palace.

Chancellor Roumiantzev, who postponed his retirement till the Emperor's return, found a great change in him. He looked slightly older than his thirty-seven years warranted. His deafness had become a little more acute. His grasp on the day's matters was firmer than ever, and there seemed an air of self-assurance never noticed before. Yet the medal struck to commemorate the most glorious war in Russian history bore the inscription, 'Not unto us, O Lord, not unto us . . .', and the people's hunger for a public recognition of all the triumphs was answered by a solemn Te Deum at the Kazan Cathedral. It was left to the Dowager Empress to honour her son's return by a stupendous banquet at Pavlovsk.

Through the whole of 1813 Alexander's letters to his intimates are charged with faith and hope. Thrown into the very heart of the war, he makes frequent allusions to peace which was now his portion. Defeats are taken as incentives to grind all further obstacles to dust. Victories are interpreted as signs of God's approval of the task. In the light of such correspondence we can almost imagine the Emperor subscribing on New Year's Eve to the entry Alfred de Vigny would make in his diary for 1831: '*L'année est écoulée. . . . Je rends grâces au ciel. . . . Je n'ai fait de mal à personne,*' and yet on New Year's Day 1814 the Margravine of Baden sat down to write to her daughter in a mood of high indignation:

'. . . *Pourquoi donc ce cher Empereur vous donne si peu de détails et en est si prodigue pour sa mère? C'est inconcevable. Car mettons de côté mari et femme; vous êtes pourtant sa meilleure amie, et qui partage avec le plus de chaleur sa gloire et ses succès . . .*'

Elizabeth was indeed her husband's '*meilleure amie*' at the time. Naryshkina had gone never to return, and there would be no other to follow her. The anxieties of 1812 had forged a link between husband and wife, and her activities during the worst moments of danger had endeared her to the people. Unlike the rest of the family, she remained tranquil, and neither meddled nor advised in matters of state importance. Yet all she gave to Alexander was forgotten once he happened to be away from her. His letters, for all their courtesy, were brief, superficial, and meagre in detail. It was from the Dowager Empress, and from a sister-in-law whom she could not respect, that Elizabeth must receive what crumbs of information they thought fit to dole out to her. It was from the impersonal dispatches, brought by couriers, that the Empress could follow the road so soon to reach its triumphant end. Her love now mingled with unbounded pride, not to say adoration, she certainly deserved much more at the hands of a man who, in his own words, 'had turned to God'. The contradiction is insoluble.

There is a puzzling letter written by Alexander to Koshelev on the eve of 1812. The Emperor asked his old friend to believe that 'the seeking after God' was of many years' standing. It may well have been so, but there is no evidence to prove it. Paul's murder in 1801 may be taken as the first great crisis in Alexander's life, but it plunged him into well-nigh pagan despair rather than into remorse. Until his final rupture with Naryshkina, his morality was certainly out of accord with Christian principles. The diplomacy both before and after Tilsit was the diplomacy of a statesman not committed to any religious profession. And if one goes further back, to the days of the Emperor's youth, there is hardly a trace of any spiritual awareness. Nor is that to be wondered at. There were no opportunities for any such development at Catherine's court; religious instruction was not one of La Harpe's duties, and Samborsky was more at home in agricultural matters than in the roots needed to foster spiritual life. Alexander had never suscribed to rationalism, and he would have been wholly at sea in the philosophies of the eighteenth century. Both as Grand Duke and as Emperor, he conformed to the Orthodox observance, but the conformity in no way prevented a deadening conviction that all the failures and griefs falling to his lot were due to his vicarious share in his father's assassination. The sense of being pursued by vengeful fates never quite left Alexander.

The turning towards God did not really begin until 1812. Early that year, with a foreboding weighing heavily on him, the Emperor began reading the Bible on the advice of Prince Alexander Golitzin, his childhood friend.[1]

It is clear that at the time the Bible was an unknown book to the Emperor. He did not even possess a copy of his own and had to ask the Empress for hers. He had to ask Golitzin's advice as to which books were to be read first.

Little by little, Alexander was drawn into a world as mysterious as it was enchanting. In February 1813 he wrote to Koshelev that his faith 'was zealous and pure. . . . Now a few words about M. A. Naryshkina's arrival in St Petersburg. I hope you know the state of my soul well enough not to be anxious on my account. . . . There is really no merit in growing indifferent to a person in view of all she has done. . . .' Indeed there could be no merit; the woman's unfaithfulness had long since been proved. She would have no successor.

The fire of Moscow, in the Emperor's own words, had enlightened him. Those flames came to him as a challenge, and the finest qualities latent in him awoke to answer it. In the very heart of the difficult campaign that followed Napoleon's débâcle, Alexander wrote to Golitzin that it would be impossible to describe all the emotions '*dont je me sentais pénétré en repassant tout ce qui s'était passé depuis un an, et où la Providence Divine nous avait conduits . . .*'

As it happened to Pierre in *War and Peace*, so it was with Alexander—with the difference that Pierre knew where to halt. Out of the flames of Moscow rose the image of the Apocalyptic beast, and the perfervid language of the proclamation issued by the Holy Synod was felt by the Emperor in all his pulses. He believed himself called to fulfil the purposes of God, and he dreamt of a quietened Europe, its wounds healed by a miraculous concord, much as a dedicated Crusader of the eleventh century dreamt of the Holy Places, and much as Blake dreamt of England. Alexander's aim, revealed, as he believed, by the Most High, was to conquer evil by

---

[1] Two people exercised a great influence on Alexander at the time. Golitzin, the Procurator of the Holy Synod, and Rodion Koshelev, a retired diplomat and a scholar, who had rooms allotted to him at the Winter Palace. Golitzin, a great worldling until 1801, was then appointed to his high office, and in the end became a true man of prayer. His integrity irreproachable, he stood head and shoulders above his contemporaries. Arakcheev hated him. Koshelev had been a disciple of Eckhartshausen, whose leading idea was that perfection consisted in the triumph of the spirit over the body and that the ultimate liberation of the spirit led to a victory over death.

good. His victories in the field made people call him 'Agamemnon'—but among his own subjects he became 'The Blessed'.

Alexander's humility shrank from the title. His faith accepted all it implied. So the French had the occasion to marvel at his piety and were moved by the Orthodox requiem sung on the very spot where twenty-one years earlier a King's head had fallen in the dust of Paris. So too the Quakers in England were even more deeply moved by Alexander's gentleness, readiness to learn, and his hunger for the things of the spirit.

Sincerity and fervour were there. But a perfect integration, which alone would have turned the Emperor's spiritual life into a living and fruitful thing, was lacking. The sense of joy came and went. Inner peace was even more fugitive. The pagan despair which had smitten him in 1801 would not return. Futile remorse would step in. Yet little of it could be discerned in 1814 when 'The Blessed' came back to his homeland.

VIII
THE ARBITER
OF EUROPE

GUNS WERE silenced in Europe in the autumn of 1814, but the
tumult in Vienna might well have been compared with the roar of
cannon. Innkeepers, pedlars, cooks, tailors, confectioners, butchers,
ladies of light virtue, purveyors of meat, fruit, cosmetics and wax
candles, all wholly indifferent to the purposes of the Congress, were
comfortably conscious that the presence of so many royal per-
sonages in Vienna had in it the making of many small fortunes. The
Congress met to decide the administrative and territorial future of a
shattered and tattered Europe, but the two emperors, four kings,
thirty reigning princes, all their wives, to say nothing of statesmen
and their attendants and a crowd of flunkeys and maids, must all
sleep, eat, dress, burn candles, have their clothes freshened for balls
and banquets, hire coaches and horses to drive them along the
engayed streets, from one brilliantly lit palace to another, so that in
the end Prince de Ligne's sarcasm was amply justified: '*Le Congrès
dance, mais ne marche pas.*'

In truth, there were far too many entertainments. Alexander and
Elizabeth must borrow Count Razumovsky's great palace for a
banquet given by them to a crowd of guests, whose number varied
from four to seven hundred, according to the imagination of
chroniclers. That banquet was long remembered in a city known to
excel all others by the glory of its entertainments. A Lucullian feast
was served at fifty tables in an enormous panelled hall, all the
porcelain and silver having come from Russia. It happened in the
very heart of winter, and it was pleasant to be able to offer such
delicacies as tiny fresh cucumbers, perfectly hearted lettuce and
cherries brought over from the hothouses of Tsarskoe Selo. The
hostess, all in shimmering silk, gauze and tiny pink roses, was
declared to be unsurpassable both for beauty and graciousness, and

many guests remarked the pride in Alexander's eyes when they fell on his wife.

His slightly jaundiced aide-de-camp, Mikhailovsky-Danilevsky, noted in his journal that not a single Russian come to Vienna had quality to match the importance of the moment. Indeed, Nesselrode and a few others could not be considered equals either in experience or in natural gifts of Metternich, Hardenberg, Castlereagh, and Talleyrand. Danilevsky failed to see that his Emperor had no need of experienced counsellors. He came to the Congress fired by a vision, determined to follow his mission which he believed to be God-given. Later, some writers would rebuke the Emperor for spending much time in gaiety. But he had fully earned his right to the gaiety. He sat at the Congress table, his mind perfectly clear on the matters in hand. If the business of the Congress dragged on, it was not Alexander who kept putting spokes in the wheel, but those who kept opposing him.

Among the major problems to be decided were the future status of Poland and the fate of Saxony. The Emperor meant to restore the Kingdom of Poland and to cede Saxony to Prussia in recompense for the devastation she had suffered during the war. The Kingdom of Poland, as its frontiers were envisaged by Alexander, would inevitably absorb some territories held by Prussia since the last Polish partition. He thought that Saxony, its behaviour treacherous all through the campaign, might well make a part of the compensation due to Prussia.

Trouble started at once. Both Britain and Austria opposed the plan. The greed of Prussia, not satisfied with the promise of Saxony, led her to insist that Polish lands along the banks of the Vistula should be added to her possessions. Austria, upheld by England, strenuously opposed any aggrandizement of Prussia. And the wily representative of a conquered France, who had come to Vienna as 'an observer', began spreading the idea that the Bourbons alone would eventually save Europe from total shipwreck. Talleyrand flattered Alexander, warned Metternich against Russia, told Hardenberg that Prussia must be on guard against Austria, and echoed Castlereagh's conviction that the Russian ideas spelt danger to Europe.

Alexander heard about the intrigues and brushed them aside. He did not know that in January 1815 a secret convention, its clauses directed against Russia, had been signed by Metternich, Castlereagh and Talleyrand, who hoped to cajole Bavaria, Württemberg and Hanover into his finely meshed net. Alexander knew about the opposition; he distrusted Metternich and guessed at the Austrian apprehension lest the re-creation of the Polish kingdom were to threaten Galicia. He did not, however, know that Talleyrand's dictum *'retablir la Pologne pour la livrer à la Russie signiferait créer un danger pour l'Europe'* went from Vienna to Paris, from Paris to London, and ended by hardening King George's government until at a session Castlereagh declared that his instructions were not to agree to the reconstruction of Poland except on condition that she would be independent of Russia. As to the cession of Saxony to Prussia, the statesmen argued themselves hoarse on the matter and could not arrive at any conclusion.

Alexander was spokesman throughout. In spite of the whirl of balls and banquets, he never came jaded into the hall of the Congress. Point by point, he pressed on with his case. His own Empire having been ravaged by the invader, he yet asked nothing for Russia. He wanted the very best for Prussia, whose greed and ingratitude must have hampered him sorely at many a turn. He kept cool enough during the sessions. In private, he felt he could afford to slip off the mask. He banged his fist on the table and lost his temper with Metternich more than once.

At last, they reached the doubtful harbour of compromise. *'Afin d'obtenir l'assentiment d'Alexandre à l'existence de la vieille Saxe,'* wrote Chateaubriand, *'il fut nécessaire d'abandonner la Pologne au Czar,'* but it would be a kingdom of Poland deprived of its ancient possessions in the Poznan Province and in Galicia.

The compromise, as was to be expected, infuriated Prussia. Hardenberg had been set on seeing his king put on the crown of Saxony. The turmoil deepened, and Talleyrand wondered if the compromise would work to any advantage of France. Castlereagh considered that the matter of Poland had been settled in the most hazardous way possible for the future of Europe's tranquillity, and Castlereagh was right. Alexander, having asked nothing for himself, had none the less won the incalculable advantage of having a vassal country set between his frontiers and the West.

Austria, certain of her future lien on Galicia, was quietened. Not so Prussia, the Saxon prize gone beyond all hope. Dissensions grew in bitterness until on a day in March a courier from France galloped into Vienna, his dispatch bringing all the statesmen to their senses.

Napoleon had landed at Cannes. Louis XVIII had fled to the Low Countries in such a hurry that most of his baggage and many state papers were left behind. From the Tuileries, once again master of Paris, Napoleon chose to send Alexander a copy of the secret treaty between Austria, Great Britain and France. No message was attached to the document, its contents, as Bonaparte hoped, being enough to make the Emperor of Russia see the sorry stuff his allies were made of. The Emperor of Russia read the paper, summoned Metternich, handed it to him, and said: '. . . *il ne doit jamais être question entre nous de cette affaire. Nous avons maintenant autre chose devant nous; notre alliance sera plus ferme que jamais. . . . Nous sommes chrétiens . . . notre sainte loi nous commande de pardonner les offenses,*' which was hardly a language to use to Metternich, but the incident illustrates Alexander's resolve not to betray 'the enlightenment' fallen to his lot. Napoleon having sent the paper out of malice, Alexander foiled his design by a most ingenious means where magnanimity and foresight marched hand in hand.

The news, having shaken Europe, at once ended the Viennese dalliance. The scent of war swept all over the allied countries. A host of some eight hundred thousand was being mustered, over one hundred thousand of them being Russians under Barclay's command, but all those regiments were in Russia. However urgent the orders, the spring had already become a memory before they could start for the west, and Barclay was not in time for Waterloo.

The Congress hurried with its business. Much red wax was melted, many papers were signed, and the newly fashioned kingdom of Poland was born—to the pleasure of Alexander and the Polish nobility, the humbler folk remaining wholly indifferent. The new kingdom, however, appeared in a somewhat altered form. His early dream attained, Alexander could afford to make minor concessions. To reconcile Prussia for Saxony, the Poznan Province, Thorn and Bromberg were given to her. Cracow was declared a free city. The Province of Veliczki together with the Tarnopol Region were ceded to Austria as a reward for her ardour in exaggerating her sacrifices.

There remained difficulties much more complicated than Prussian rapacity or Austrian sullenness. The very idea of a constitution being given to Poland by the Emperor of Russia, in whose dominions electoral representation remained the dream of a few, seemed an absurdity, and Pozzo di Borgo had enough courage to point out that it would tease Alexander's subjects into dangerous discontent. Alexander made no reply. Pozzo di Borgo, having served him so well, thereby lost the imperial favour.

Alexander's mistakes were rather obvious. Czartorizky had hoped to be appointed Viceroy in Poland. The Emperor nominated some-one else. The open letter to the President of the Polish Senate caused bewilderment and indignation in Russia.[1]

What, Nesselrode was asked on his return to St Petersburg, were the advantages of the great victory for Russia? To have an inimical neighbour incorporated into the Empire under conditions as yet unachieved in the Empire seemed a shabby return for all the sacrifices borne by Russia.

It was not so to Alexander, however. Two ideas were clear in his mind: to ensure peace in Europe and to establish Russia's place in the West. The grant of a constitution to an ancient enemy was not wholly a gesture of pure Christian chivalry. It was a well-calculated measure. It offered a proof of a level reached by Russia, a level which amply justified her full admittance into the comity of European nations. In that sense it becomes possible to endorse Madame de Staël's encomium: '. . . *seul entre les souverains,* [*Alexandre*] *marche dans le sens de la postérité.*' Nothing need be said here of the lesser German potentates, but neither Francis I of Austria nor Frederick William III of Prussia came up to Alexander's stature, nor can an exemplar be found among the predecessors of his own dynasty.

The Congress, galvanized into energy by Napoleon's escape, kept the Emperor busy enough but, with the shock receding, he found himself facing a legion of doubts. 'I do not want to see Russian blood shed again', he is supposed to have said, and though most urgent orders were sent to Barclay, the Emperor does not seem to have had much concern about their reaching Europe in time. There still remained a few lesser matters for the Congress to deal with, but Alexander felt spent. The Empress having returned to Russia, he left Vienna for Heilbronn.

[1] For full text see Grand Duke Nicholas, *The Emperor Alexander I*, Vol. I, p. 172. '*Si le grand intérêt du repos général n'a pas permis que tous les Polonais soient réunis sous le même sceptre, je me suis efforcé du moins d'adoucir, autant que possible, les rigueurs de leur séparation et de leur obtenir partout la jouissance possible de leur nationalité.*'

There a mood he had been prone to all his life engulfed him utterly. After the deafening maelstrom of Vienna, Heilbronn should have brought refreshment. Instead, Alexander's unruly imagination presented Napoleon's escape in terms of a revenge. He had prayed for a victory over 'the foe of mankind', but his prayers had not been answered. Now even the Bible could not sweeten the bitterness, and memories of a March night in 1801 filled his mind again. Alexander had never been wholly free of that cancer, but now, his thought, grown accustomed to interpretative journeys into obscure texts of the Apocalypse, saw in Napoleon's bid for the power he had lost something like God's answer to the daring which had ventured to vanquish one evil by the means of an earlier one.

'My heart felt so heavy,' the Emperor wrote to Mademoiselle Sturdza, his wife's lady-in-waiting, with whom he would correspond on mystical themes, 'and I had to leave the Bible alone. Then I remembered what you had told me about Madame de Krüdener. Where is she now, I wondered, and where could I meet her? Here I heard a knock at the door, and in came Prince Volkonsky, looking rather ill at ease. He said he could not help disturbing me because he did not know how to get rid of a woman who insisted on seeing me. To my amazement he named Madame de Krüdener. I received her at once. She, apparently reading all my thoughts, brought me much comfort.'

To the dismay of the household, the lady stayed three hours with the Emperor, her first words being a passionate admonition that he should acknowledge his sins if he desired to obtain peace. Alexander knew that Roxanna Sturdza had met the lady at Karlsruhe earlier that summer and been greatly impressed by her eloquence. Alexander did not know that his whereabouts on leaving Vienna were made known to the Baroness who, before going to Heilbronn, wrote to Mademoiselle Sturdza that it was essential for her, Julie Krüdener, to meet the Emperor privately—'*j'ai d'immenses choses à lui dire car j'ai beaucoup éprouvé à son sujet.*'

Born in 1764, Julie Fittinhof came of petty Baltic gentry, her father having amassed a fortune by clever speculations in corn and alcohol. She had a dowry and she had looks. French was her second mother-tongue, its study beginning and ending her education. Her most striking attribute was an intense interest in her own self. At eighteen she married Baron Krüdener, her senior by twenty-odd years, and she had two children, whose arrival was not allowed to interfere with her way of life. She would leave the Baron when it pleased her and then return to him when her resources were depleted. Her autobiography was in reality a romance. 'I was always close to nature . . .'—the lady could not tell elm from oak. 'Pleasures of society meant nothing to me, and I have always clung to simplicity . . .'—wherever she lived, Julie Krüdener formed a salon, and a three months' stay in Paris ended with an enormous account at the most fashionable modiste's. Julie Krüdener made it her business to meet anyone worth knowing in most European capitals. Doors were open to her; she bore a good name, had a wonderful conversational facility, and enough discretion not to make a vulgar display of her lapses from conventional virtue.

In 1804, a widow, her circumstances crippled by extravagances and by lawsuits, the Baroness was at Riga. A chance encounter with a shoemaker, who belonged to the Moravian Brethren, decided her fate. Imagination, unacquainted with any discipline, leapt high, and within a few months Julie Krüdener knew herself to be one of the elect, her mission being to transform the kingdoms of the world into the Kingdom of God. Those who crossed her path either damned her or exalted her. The Emperor of Russia proved to be the greatest fish in her net.

At the time of the Vienna Congress, she was in Switzerland, preaching, praying and prophesying. From there she made her way to Baden. Her coming to Heilbronn was a carefully calculated step, and she won the first round brilliantly.

'We do not value her merits very highly,' said Grand Duke Nicholas in his *Alexander I*, 'and her sincerity is more than doubtful.' The last words should be slightly qualified. Krüdener believed passionately that she was a messenger of God; she gave herself up to prayer and maintained that on occasions she was in direct communication with her Maker. But the nineteenth century afforded no background comparable to the biblical days: prophets had to take some thought for the morrow. Straitened finances mapped much of Krüdener's way; Alexander could well afford to be generous as is evidenced by many of his letters to Golitzin. He made her many gifts. The prophetess, however, soon began considering them as her due.

Her hold on the Emperor lasted little more than a year. She ended by boring him—but not before some harm had been done. Golitzin and Koshelev had certainly influenced the Emperor; they had put the Bible into his hands and done much to awaken his spiritual consciousness. But neither of them had any intention of 'possessing' or 'directing' Alexander's soul. The Baroness, having captured him by her eloquence at Heilbronn, proceeded to write: '*Si vous saviez combien Il vous aime, vous ne pourriez Lui résister en rien.*' Nor did she stop there. She alleged that none except herself was given the grace to know that Alexander was '*un des élus, et votre coeur fut déjà préparé par de grands sacrifices et d'énormes douleurs à être capable de devenir la joie . . . de notre Dieu . . .*'[1]

She went on to explain that Napoleon and all the ravages by him committed were so many expressions of God's will, an instrument in God's hand whereby Alexander's triumph might be manifested to the expectant, wearied world. Yet the attainment of that final triumph must be girdled by certain conditions. '. . . *dans nos relations, votre réserve coupe tout . . . Il faut que vous deveniez un enfant. . . . Toutes les voies humaines ne peuvent rien vous apprendre—il faut l'oeil divin . . . il faut cette femme* [she refers to herself] *habituée à vivre aux pieds de Christ . . .*' She was writing those letters at the time when the wounds, the uprootings and the jealousies caused by Napoleon's invasions had not had the time to heal. Out of those clouds Krüdener envisaged Europe as one vast temple dedicated to contemplation, with the Emperor as its high priest and herself his vicaress, always at hand to interpret the will of God to his far less enlightened understanding.

'[*Je*] *m'attache à vous comme une mère tendre qui surveille son enfant avec anxiété.*' It was wrong for the Emperor to be so burdened with purely congressional business. A far loftier task awaited him. '*Les liens de la nature, ceux des Empires . . . ne sont que les secondaires lorsqu'il s'agit de Vous, Seigneur,*' and then she asked Alexander: '*Où trouveriez-vous l'être qui peut être pour vous ce que je suis? Je vous dis sans crainte, vous ne pourrez avancer sans moi autant que Dieu veut que ce soît moi. . . .*' Brazen vanity could hardly go further.

Krüdener failed in making her influence felt in matters of real importance. That, in spite of the triumphant paeans in her letters,

---

[1] All the quotations from Baroness Krüdener's letters to the Emperor are taken from Grand Duke Nicholas's *Alexander I*, Vol. II, p. 215 et seq.

she deepened his sense of sin and therefore helped to pave the way to even deeper melancholy, is unhappily true. The root of the harm lay in one diseased imagination so playing on another that little by little Alexander's sense of reality would come to be blurred. The process was gradual. Nothing but a seed was planted in 1815.

That autumn Krüdener installed herself in Paris, prophesying and praying with greater intensity than ever before, and Alexander saw much of her, but even Empeytas, her most ardent panegyrist, dared not assert that the Baroness was responsible for the instrument of the Holy Alliance, though it is true that during his three months' stay in Paris the Emperor spent his free evenings in Krüdener's salon where they read the Bible, prayed, recounted their dreams and visions, and on occasions listened to the hostess's prophecies. The Baroness was certainly a success, and those meetings were often crowded.

Yet even then there came awkward interludes. Krüdener claimed the gift of knowing things which happened at a distance. A guest entered her salon one evening at the moment when she was saying loudly and slowly, graving each word with a peculiar emphasis: 'Momentous things will soon happen all over the world, and it is good that a severe fast is being kept all over Paris this evening.' The guest, having just come from a succulent banquet at the Palais Royal, felt nonplussed, and later shared his bewilderment with many. But Krüdener, even if confronted with the discrepancy, would not have been at a loss for an answer: all sense of time being denied in her visions, the rigid fast might well have been held already, or else it would be kept at some time not yet defined.

Some time in 1816 the Emperor got tired of those spiritual apron strings and told Princess Mecherskaya that he thought the Baroness's 'light' was an *ignis fatuus*. Krüdener's disciples at once blamed Metternich for the estrangement and explained that the prophetess was too spiritually minded to take notice of intrigues against her.

The rest of the sordid story can be told here. The Baroness began carrying her evangel all over Switzerland and the German states; she did not avoid publicity, and soon enough made a nuisance of herself. The Swiss police handed her over to the Bavarian authorities, and those passed her on to Württemberg. Her sermons brushed against all the social ills of the hour, and she kept promising her listeners that all the darkness in their lives would vanish once the Kingdom of God was established among them; but authorities, absorbed in their task of restoring a normal rhythm of life, had small use for a lady who moved people to discontent, offered no tangible remedies, and seldom had enough money to settle her bill at the inn.

All that time Krüdener kept sending stilted, repetitive letters to the Emperor, where spiritual texts were interwoven with descriptions of her own visions and cloying flattery was neighboured by obscurely worded warnings of burdens soon to fall on Alexander's shoulders. Gradually her letters were crowded with sour complaints and reproaches. In her mind, the Holy Alliance became a thing of nought since nothing was being done to ease anyone's lot. '*On nous a forcés de partir de Bade,*' she wrote from Leipzig on Christmas Eve 1817, '*sans un sou d'argent. . . . Enfin on se demande, à quoi sert la Sainte Alliance et si on ose croire qu'elle n'est un simple son. . . . Les chrétiens dorment. Nous avons plaidé la cause des opprimés et nous avons dû être persécutés. . . . En Prusse, on nous a traités comme des malfaiteurs . . .*' and here the Baroness added a sentence which, when we remember Alexander's opinion about the King of Saxony, was not likely to move the Emperor to compassion: '*le roi de Saxe a été seul humain envers nous . . .*'

Her crusade come to an inglorious end, beset by creditors, facing a bleak evening, the lady returned to her native Baltic coast, to resume from there her interminable letters to the Emperor. She had not met him until she was over fifty, but it did not prevent her from maintaining that her entire life had been devoted to him and even more: the Emperor owed her, Julie Krüdener, an incalculable debt: '*je vous ai proclamé aux peuples et aux états comme l'Elu du Seigneur,*' but the extravagant claim received no recognition in St Petersburg. The letters were not answered. Alexander was occupied with matters of far graver moment both at home and abroad. In spite of his silence, the Baroness would not give up hope. Her epistles grew in number, length and absurdity. Now she insisted that the Emperor must occupy himself with internal affairs of this or that country according to the vision given her. Now she complained that all her efforts with his soul were being wasted for the number of the tasks he kept taking on. At the end of 1818 she came to Russia and stayed in St Petersburg, but no audience was accorded to her, and her last letter in September 1819, written from a small town in the south of Russia, can speak for itself:

'The time has come when I must speak plainly. I have struggled hard, forsaken by the one man who should have been my companion at the foot of the Cross. Calumniated and persecuted, I crossed the whole of Europe, fighting for the noblest cause anyone could embrace, and I fought for that cause, not a single grain of self-interest in my mind. . . . Then I came to Russia—I was so near your home—banished from it by an intrigue . . . I had offered up my whole life to you and now, having come to your great Empire, I did not have a single flower given me . . . not even a cup of cold water— the only thing I could accept from you. . . . And I wept over the ills of Russia, I, God's servant, condemned by the shameful intrigues of politicians . . .'

The Emperor refused to meet her again, but the Baroness did not scruple to receive more than 'a cup of cold water' at the hands of 'the intriguing politicians'. Her wanderings ended, her comfort assured, she died a few years later.

It is an ignoble and sad story, and the blame cannot be wholly laid at the Baroness's door. At Heilbronn and in Paris she received most exaggerated encouragement from Alexander. However fatuous her later letters, there had been a time when he would listen to her, pray together with her, find comfort in her words, ask for her counsel, and follow with something like pleasure the undisciplined drift of her utterances. Julie Krüdener had praised an image built in her own imagination: She had never learned the man, but her mistakes and extravagances together cannot quite justify the Emperor's manner of sundering a link he had been the first to fashion.

According to Alexander Sturdza, one of the Emperor's secretaries, the Act of the Holy Alliance was originally written in pencil by Alexander's own hand. In making a fair copy Capo d'Istria and Sturdza slightly amended the style, but they did not alter the meaning of a single paragraph.

The basic idea was not original. The really novel element lay in Alexander's conviction that the idea and the time complemented each other, that Europe, rescued from Napoleon, was ready to form a federal union based on inviolable principles of justice and mutual trust. Charlemagne's imperial concept had mirrored the same design—and, however varied in form, it had lasted until the sixteenth century, when the Reformation dealt a death blow to the Holy Roman Empire by cleaving its body asunder. A little later Grotius put forward his theory that international relationships should be based on the assumption of legal equality among all the states. But the theory failed to answer in practice. By the eighteenth century, power lay in the hands of five states—Britain, Prussia, France, Austria and Russia. Sovereignty without the backing of wealth, great territorial possessions and a strong army ceased to count. The King of Denmark, the Margrave of Baden and the Grand Duke of Tuscany could indeed sign treaties and choose their friends from among the mighty, but they were never allowed to forget that trout had precedence over the minnows.

In his youth Alexander had read Sully, whose *Grand Dessein* could not fail to capture his imagination. The purpose of the federal union was 'to deliver Europe for ever from the bloody catastrophe of war and to secure an unalterable peace so that all the princes might henceforth live together in concord . . .' But Alexander's plan was no mere echo of Sully's *Dessein*. The latter was rooted in the commonalty of statesmanship. The Emperor's 'Act' aimed at introducing conscience into the business of governing. The signatories were invited 'to publish their firm determination . . . to take for their sole guide the precepts of the Holy Religion, of justice, Christian charity and peace . . . which . . . must have an immediate influence on the counsels of princes . . . being the only means of firmly establishing human institutions and correcting their imperfections.' These ideas were embodied in the three articles of the Act, which committed the signatories to form a union of brotherly friendship, to consider themselves members of a single Christian race, and to invite others to join the Alliance.

Alexander's idea, so compelling in its simplicity, could not but remain an ideal. He believed the moment to be most propitious for its realization. In hard truth, the moment was no more and no less propitious than any other moment in history. Europe was outwardly at peace; no armies crashed across any frontiers, no unremarked fields leapt into chronicles because of fearful battles fought on their breast, no councils of war were summoned at wayside inns or in peasants' huts. But there was no inner peace, and the same conditions which had shaped the Napoleonic era could be evoked again—even with a far less menacing Napoleon to direct their course—because of famine, disease, lack of justice in the courts, bad harvests, epidemics among the cattle, mistrust of a language not understood beyond a frontier, and the sullen discontent thickening among the numberless have-nots. 1815 held all those and many more in its womb.

Again Alexander's aim was to establish a pattern according to 'the precepts of the Holy Religion'. Here he thought and planned within the light to him accorded, and that light was no flicker of a tallow candle. He had friends among the Quakers, he forbade the Holy Synod to persecute any dissenters in his own Empire, he allowed many of his Orthodox subjects to become Roman Catholics, he was gracious alike to Lutheran and to Calvinist, and jealously safeguarded the interests of his Muslim subjects. But that very tolerance displayed by him on so many occasions stirred mistrust in the West. 'Holy Religion' meant one thing to the King of Prussia and quite another to the Emperor of Austria. The divisions in Christendom had never before troubled Alexander. Now he was to feel their bitterness.

Frederick William III approved of the Act, and Hardenberg signed it on his king's behalf. The Emperor Francis was rather unsure of the commitments it involved. In the end Metternich was allowed to append his signature to the document he called contemptuously 'vide et sonore'. Castlereagh condemned it outright, and 'the piece of sublime mysticism and nonsense' never received the British signature, though the Regent sent a personal letter to Alexander with polite assurances of his personal agreement with the lofty principles embodied in the Act.

In late autumn of 1815, all allusions to 'the precepts of the Holy Religion' studiedly avoided, the Allies signed a Treaty of Alliance. Its sixth article might be taken as an inauguration of the brief congressional era.

In spite of the attitude of Great Britain and Austria, the echoes of the Holy Alliance still lingered over Europe, and the resolve embodied in the short Act became the hope of many. To quote Sorel[1]—'*Alexandre se montra tout à la fois ce qu'il était et ce qu'il voulait paraître, politique et magnanime. Cette grandeur d'âme dont il se sentait capable, dont il se faisait depuis sa jeunesse un idéal, il l'avait plutôt mise en scène et s'en étant plutôt donné le spectacle en 1814 qu'il n'en avait éprouvé l'efficace et opéré l'action. En 1815 il vit*

[1] *Napoléon et Alexandre,* 172.

de haut, il vit clair, il vit loins, et il agit avec autant de simplicité et de droiture que d'énergie et d'habileté.'

Alexander's sole enemy had been Napoleon. Again and again he would stress the fact that he regarded the people of France as his friends, but the Prussians thought differently. France lying prostrate, it was surely the moment for the conquerors to fall upon her body. So Prussia, all shame forgotten, raised her voice to demand the cession of Alsace-Lorraine. One evening, alone with the Duc de Richelieu, Alexander unfolded a map of France and, pencil in hand, traced all the territorial sacrifices demanded of France by the Allies and said to the duke: *'Voilà la France telle que mes alliés veulent la faire. Il n'y manque que ma signature et je vous promets qu'elle y manquera toujours.'*

In December 1815 the Emperor was back in St Petersburg. Elizabeth saw little of him. *'J'y suis tout résignée,'* she wrote to her mother, *'sachant combien il est tarabusté, occupé, accablé d'affaires.'*

In Alexander's armies there were many men like Arakcheev, who could travel through the length and breadth of Europe and return home to make no more revealing comment than that the German and French soups were greatly inferior to the Russian. But there were also numbers of others, who, remarking all the evidence left in the wake of invasions, knew they had crossed the frontier in more senses than one, that they were in a Europe where a mighty effort for individual liberty had been made and made successfully less than a generation before. Inevitably, such men began making comparisons between the familiar landscape at home and the infinitely more inviting conditions of life they saw all about them. On their eventual return to Russia, such men carried anguish in their hearts and daring thoughts of liberty in their minds. Pypin quotes[1] from the diary of Ivan Yakushkin, an officer in the Guards and later a Decembrist: 'The first brigade [of Guards] landed at Oranienbaum, and a vast crowd had collected to welcome us. A solemn Te Deum was sung out in the open as soon as we came ashore. All through the service numbers of policemen continued kicking and beating those civilians who tried to get nearer to the soldiers. . . . What a sad and sickening impression it made on us. . . . And the episode was followed by many similar ones . . .'

[1] op. cit., p. 34.

Such an impression would have glanced off the men's minds, but among the officers it increased the consciousness of the general rottenness in their country. It did not matter so much that European peasants were not compelled to share their roof with livestock and poultry. It certainly mattered that they were not serfs and that the feudal crust in many German states was being broken up by the onrush of new ideas. But in Russia the common folk went by the name of 'black folk' —at the mercy of every policeman and every clerk in a Government office.

Discontent spread. It had other causes over and above insidious comparisons. They still called Alexander 'The Blessed' and were proud of the leading part played by him in the councils of Europe. But they were no longer in 1812 or even in 1814. They asked themselves why the Emperor should have so exerted himself on behalf of Poland, an ancient enemy, and of France, which they had vanquished. Taxes in Russia rose alarmingly. So did the cost of living. The Treasury was supposed to be almost empty, and nobody, as they saw, was prepared to offer them the means whereby they might rebuild their ruined cities. The bestowal of a constitution on Poland deepened the growing unrest, and there reactionaries and liberals, however varied their reasons, met on common ground. It seemed unjust that so much should be done for the foreigner when so many national needs remained unanswered. Already in September 1816, the French ambassador, de Noailles, wrote to Paris about the increasing financial embarrassment in the Empire and also about '*le mécontentement qui en est la suite . . . si cette fumée se dissipait, je ne sais ce que deviendrait ce grand Empire . . .*' Admittedly, this was a foreigner's opinion, but de Noailles's powers of observation were far above the average. It did not take him long to discover the mutual dislike between the throne and the nobility and to adjudge Alexander's care for the army in a novel way. '*L'Empereur se croit assez fort avec son armée . . . pour se mesurer . . . contre tout ennemi intérieur. . . . L'armée est constamment l'objet de ses soins.*'

As usual, criticism leapt into grotesque exaggerations. 'Nothing is being done for the country,' wailed the chorus of pessimists recruited from among every school of opinion. Yet things were being done. The educational reforms proceeded apace and that in spite of depleted national resources. Men were still working at the notes left by Speransky. Alexander had not yet shelved the question of emancipation and invited many landowners to submit their views on the reform. From Vienna he had written to Koshelev about a great task awaiting him at home. He meant to devote himself to it 'coûte que coûte'. That task was very possibly emancipation. Just at that time two or three men, who had studied the problem for some years, submitted their detailed reports to the Emperor. General Kisselev was among them.

Irritated by the false interpretations given, so the Emperor thought, to the aims of the Holy Alliance by British spokesmen, he wrote a letter to his ambassador at St James's. Its contents were to be made known to the Regent and Castlereagh. They must have bemused the former and done little more than to confirm the latter in his earlier opinion of the Alliance.

Now that Napoleon was conquered once and for all, wrote the Emperor, another and an even more deadly enemy was working towards the annulment of the triumph achieved by the Allies. '*Le génie du mal, terrassé par l'action supérieure de la Providence . . . semble faire de nouveaux efforts*'—all in order to wreck the Holy Alliance.

The spirit of evil would, as time went on, be manifested in numberless ways—from the mutinous behaviour of German university students to a careless answer given by a Russian soldier to his company sergeant. What Alexander firmly believed to be its manifestations would be fought not by prayer and fasting but by the sickening zeal of his own secret police carrying out repressive measures, many of which would be suggested to the Emperor by Metternich.

But in 1816 the only expression was found in the letter to Lieven. Alexander's mood was heightened by the homage they paid him in Europe. He kept stressing that Russia had no territorial hunger and he was believed. 'The Gulf of Bothnia is something of a wall now that Finland belongs to us. Poland stands between us and the West, and we enjoy the privileges afforded by many ports on the Baltic. Turkey is a safe enough neighbour because she is weak, and we have no axe to grind in Europe.' Alexander had accomplished his mission brilliantly. Now he told himself that he must not stay idle. '*Le génie du mal*' and its fearful challenge must be fought.

In 1816 the Emperor's twilight was still some two or three years distant. But the seed was implanted in his thought. There was nothing to wonder at: an impressionable mind, leaping from the heights of enthusiasm into an abyss of melancholy, had taken a plunge into the waters of the other-worldly, neither rudder nor compass to guide his course. Such a plunge necessarily demands a lengthy preparation and a total dedication. Alexander had had none of the former. Being an autocrat and harassed by all the affairs of state, he could not possibly afford the latter. There was nobody to warn him that the powers of evil can and do use a half-dedicated soul for their own purposes. Alexander's twilight and midnight cannot be explained in any other way. A passionate neophyte, he ran along a path where he should have walked with the utmost circumspection.

The project of the so-called military settlements had already been foreshadowed in the Manifesto of November 1814. '... and we hope that the firm establishment of peace and tranquillity will enable us to find the means whereby the living conditions of the men in our forces might be greatly improved, and a way be found to have them settled in the country and be no longer separated from their wives and families.' It should here be noted that the idea belonged wholly to the Emperor. Contrary to many contemporary opinions, it did not come from Arakcheev. In point of fact, he strongly opposed it at the beginning.

Service conditions in Alexander's Empire were harsh in the extreme. There was no regular conscription, the Government having recourse to recruitment whenever it answered their purpose, and little by little recruitment became a more or less regular annual feature—to the great resentment of landowners. In common parlance, military service bore the name of '*kátorga*', i.e. 'penal servitude.' In theory, the term lasted twenty-five years. In grim practice, it ended when a man was no longer fighting fit. On being forced into the army, a recruit must say goodbye—often for ever— to his parents, his wife and children, and his home fields. There was no leave even in peace-time, nor was there any provision made for the permanently disabled. If the cruel discipline and the enemy cannon balls did not succeed in killing a man, he would come back to his village and get no welcome from anyone, least of all from his kin—if he had any left. Whether crippled or not, such a man was no longer regarded as a member of the community. Twenty-five or more years of soldiering would have divorced him from the plough and harrow, and drones were not particularly cherished in the countryside. His master might or might not have compassion on his old age. The *mir*, i.e. 'commune', would grudge him a crust or a rag. All in all, the plight of army veterans was such that many a man, on returning home, had reason to regret that the enemy bullets had spared him.

Alexander was determined to make an end of it. In time of peace, his soldiers, reunited to their families, would live in the country, work the land to them allotted, and incidentally lighten the financial burdens of the War Ministry. So in 1815 one battalion of Grenadier Guards was 'settled' at Vissotzk in the Novgorod Province. In the following year many more military units were 'settled' between St Petersburg and Kaluga.

Alexander's sincerity in wishing to ease his soldiers' lot could not be doubted. Arakcheev opposed the idea on the grounds that it was not practical, and he suggested an alternative: the term of military service should be shortened by eight years. But the Emperor turned it down, and he ended by persuading his 'dear friend' to see his point of view, and 'the dear friend' became Commander-in-Chief of all the military settlements in Russia. Nothing was made public. There were no official announcements that such and such a regiment was being 'settled' in such and such a province. The Emperor willed it, and Arakcheev obeyed the command.

The late Grand Duke Nicholas thought that there existed a link between the military settlements and the development of Alexander's religious mania[1]. To admit such a link would lead to a confusion of issues. Most certainly, Alexander was a romantic, and he had read Karamzin's note on 'Ancient and Modern Russia' with its moving picture of a labourer seated on the lush silken grass and enjoying the evening landscape in his wife's company—as though any labourer in Russia had any leisure or inclination to enjoy any landscape. But there was not a trace of romanticism in the development of military settlements. It was a healthy, practical idea, void of any sugared sentimentality. It was a mixture of humaneness and economic foresight: there were the men to work the land, and the War Ministry, though retaining their services in case of a national need, was no longer responsible for their keep.

[1] cf. op. cit., *The Emperor Alexander I*, Vol. I, p. 228.

A poisonous plant grew out of that good seed.

Arakcheev was busy enough at the time, and Alexander might have called on many of his generals who, unlike Arakcheev, knew every aspect of a soldier's life in barracks. There were Dokhturov and Konovnitzin, to name but two, men whose natural gifts together with their experience enabled them to follow a rigid discipline without letting its demands petrify into soullessness. But Alexander chose to entrust the task to Arakcheev, who was an expert on ballistics, knew the army regulations by heart and was at home on the parade ground, and who regarded the men as so many uniformed marionettes. To him, the army was a gigantic mechanism, and he prided himself on his knowledge of every cog, bolt and nut in it. In his hands, military settlements would gradually become so many forerunners of concentration camps. Far from easing a soldier's lot, Arakcheev embittered it beyond telling. Peasants passed over by recruiting officers were now forced into uniform and made subject to the army discipline. Little boys, accustomed to brief shirts in the summer and rough sheepskins in the winter, were dressed as soldiers. Days began and ended with the roll call. They marched to their work in the fields and they marched back again. Every day was 'regulated' from sunrise to sunset. The little huts, apparently so pleasant and inviting, were in reality so many barracks in miniature. The housewife must have so many pots, platters and mugs, and keep them on a shelf according to the regulations. She was fined if she served fish to her family on the day when broth was appointed for dinner. If she did her washing on Tuesday instead of on Monday, she was haled before the military tribunal. Men at eighteen and girls at sixteen were married by drawing lots. Widows who were not past child-bearing were forced to re-marry. The least murmur of dissent led to sickening reprisals.

None of it reached the Emperor's ears. His frequent visits to various settlements gave him an impression of happy and well-ordered activity. Arakcheev was as limited as cruel people only can be limited, but he was no fool. Alexander's visits being known beforehand, the favourite left nothing to chance and presented a well-nigh paradisical landscape to the august visitor.

How, it can well be asked, could it happen that a humane and sensitive man like Alexander should have so cherished a sadistic bully and should have drawn him nearer and nearer the throne until the favourite's power seemed almost to brush against the fringe of autocracy and the years of his sway came to be called '*arakcheev-china*'. There was nothing endearing in the man. Apart from his knowledge of ballistics, his mind was like a shrivelled pea. He would take offence without provocation and carry his sulks to Gruzino there to indulge in a prolonged spell of self-commiseration whilst important matters must needs hang fire in St Petersburg. He had neither manners nor education. His piety was a nauseating mockery. He was loathed and feared by everybody in the land. The imperial family detested him. Alexander's brothers stood in awe of him.

But to the Emperor, Arakcheev was his 'dear and estimable Alexey Andreevich'. Arakcheev's asthma and insomnia were matters of grave concern to Alexander. All the letters written to him are charged with deep affection and boundless trust. The gifts of asthma pastilles, very special bilberry jam, little cushions stuffed with aromatic herbs, snuffboxes, pills to conquer insomnia, all those innumerable presents sent from the palace spoke of an intimacy which entered every detail of Arakcheev's life and often forestalled his needs. Where is the clue to the tie between 'The Blessed' and 'the accursed serpent', as Prince Peter Volkonsky and many others called Arakcheev? How to explain Alexander's delight in those visits to Gruzino where the host's conversation could neither amuse nor enlighten, and where the host's drunken slut of a mistress must needs be hidden out of sight during the Emperor's sojourn under her lover's roof?

Paul's ghost is the only possible clue to the enigma.

In Alexander's youth, 'the Gatchina sergeant-major' would often screen him from his father's wrath. Later, Arakcheev's loyalty to the father was transferred to the son. Alexander was convinced that if Arakcheev had been there, something would have prevented his father from being murdered. Arakcheev refused to believe in Alexander's share in the murder. In the Emperor's later life, he alone screened him, as it were, from his father's ghost. In his presence, particularly at Gruzino, Alexander felt easier, as though Arakcheev's obdurate faith in him drew—however fleetingly—some poison out of the memory.

In January 1817 the Empress Elizabeth wrote to Baden that '*les manières de l'empereur pour moi sont devenues tout à fait amicales*,' and the people in the capital and at Tsarskoe Selo were heartened to see the imperial couple often appearing together.

The engagement of the Emperor's younger brother, Grand Duke Nicholas, to Princess Charlotte of Prussia led to a spate of furtive speculations. Grand Duke Constantine, still styled the heir, was then living with Johanna Grudzinska, a Polish lady whom he hoped to marry. People knew, or thought that they knew, that Constantine had no wish to succeed his brother. Nicholas was but little known to the nation. Spoilt by his mother since childhood, even more handsome than Alexander, the young Grand Duke was supposed to be cold and arrogant. A letter sent by him to his fiancée before her arrival in Russia affords a telling revelation of the split in the imperial family. Princess Charlotte was to pay every attention, courtesy and respect to the Empress Elizabeth—'mais pas la moindre confiance—en aucun cas. Pour l'empereur, tout respect, confiance entière et la plus grande amitié.' The girl's mind thus prejudiced before she left Potsdam, she quickly became 'das Herzblatt der Kaiserin Mutter'. The two imperial camps continued to dispense outward courtesy to each other and no more. The Dowager Empress never lost an opportunity to interfere or to criticize. The formation of the new Ministry of Spiritual Affairs, with Prince Alexander Golitzin at the head, called by Karamzin 'the Ministry of Eclipse', caused Marie to remind her son that he would have little time for the real business of government if he allowed himself to be absorbed in religious matters. It was true, but it might have been expressed with less crudity.

Elizabeth, disliking Baroness Krüdener and all the others of the same colour, erred in an opposite direction. She would not criticize even where criticism was necessary. The Empress Marie, her own spiritual needs about as deep as a saucer, disapproved without having the least idea of the matter in hand. Elizabeth might have served Alexander far better if, herself much more at home in such things than her mundane mother-in-law, she could have steeled herself to check her husband's growing preoccupation with pseudo-mysticism. She never did—so afraid was she of again running into the cold waters of his neglect.

The opening of the first Polish Sejm in March 1818 sharpened the family dissensions. Marie, her daughter Catherine, Constantine and even Nicholas, were appalled by the Emperor's speech. He told the

Poles that he considered all his pledges to them were carried out. . . . 'The level of culture in your country having enabled me to put liberal principles into practice. . . . I still hope that their salutary influence may be felt throughout all my dominions . . .' Young Grand Duchess Nicholas echoed Marie's verdict that the speech 'would give rise to many false hopes in Russia'. The Empress Elizabeth's undisguised pleasure and pride served for nothing but to enhance her outsider's position in the family.

✓ The speech led to a multitude of reactions in Russia. The diehards were indignant at the damaging comparison made between the two countries. The liberals gave a qualified approval, though it irked them to realize that a constitution so freely granted to an ancient enemy was not even in an embryo state in Russia. The young rejoiced to see in the Emperor's speech an earnest of their own liberties to come. Karamzin wrote sorrowfully to Dimitriev, the old poet, 'the news from Warsaw has greatly troubled all the young minds in the capital. They sleep and dream of the glorious constitution.' The lesser gentry throughout the Empire were disturbed, someone having said that constitution and emancipation were bedfellows.

Alexander wrote to Koshelev that the speech had come from his heart, and he did not even suspect that his liberalism so richly proved beyond the Russian frontiers had done much to irritate his Russian subjects. On leaving Warsaw, he travelled from one province to another, and faint ripples of discontent puzzled him. The cause being to him unknown, he was none the less disturbed. Only at Gruzino, under his favourite's hospitable roof, sipping a raspberry cordial and listening to the host's adenoidal voice recounting the day's ordinary happenings, did Alexander find rest from all the troubles and doubts fretting his mind. The Sovereign and the favourite went to the cathedral-like church of Gruzino there to attend a beautifully sung requiem for the repose of the soul of the Emperor Paul, and Paul's son left Gruzino refreshed and quietened.

In the autumn, on the eve of his leaving for the Congress to be held at Aix-la-Chapelle, the Emperor said to the French ambassador: '*La France et l'Europe renferment une éspèce d'hommes dangereux qui ont horreur de l'ordre . . . et qui s'accomodent bien à un régime qui satisfait toutes les passions basses. . . . Il ne faudra pas que votre gouvernement, affranchi de la surveillance des armées alliées, s'endorme sur ces dangers . . .'*

De Noailles took it to mean that the Emperor was still disturbed by the ghosts of 1789. He replied that he believed his government was strong enough to deal with any revolutionary movement. Alexander did not smile. He did not mean the revolution, as such, he explained. The devil had a well-equipped armoury at his disposal, and revolution was but one of the many weapons. There existed a powerful secret organization, vowed to chaos and destruction, and ready to pounce upon Europe. De Noailles, remembering the Emperor's speech in Warsaw, looked perplexed. 'We are all prepared for the battle,' Alexander assured him.

There were neither empresses nor queens at Aix-la-Chapelle to lend gaiety to the second Congress. There was nothing but hard work. The main issue was the Allied occupation of France, but there was a host of minor affairs for the Congress to settle one way or another. There were difficulties between Sweden and Denmark; the Elector of Hesse was asking to be recognized as King; there was a complaint of Monaco against its Prince; the disputed succession to the Duchy of Baden; and the Jewish problem in Prussia and Austria. It seemed a crowded agenda.

Great men were gathered together at Aix: Wellington, Richelieu, Castlereagh, Metternich, Hardenberg and Nesselrode. Once again, the Emperor of Russia proved an acknowledged leader. He neither danced nor indulged in delicate dalliances with the ladies of Aix. He did not say anything about '*le genié du mal.*' He worked. He made one fiery speech after another, convincing the Congress that the Allied troops should evacuate France at the earliest possible opportunity since it was essential for the health of Europe that France should be a fully fledged member of the Alliance. Alexander won on the major point, but there was little enough accord about other matters awaiting the Congress. Argument followed argument. Russia and Prussia wanted an international fleet to patrol the Mediterranean to check the Barbary pirates, but Britain turned it down. About the only point passed unanimously was the decision not to recognize the Elector of Hesse as King.

The Congress was nearing its closure when the Emperor came out with a bombshell of a proposal. His mind turning back to '*le génie du mal*', he suggested that a declaration should be signed to guarantee the rights of princes to all existing territorial settlements—in case the latter were menaced by an untoward twist in the European situation. Hardenberg and Metternich applauded it. Such a measure, as they saw clearly, would compel the signatories to common action against any uprising and check the flow of any changes. Castlereagh defeated the proposal, saying that the Alliance was 'never intended as a union for the government of the world, or for the superintendence of the internal affairs in other countries.' France supported Great Britain.

IX
THE TWILIGHT

IN JANUARY 1819 the court went into mourning for Grand Duchess Catherine, Queen of Württemberg, who died very suddenly from an attack of erysipelas in her thirty-first year. Her death smote at Alexander with a flail. She was his favourite sister; she enjoyed good health, and in the abruptness of her going he saw but another proof of God's displeasure with him. Catherine's vagaries had been many, her political game a mixture of tiresome childishness and dangerous intrigue. She delighted in creating gulfs in the family, and her dislike of the Empress Elizabeth was so evident that some people held her responsible for the long estrangement between husband and wife. Taste and discretion entirely lacking in her, the Grand Duchess bestowed friendship without considering the consequences. She could be strikingly vulgar, and at the death of her first husband, Prince George of Oldenburg, she was supposed to have said that she did not regret being a widow because black became her. None the less, she had a definite colour of her own, was interested in literature, and seemed far more enlightened than all her other sisters.

In the last few years of her life Catherine showed a growing affection for Nicholas, her younger brother. She approved his marriage and was markedly attentive to his bride.

Grand Duke Nicholas was twenty-three. Badly educated, the apple of his mother's eye, he might have been a son of Arakcheev's because '*l'affaire militaire*' absorbed him to the exclusion of all else—with the sole exception of the Dowager Empress's entertainments. He had been abroad, but his travels had not widened his horizons. His horsemanship was impeccable. In what concerned family relations, he and his younger brother, Michael, faithfully followed the lead given by the Empress Marie.

The summer of 1819 saw the usual manoeuvres at Krasnoe Selo attended by the Emperor. Nicholas so acquitted himself that his brother praised him on more than one occasion and sometimes spent an evening at Nicholas's villa in the neighbourhood. It pleased Alexander to relax in the presence of his young sister-in-law, who reminded him of Memel and Potsdam and the delicate platonic dalliance with her mother. By 1819 Grand Duchess Nicholas had acquired her own importance: she was the mother of a son on whom rested all the hopes of the dynasty. The Emperor's attention could not but please her.

One evening Alexander dined with them. The meal over, he told the Grand Duke that he wished to have a private conversation with him and his wife. Members of the household and servants left the room. The Emperor, seated on a sofa between husband and wife, told them that he looked upon Nicholas as his successor and that the change 'might happen much sooner than anyone imagined because it would take place in his, Alexander's, lifetime,' as the Grand Duchess recorded in her journal.

'. . . we sat, the Emperor between us, like two statues, wide-eyed and speechless. The Emperor went on: "Constantine, who has never wished to follow me, is more than ever determined to renounce his rights. . . . Never before has Europe stood in such a need of young sovereigns in the plenitude of their strength . . . I am no longer the man I was, and I think it will be my duty to retire . . ." ' Nicholas looked stupefied, Alexandra burst into tears. 'The Emperor tried to comfort us by saying that some years would have to pass before his plan was carried out.' The Grand Duchess did not mention if Alexander impressed secrecy on them, but it was obvious that he would have done so.

The incident could not have been invented by the Grand Duchess, but the reaction she described strikes a false note. By that time, both she and her husband knew what the court and society, still less the masses, did not know, namely, that Constantine would never reign. The Emperor's idea of abdication may well have surprised them, but it is unlikely that either should have been in need of comfort. They were pleased. *'Nicolas n'a qu'une idée en tête— de régner . . .'* said the Empress Elizabeth, and the young Grand Duke's behaviour did not belie the words. The third gentleman in the land never allowed himself to criticize his brother's liberal ideas, but all the reactionaries knew that Nicholas was whole-heartedly committed to their point of view.

In 1819 Alexander was in his forty-second year, but a decade of wars and anxieties, to say nothing of the work he must do day by day, was beginning to tell. The deafness increased; the leg injured in an accident gave occasional trouble; and a look in his eyes sometimes betrayed his fatigue. The idea of abdication put before his brother had occupied him for some time, and fairly revealing hints had been given now to one intimate, now to another, all of whom kept his confidence.

The manoeuvres were ended at Krasnoe, but the Emperor did not return to Tsarskoe Selo. A mood of restlessness falling on him, he left for Finland and the northern provinces, having first commanded that there were to be no official receptions anywhere and that no flags and drums were to mark his comings and goings.

Somewhat refreshed, he returned to St Petersburg there to find Karamzin's booklet *The Opinion of a Russian Citizen* waiting for him. The historian argued that the restoration of the Kingdom of Poland was against prudence in general and Russian interests in particular. Alexander summoned him to the Winter Palace. After a very long talk, Karamzin was left with the consciousness that he and his sovereign 'had parted in spirit'.

They did not discuss the Polish question alone.

'I was quite frank about the heavy taxation, "The Ministry of Eclipse", military settlements, the delayed reform of the law, our poor ways of communication, the matter of Poland and the rest,' Karamzin wrote to a friend.[1]

Such candour needed rare courage. The Emperor listened courteously. Every point raised by the historian could—in Alexander's opinion—be explained by circumstances which left no alternative for a different course. Alexander had a great respect for his historiographer, but the lengthy session proved wholly barren, and even a less imaginative man than Karamzin could not have escaped the sense of frustration when his sovereign kept reducing all the points made to one common denominator: '*l'empire du mal*.' The great study with its several windows overlooking the Neva was as usual meticulously tidy. The innumerable drawers held masses of papers all neatly arranged and marked 'for future reference'. Those

[1] cf. Schilder, op. cit., Vol. IV, 468.

drawers were so many burial places for plans out of accord with the imperial will.

By 1819 the matter of Poland was in a sorry tangle. To subject a constitutional government to an autocratic supervision was stultifying enough. To have its business tampered with by the autocrat's brother, who, Viceroy of Poland and Grand Duke of Russia, regarded the constitutional pattern as some fungoid growth, was an absurdity fit to be included into *The Rose and the Ring*. Unfortunately Poland was no Paflagonia, and the situation already carried the seeds of the tragedy to come. But Alexander could see none of it. Year by year, his words to the Poles rang a harsher note, and he felt that the thickening discontent among the Poles was black ingratitude after all the blessings granted to them. When, in the autumn of 1819, some members of the Sejm protested against the violation of their constitutional rights, the Emperor's manner became icy. In his mind, such speeches rang with the echoes of 1789.

Dismal colours crept into the Russian landscape during that year. Even the opening of the university in St Petersburg did not lighten the mood. People's patience was badly frayed. Delayed reforms, the sovereign's frequent absences, Arakcheev's pre-eminence, ever increasing taxes and much else served to deepen the anxiety. The liberals still nursed their hopes, but they had griefs of their own. Count Kotchubey, once a zealous supporter of all liberal aims, was now known to be in warm accord with Arakcheev. Diplomats' reports hardly exaggerated the general disillusionment creeping into the national life. '*On attaque sans cesse l'empire que les idées réligieuses exercent sur le monarque,*' wrote Chevalier de Malvirade. '*Il est certain que jamais la société de Pétersburg ne s'est trouvée frappée par plus de privations que depuis que ces idées se sont développées avec la force où elles existent aujourd'hui . . .*' The Emperor, hungry for peace and frenziedly pursuing the means which would enable him to quieten his conscience, expected the entire nation to carry its share in the expiatory process.

That autumn visit to Warsaw brought no reassurance to the Poles and deepened the Emperor's gloom. Schilder recorded an episode,[1] its provenance rather clouded. An equerry of Alexander's,

[1] cf. op. cit., IV, 465.

Mikhailovsky-Danilevsky, recorded it in his diary from the remarks made by General Kisselev who, in his turn, was supposed to hear it from Grand Duke Constantine. Now, Danilevsky was by no means a reliable chronicler, and all too often painted his own importance in imaginary colours. He was an equerry of no particular standing. He may well have been present during General Kisselev's conversation with someone else.

When in Warsaw, the Emperor was supposed to have a private conversation with his brother. Alexander's alleged words were: 'I want to abdicate. I am tired and cannot bear my burdens any longer. I give you warning of my intention.' Constantine's supposed reply was facetious. 'Then I will become one of your valets and polish your boots.' The Emperor ignored the flippancy and went on: 'When that moment comes, I will let you know so that you can write to my mother about your own plans,' this being a reference to the necessity of asking the Dowager Empress's consent to the annulment of Constantine's first marriage.

The story is here given for what it is worth. It is true that within less than six months Constantine's marriage to Grand Duchess Anna (Princess Julie of Coburg) was publicly annulled. In May 1820 he married his mistress, Johanna Grudzinska, raised by the Emperor to the rank of a princess. The heir's marriage to a commoner brought the thorny problem of succession to the foreground. Yet Constantine still bore the title of 'Cezarevich' and social curiosity was left unsatisfied. Most wild conjectures were made on all sides, and there were sullen ripples in the imperial family. Grand Duchess Nicholas was alleged to wonder why her husband—in view of his brother's morganatic marriage—was not given the heir's proper title. The Grand Duchess's remark was reported to the Emperor, who took great exception to it. 'Alexander, who had been so kind to me,' she wrote in her journal, 'now causes me much distress'—and she went on, 'he often imagines that he is being held up to ridicule. . . . Never had I imagined how suspicious he could be. . . . Some of his ideas are so silly that it hurts one to find so much pettiness in a man of such remarkable qualities of heart and mind . . .'

The Empress Elizabeth alone forbore to criticize. She considered her husband to be a victim of brotherly affection. Constantine's second marriage deeply shocked her. '[*Alexandre*] *n'a pas pu s'opposer à ce que son frère lui représentait comme non seulement nécessaire à son bonheur, mais même au repos de sa conscience, ne voulant plus, disait-il, vivre en désordre,*' the Empress wrote to her mother in the early summer of 1820. '*Tout le monde cependant ne jugera pas l'Empereur comme moi: il y aura bien du blâme . . .*' There was, but there should not have been. Not one of Alexander's brothers had taken the trouble to win the people's affection and to ensure public concern on their behalf.

The murder of the Duc de Berri confirmed Alexander's conviction that the revolutionary leaven was far from being dead in France. Insurrections in Germany, northern Italy, Spain and Naples led to a further hardening of his belief. That autumn, addressing the Polish Sejm, the Emperor threatened to withdraw all Polish liberties if discontent were allowed to spread among them.

His speech bewildered many people outside the Polish frontiers. His listeners had hoped to hear about their agragrian future, some easing of taxation and changes in trade tariffs. Instead they were urged to recognize that the hour of the Prince of Darkness had struck in various parts of Europe and that it was their duty to gird up their loins for the battle.

The small and hitherto unregarded town of Troppau in Silesia came to be the burial ground of the original aims of the Holy Alliance. Alexander, being spokesman, gave the Congress his reasons for refusing to recognize the revolutionary government set up in Naples, and Metternich heard the Emperor's arguments with pleasure. Prussia, her own unrest growing from month to month, prepared to follow Alexander's lead, but the British and French representatives adopted a different course. Castlereagh's reply was unequivocal. He argued that the Neapolitan troubles could indeed provide a case for Austria's intervention to protect her sovereignty in other parts of Italy but no other power had the right to intervene in a Neapolitan home affair.

The Emperor argued that the revolution in Naples was the common concern of Europe in that it menaced the peace of every country, but Castlereagh held his ground. In the end, the so-called Troppau Protocol, embodying Alexander's idea that the Great Powers should use all their resources to check the spread of revolutionary movements, was not signed either by Great Britain or by France.

The Emperor's letter to Princess Sophie Metcherskaya[1] may well be taken as an affirmation of a policy which was no policy in the accepted sense of the word. The Holy Alliance was being reshaped into the Holy Inquisition. Alexander had learned nothing from the Napoleonic lessons; he refused to admit that an era so full of tumults and uncertainties was the spring-board for fresh ideas, for a heightened consciousness of a national hearth, a new appraisal of social values, and the inevitable discarding of patterns proved useless during the long struggle. He observed the day's landscape through glasses so tinted that a sunrise over the Alps could be turned into the angry flames of a revolutionary bonfire. Behind the blurred vision stood his private conviction that, having once, however unwittingly, been Satan's accomplice, he must now spend himself utterly in fighting the same Satan at whose persuasion an anointed of the Lord—and that anointed his own father—had met a ghastly death in March 1801. The Empress's letter to her mother now proved to be a tragic prophecy: '*Son coeur en restera déchiré à jamais.*'

So from Troppau he wrote to Princess Metcherskaya that they were all engaged in a most important and difficult business. '*Il s'agit de porter remède contre l'empire du mal qui s'étend avec célérité et par tous les moyens occultes dont se sert le génie satanique qui le dirige.* . . . *Ce remède que nous cherchons, hélàs, est au-dessus de notre chétif pouvoir humain* . . . *Le Sauveur seul* . . . *peut fournir ce moyen.* . . . *Invoquons-le donc de toute la ferveur de nos coeurs pourqu'il daigne répandre son Esprit Saint sur nous et nous faire marche—dans la voie qui seule peut lui plaire et qui seule peut nous conduire au salut.*'

The remedy thus fervently sought was embodied within the Protocol envisaging the creation of a European police force.

When still at Troppau, Alexander received the report of a mutiny in the Semenovsky Guards regiment. Seen in sane proportions, the incident was hardly an affair of national importance. Goaded by the cruelties of the commanding officer, a certain Colonel Schwartz, two or three companies refused to obey the orders given first by sergeants and later by officers. The Empire being at peace, martial law could not in justice be applied. There was much shouting, a few scuffles, but no bloodshed. On being arrested none of the men

[1] cf. Schilder, op. cit., Vol. IV, 470 and Grand Duke Nicholas, *The Emperor Alexander I*, Vol. I, p. 251.

offered the least resistance. The report sent the Emperor into a panic. The disobedience at a St Petersburg barracks was at once related to the activities of revolutionary groups in Europe, as the Emperor wrote to Arakcheev and others. When the findings and the sentences of the military court reached Troppau, Alexander not only endorsed but in some cases increased the savage penalties to such a point that to read the document today is to be haunted by an appalling instance of man's studied cruelty to man.

The episode had one odd consequence. So badly was Alexander shaken by the report that he poured himself out to Metternich. The latter at once agreed that the mutiny had sprung out of a revolutionary impulse and approved the savagery of the sentences, and Alexander was deeply gratified by his listener's understanding. A promise was given to help Austria in her Italian involvements, and the Emperor wrote to General Wassilchikov in St Petersburg that 'we must decide on really serious measures to counteract the flames spread all over the south of Europe. Austria is sending troops to Naples to rescue the King from the clutches of *carbonari*, and I am convinced that we should help them. An Austrian success will heighten the morale in Spain and Portugal.'

At Troppau all sense of logic seems to have forsaken Alexander. He had expressed his conviction about the link between the Guards mutiny and the revolutionaries, but when some of his ministers hoped that he would return so as to guide an extended inquiry into the affair, the Emperor replied: 'Were I to hurry back to Russia now, the underground enemies in Europe might imagine that there is something wrong with my own Empire and that they have succeeded in introducing their ideas there.'

About that time a curious and most unpleasant figure stepped into the foreground of the Russian scene. It is tempting to compare Photius with Rasputin, but the comparison does not answer except in one detail: both 'the mad monk' and 'the Siberian *moujik*' were endowed with extraordinary magnetic powers and both knew how to use them. No other country, Russia excepted, could so shape their courses that their influence ended by being exercised under the roof of the palace.

Miropolsky, Photius' biographer[1] says that 'a combination of

---

[1] *The Archimandrite Photius*, St Petersburg, 1878.

circumstances brought [him] forward, a man of no importance or natural gifts, sketchily educated . . . a frenzied fanatic, who would have faced the stake for his beliefs. . . He was rude, aggressive and violent . . .' Photius also possessed a curious blend of fiendish cunning and well-nigh wooden stupidity, the latter enabling the high-placed reactionaries to use him as their tool.

Photius left his own autobiography where he recounted many combats with devils and gave many details about his mortifications, the hair shirts and the iron chains he wore, the cold and the hunger he suffered since 'all such things are useful as whips and scorpions to beat Satan with'. Photius was no hermit, but Dostoevsky may well have had him in mind when he created his Ferapont in *The Brothers Karamazov*.

About 1817 the days of Photius's obscurity were ended, a prelate remarking his extraordinary piety. The prelate being a friend of Arakcheev's, Photius' future was assured. The monk did not suffer from false modesty: he declared himself to be one of God's elect, his purpose being to fight atheism, revolution and freemasonry, and he told the Archbishops that he considered the Emperor's tolerance of other creeds was an insult to pure orthodoxy and a sin against the Holy Ghost. Such words were dangerous. But Photius knew that he was speaking to men who agreed with him in their hearts.

At that time St Petersburg was going through a phase of a super-charged interest in other-worldly matters. Side by side with the tranquil and sincere preoccupation of men like Prince Golitzin, Koshelev and Labzin, there were Tatarinova and her 'holy' dances, Krüdener and her prophecies, excited gentlemen from Denmark and Prussia, to whom the Bible meant little more than their own fantastic interpretation of the Apocalypse; there were monks and lay pilgrims with their stories of the latest miracles at this or that shrine, and their assertions that God's will could be known by them and them alone. Society ladies toyed with the occult, sat at the feet of Roman Catholic preachers, or joined one or other of the many offshoots of Orthodoxy. In all that motley crowd, Photius was somewhat singular. Priest and monk, he stood for untainted Orthodoxy. Roman Catholicism, the occult, and the evangel preached by Baroness Krüdener were all one to him, all to be consigned to the nethermost flames. He used the pulpit as no other could in his generation. He preached no common sermons. With him, any pulpit became a volcano in full eruption. The brimstone, fire and sulphur of his words terrified and yet compelled his congregation until Seraphim, Metropolitan of St Petersburg, called Photius 'God's messenger'. He attacked everybody 'in the name of the Lord God of Sabaoth'. His vehemence outrivalled Abbakum's, and society ladies vied with one another in showering gifts on 'God's elect'. Hair shirts, rigid fasts and all, Photius did not despise valuable presents.

In the end it was the wealthy Countess Anna Orlova who brought the man into the palace there to thunder his denunciations of atheism, revolution and freemasonry, and so influence the Emperor that the very last flickers of liberal intentions died, never to rise again. Masonic lodges were closed down; police inspectors instructed by clergy wormed their way into all educational establishments suspected of 'heresy'; censors were ordered to exercise a greater severity; Pushkin was exiled into the country; and Golitzin was dismissed from the Ministry—to Arakcheev's great joy.

Photius strides across the Russian scene much in the manner of a revenant from the fifteenth century, a frenzied zealot who saw his country as a third Rome and the true cradle of pure Orthodoxy. One of the Emperor's presents—a diamond pectoral cross—went with the man to St George's Abbey in Novgorod, Arakcheev's Gruzino being in the neighbourhood, where the two bigotries—ecclesiastical and lay—met in wondrous accord. The Abbey, lavishly endowed by Anna Orlova, began drawing crowds of pilgrims.[1]

Photius' education having been most sketchy, it is doubtful if he could have used arguments powerful enough to make the Emperor turn away from 'all Western poison'. That he influenced Alexander in other ways is proved by the spate of restrictive measures which followed the man's climb to recognition. The common ground between Sovereign and subject was '*der Drang nach Gott*', though

[1] Anna Orlova, reputed to be the richest woman in the Empire, was called by Photius his 'maiden daughter' (*dtcher-dievitza*), 'a vessel of grace' and 'a humble servant of the Lord'. Schilder (op. cit., Vol. IV, p. 261) gives a reproduction of a portrait of 'the vessel of grace'. Elaborate curls escaping from under the wide brim of a huge velvet hat trimmed with ostrich feathers, pearls at her throat and bracelets on her wrists, a gown cut fashionably low, together with an expression of deep self-satisfaction, all of it together is in eloquent disaccord with Photius' description of Anna Orlova. He dissuaded her from marriage in a treatise of 170 pages written to prove that virginity was the strongest weapon against the wiles of Satan.

the process meant something different to each. The Emperor's piety, for all his outward conformity to the Church, was not rooted in doctrinal Orthodoxy. To Photius, the least deviation from the Orthodox path meant a sin against the Holy Ghost, though even such transgressions could be conveniently graded when committed by God's anointed. The two wholly agreed about the dominion of Satan, and Alexander was certainly satisfied by the monk's assertion that the struggle against evil was an autocrat's most important business.

The Neapolitan revolutionaries were crushed by the Austrians without Russian help, but the Piedmontese rose in revolt, and indignation broke out in St Petersburg on hearing about the Emperor's offer to send an army one hundred thousand strong, commanded by General Ermolov, into Italy. In the end, the Emperor was dissuaded from confirming the order and the Russians did not go, but Alexander was angry with his advisers. He had forgotten his grandmother's words to his own father when Paul argued that Russian troops should be employed to defeat 'the seven-headed hydra in Paris'. 'No single soldier of mine goes abroad,' said Catherine the Great. 'It is futile to try and fight ideas with guns.' But those words, even if remembered, would have meant nothing to a man who held that *'le mal actuel est d'un genre plus dangereux encore que ne l'était le despotisme dévastateur de Napoléon, puisque les doctrines actuelles sont bien plus séduisantes pour la multitude que le joug militaire sous lequel il la tenait,'* a sentence summing up so tragically the sunset years of Alexander's reign.

What may well be called the high tide of obscurantism and a bitter humiliation for the Russians came with the Greek uprising in 1821 when Prince Ypsilanti, still an officer in Alexander's army, raised his standard, gathered thousands of adherents, crossed the Pruth, and entered Jassy. The revolt spread like a tongue of flame over dry stubble, engulfing the Morea and the whole of the archipelago. The Turks answered by immediate reprisals. Great numbers of Greek men, women and children were butchered. In Constantinople, on Easter Day, the aged Patriarch Gregory was dragged from the altar and hanged in full vestments in the porch of his cathedral.

Russia's anger leapt high. War with Turkey appeared a foregone conclusion, but the Emperor hesitated. The actual *casus belli* was incontrovertible: by the terms of the Kutchuk-Kainardji Treaty of 1774 Russia had the right to safeguard the interests of the Sultan's Christian subjects, though the public mood did not concern itself with the provisions of any treaty. It was the plain duty of Russia to rush to the help of her Orthodox brethren. The two capitals became wildly pro-Hellenic, and even Grand Duchess Nicholas had the courage to write to her brother-in-law and say that the Greeks certainly had a case.

Alexander's hesitancy was resolved soon enough. Metternich's remark that a war with Turkey would certainly make '*une brèche affreuse*' and help spread 'dangerous ideas' turned the scales in Alexander's mind. Now he decided that the Greeks were up in arms against lawful authority, and in that twilight of his mind the revolt was at once joined with the activities of '*le génie du mal*'. He blamed France for having fanned the flames in Greece. '*Le centre est chez vous,*' he said heatedly to La Ferronays; '*les révolutionnaires français ont suscité l'affaire de Grèce,*' and he added that he knew Prince Ypsilanti had been in touch with the French Government. When Baroness Krüdener, talking sense for once, wrote imploring Alexander not to betray his high vocation of a Christian prince, he had her exiled from the capital. The press muzzled by censorship dared not be articulate, though Pushkin's fiery lines about the banners of honour came to be widely known in manuscript. With the exception of Nesselrode, who maintained that the Empire should preserve peace, Alexander was about the only man in Russia who stood against fighting Turkey and that at a time when his own forces might have crushed the Sultan's army in a month. When Britain's voice rose in support of the Greeks, the Emperor explained it by the influence of freemasons.

Austria and Prussia upheld the shameful policy, and Europe must watch the curious and unpleasing spectacle presented by an alliance of Christian princes ready to defend a Mahommedan throne against Christians. La Harpe sent a heartbreaking letter to his pupil. '*Je suis profondément navré de ce qui se passe*', he wrote to Alexander from Lausanne. The letter remained without a reply and marked the end of a lifelong correspondence.

In 1814, Gentz, a well-known Austrian publicist of the day,

wrote that the Emperor of Russia was the only sovereign in Europe capable of carrying out any plans of major importance. Nothing could withstand the onslaught of his armies. No obstacles restraining other rulers existed for him. 'What he plans today may well be achieved tomorrow, and all his purposes are aimed towards the good of the nations. His personal charm conquers everybody . . .' Gentz might have added that Alexander's courage and the clarity of his vision broke upon a tired Europe like a dawn following a long wintry night. There he stood—to offer justice and comfort to the wounded nations, 'The Blessed,' 'The Agamemnon of our time', 'the pride and hope of all'.

In less than seven years the triumph was forgotten, as though it had never been. All the faults, screened so adroitly by the imperious commands of an emergency, leapt into daylight again, and the triumphant outcome of the war deepened the colour of every fault and every weakness. Once a leader, Alexander, as Metternich said, 'was now led by the Austrians'. Mistrusted by Britain, loathed by all the liberals in Europe, and, what was worse, feared by his own people, Alexander became a prisoner of his own fears, doubts and remorse. He resembled a man who, having locked himself into his house, lost the key and refused to believe that windows could be opened. Swayed this way and that, his course following any newcomer's dark prophecies, lulled by Arakcheev's parrot-like repetition that a Tsar could do no wrong, latticing his mind against all fresh breaths in the world, using the services of ignoble puppets like Magnitzky and others to carry out his campaign against all the liberties of the mind, the Emperor was to be pitied by the least fortunate vagrant in his Empire, and even his wife—for all her devotion—had not the courage to tell him about the futility of a lifelong remorse for the catastrophe of 1801.

There, Alexander's guilt, however apportioned, had its limits. But his guilt before his people surpassed all frontiers in that he dragged them with him into the same twilight.

He still worked hard, spending hours over a mass of administrative trivia, writing to Arakcheev and Photius, to Frederick William and to Metternich, reading his ambassadors' reports, studying Galignani and any other available foreign papers always to discover more proofs that '*le génie du mal*' was gaining ground in the West. He remained ignorant of what was happening in his own dominions.

Alexander Turgenev[1] remembered Count Kotchubey saying to him half bitterly, half mockingly: ' "Just imagine—the Emperor is convinced that serfs have not been sold separately ever since his accession!" What was there for me to say when both of us knew that within a stone's throw of the Winter Palace, at the City Hall, human flesh was being put up for sale with full permission of the authorities . . . children wrenched away from their parents and husbands from wives. At an auction an old peasant woman was sold for two roubles fifty copecks—almost on the doorstep of the autocrat who thought that all individual sales of men and women were illegal.'

The new ideas brought from the West by the Emperor's officers led to the formation of the Benevolent Union, its aims wholly moral and philanthropic. Members met in one another's houses to discuss emancipation, then a topic greatly favoured by Alexander himself, the end of vagrancy, prison reform, and educational problems. But 1821 saw the end of that union, and moral and philanthropic problems gave way to a sharpened political hunger. Liberals became radicals. In the end, the iron-gauntleted hand of reaction was responsible for the creation of secret societies, one in the north and the other in the south, their members pledged to struggle against the police state envisaged by Alexander's utterances at Troppau. The Northern Society, led by Mouraviev-Apostol and the poet Ryeleev, planned for a constitutional government. The Southern Society, headed by Paul Pestel, aimed at a republic.

One day in January 1822 the Empress Elizabeth wrote to her mother from Tsarskoe Selo that she felt she was almost in a fairy-tale: '. . . *moi même, je ne me reconnais pas; il me semble que je suis en voyage et arrivée chez un Prince étranger, comme je viens de le dire à l'Empereur, tant il a mis de recherche aux attentions avec lesquelles il me reçoit . . .*' Elizabeth, forgiving and forgetting, was indeed in a strange land unvisited for more than twenty years. Alexander's travels took him more and more away from home, yet now they were together. At Tsarskoe he ordered some rooms to be furnished for her—next to his own apartments—three rooms described by Elizabeth as being '*parfaitement élegantes*'. They dined and supped *tête-à-tête*, not even servants attending on them. They went for

[1] *La Russie*, Vol. II, p. 107.

drives together. He would plan sudden little excursions for her. They spent evenings in companionable silence, nobody daring to break their peace. Her tastes were consulted, her desires forestalled, her little foibles allowed for.

Tsarskoe Selo became an island of tranquillity. At Pavlovsk was the deafening bustle of her mother-in-law's court and of 'the young court' of Grand Duke and Grand Duchess Nicholas, who did not seem to be happy unless they were caught into a whirl of ceaseless activity and entertainment '. . . *tout cela produit un ton qui choque. . . . Ceci n'est qu'une de mille choses qu'il faut voir sans pouvoir y rémedier . . .*' She, Elizabeth, had deplored it for years, but now she was not alone. '*Nous en gémissons souvent avec l'Empereur.*' She quoted her sister-in-law's words about the Dowager Empress—' "*Was ich so liebe in der Kaiserin Mutter ist, dass sie mit dem Geist der Zeit vorshreitet, es ist sogar keine Etiquette und Gêne bei ihr . . .*" *Courir et se dépêcher, voilà la dévise de la famille impériale—voilà comme la vie s'en va—sans profit pour qui que se soit,*'—but Elizabeth could now watch that noisy, impatient measure from a distance: it kept away from Tsarskoe Selo, and there she held her husband again.

Alexander's return was late in time, almost too late to make up for many years of estrangement. But to Elizabeth it brought a second spring. It all seemed little enough on the surface—a few meals with him, a few drives, some shared silences and conversation, but she treasured each little thing enjoyed in common. The tiresome, demanding family were still there with their intrusions and their insistence on wearying gaiety which Elizabeth's undermined health could not endure, but even the frequent invasions of the family now mattered less to her: she had Alexander, and she asked for no more.

The man who returned to her was not the man who had left her in 1803. His policy she would neither criticize nor interfere with. His religious abandon must have puzzled and saddened her, whose own inward life ran along a deep and quiet course. She had refused to meet Baroness Krüdener, and there is no record that Photius was ever received by her. Alexander's attachment to Arakcheev was again one of the things she could not share. But Elizabeth did not feel that she welcomed a stranger. There were still a few notes familiar to her ear alone. To be permitted to listen to them again was more than she had hoped for.

In the autumn of 1822 Alexander left her for Italy. At Verona, Chateaubriand and others noticed his great weariness. All fire seemed gone out of his speech. He left for Russia early in 1823 never to appear in Europe again.

X
THE
MIDNIGHT HOUR

ON HIS return from the Congress of Troppau Metternich said complacently: 'The Emperor Alexander is no longer a leader. In fact, it is we who lead him now . . .' These words were not altogether accurate. If the Emperor refused his help to the Greek rebels, he did not offer it to France to strengthen her hand in suppressing the revolt in Spain. The liberation of Greece produced very little effect on him. His own crusade being over, he was not at all inclined to join his banner to that of Austria. His interest in Western matters waned month by month as though his consciousness of the need for expiation were concentrated on its purely personal aspect. More and more often he would hint that it was time for him to take off the purple and to spend the remainder of his days in prayer and contrition for his sins.

After his return from Verona, court life continued its habitual rhythm only at Gatchina and Pavlovsk, with the tireless Dowager Empress doing the imperial honours, Nicholas and his wife only too ready to help her. There were hardly any great occasions at Alexander's own court. One diplomat after another complained that the Emperor gave fewer and fewer audiences. He would receive Nesselrode and other ministers at the appointed times and conscientiously listen to their reports, but the matter of Europe no longer enflamed him.

Moreover, he was very little at home. In the last two years of his reign, Alexander's restlessness reached a peak. Travelling up and down his Empire grew into a hunger which must be satisfied even if the skies fell. In an open carriage, accompanied by a doctor, two equerries and a valet, the Emperor went from north to south, from west to east, forbidding any formal receptions, shunning the welcome of notabilities, halting at many villages there to talk to peasants, break bread with them, join his voice to theirs in many a humble wooden church. His itineraries were complicated, kept secret from all except a few intimates, and subject to sudden changes. It pleased Alexander to think that he was getting acquainted with the real rural life of Russia. The administrative landscape, made so ugly by shocking abuses and worse, he utterly ignored.

In one sense, therefore, those journeys were futile. But they answered the Emperor's hidden need and strengthened the link between the people and himself. His arrival at any village created an immediate sense of an unexpected holiday from the unceasing daily treadmill of labour and care. He was 'The Blessed', '*Blagoslavénny*', among them. Grievances were not brought to him, and that not only out of fear of later reprisals by local authorities but largely because the peasants chose to turn their back on the day's burden. In the Emperor's person they lived again through the horror and the triumph of 1812, and all that came later could not rob them of their pride in him. The twilit moods of disillusionment and remorse were left behind in St Petersburg. The charm, the smile, 'the golden benevolence' remained. An elderly, bearded Ivan, asked a question about his rye yield or his livestock, would never know that his stammered answer was forgotten as soon as heard. The grace of the question carried enough strength to lighten many a wintry evening for Ivan and his family.

But away from such occasions, shadows thickened more and more. Arakcheev's iron hand lay on everything. Ministers rose and fell from favour according to his pleasure. Of all the ministerial appointments the only one to bring good to the country was Kankrin's at the Ministry of Finance. The rest were pallid nonentities anxious to steer their courses by the light which came from Gruzino. Nowhere was the situation so tragic as at the Ministry of Education. Magnitzky's appointment as governor of all colleges and schools in the Kazan Province resulted in the reactionary policy being turned into a sledge hammer throughout the province. Numbers of professors lost their chairs for criticizing Magnitzky's views, and thousands of valuable books were destroyed because they dealt with matters unnecessary 'for a pious Christian'.

Kazan University came to resemble a mediaeval monastery. Any student, breaking the least rule, ran the risk of being recruited into the ranks. Nikolsky, the Rector, lectured on geometry 'in strict accordance with the teaching of the Holy Church'. He taught that a triangle was an emblem representing the power, action and consequence of God's grace. 'The hypotenuse must be understood as the union of truth and of peace, of justice and of love through the One Mediator between God and man.'

In St Petersburg, Runich, another creature of Arakcheev's, dreamt of a truly Orthodox university, and the study of statistics was not encouraged because the Canons of the Church made no mention of it. The persecution of professors lecturing on history and philosophy, begun in 1821, reached its peak in 1824. From Derpt, Parrott wrote to the Emperor that he, Parrott, would consider himself a criminal if he did not draw his Sovereign's attention to '*l'âbime au bord duquel se trouve l'instruction publique de l'Empire et que l'on prend tant de soin à Vous cacher . . .!* but Parrott's was a voice in the desert; it found no echo in St Petersburg and it is doubtful that Alexander ever received the letter. It could not, however, be said that 'the abyss' was hidden from him: he saw it clearly enough, but he had no strength to check the movement towards it.

Shishkov had sole charge of the Censorship Office. He considered that 'the great majority of novels and other works of polite literature were harmful in that they perverted thought and taste'. A Russian translation of an English book on constitutional theory was banned on the grounds that 'there was neither need of nor decency in discussing constitutional theory in a country prosperous and happy under an autocracy'. Shishkov, Metropolitan Seraphim and Photius together worked against the Bible Society, and Shishkov urged that the translation of the Bible into the vernacular would bring untold harm to the masses. 'The language of the Church will give place to the language of the theatre and the spread of Holy Writ among the masses would be worse than fire and flood.' He argued that 'the Bible Society came to Russia through the English Methodists. How can such people, not having any faith of their own, teach us anything about Christianity?'[1]

There, however, the Emperor refused to give in, and the translation of the Bible into Russian was continued for a space, though Photius scored a major victory with Prince Golitzin's dismissal from the Ministry of Religions and the closure of all the masonic lodges in the Empire. Photius wrote in triumph to his maiden daughter:

[1] cf. Pypin, op. cit., p. 239.

'The hour has struck and all the blasphemers will fall into the pit their madness has dug.' His 'Note' to the Emperor about 'the new religion of Antichrists, freemasons and revolutionaries' shows that the phantom of a gigantic secret conspiracy which haunted Alexander's waking hours was well used by Photius.

In the end Nesselrode was the only minister to be left in peace, foreign affairs being utterly beyond Arakcheev's comprehension, nor did the dictator ever acquire a single sycophant capable of dealing with the diplomatic corps. One Tatitchev went to the War Ministry, a man distinguished by his physical bulk and an utter absence of administrative ability. At the General Staff, Prince Volkonsky, the Emperor's intimate friend and counsellor, paid a high price for his undisguised loathing of Arakcheev. Volkonsky's summary dismissal was followed by the appointment of Dibitch, a Prussian of humble origins and no great talents, who considered the Emperor to be the true inheritor of the tradition founded by Frederick the Great. Dibitch wormed his way into the Ministry by means of sycophantic flattery. 'The military settlements are a paradise in little'—such phrases never failed to win Arakcheev's good graces.

So Prince Volkonsky went abroad, asking his friends for frequent letters, but 'these should never go through ordinary channels. The censors would be only too glad of them. . . . Surely, the day cannot be far off when the Emperor's eyes will be opened to all the unspeakable enormities committed by that beast. . . .' That day, alas, was not to come, though even Arakcheev could not prevent Volkonsky from returning to Russia in the spring of 1824. He came back to court, and the Emperor was sincerely glad of him and honoured him by the bestowal of St Andrew's star. In the summer of 1825 the Prince would accompany Alexander to Taganrog.

Yet in a sense both Parrott and Volkonsky were wrong: Alexander knew far more than they thought and he acquiesced in it all. Rather, he lulled himself into believing that the brutal policy followed by Arakcheev was for the good of the country and that each repressive measure erected yet another barrier between Russia and the red-flecked menace from the West. Everything ordained by Arakcheev—from the military settlements to the stranglehold of censorship—ran counter to the popular ideas about Alexander, whose gentleness had become a legend and whose tenderness and compassion were almost feminine. But the popular idea about the Emperor stopped, as it were, at the threshold of his house. Even his intimates confessed themselves unable to read him. That Arakcheev became his necessity is self-evident. Why he should have become one is a problem with many possible solutions. It is hardly enough to say that sheer weariness made the Emperor delegate his authority in a manner which defied analysis then and later. It is likely that the true answer lies in the fact that Arakcheev alone remained convinced that the regicide of 1801 had been committed without Alexander's consent. A man lost in a pseudo-mystical twilight, tormented by remorse and by a hunger for peace, could hardly turn away from someone who kept telling him that peace was well within his reach and that all the rest came from the insinuations of the Devil.

In 1823 the question of succession was resolved. The Empress Elizabeth still thought that '*Nicolas n'a qu'une idée en tête—c'est de régner*,' a phrase which makes it obvious that she was fully in the Emperor's confidence and knew that he meant Grand Duke Nicholas to succeed him. The Dowager Empress would have been the first to realize the implications of Constantine's marriage with a commoner. But Alexander wished the matter to be kept absolutely secret 'to avoid unnecessary gossip and harmful rumours'.

The Succession Manifesto, which nominated Nicholas as the heir, was signed by the Emperor in the late summer of 1823. Three copies were made, sealed, and left in the care of the Senate, not a Senator knowing anything about the contents. The original had its outer cover marked in Alexander's own hand—'to be kept in the sanctuary of the Assumption Cathedral and to be opened on my death by the Metropolitan of Moscow in the presence of the Governor General of Moscow.'[1]

All through that year the Emperor's restlessness kept increasing. He travelled from one province to another as though constant movement brought him nearer to a desired harbour. He spent a little time with Arakcheev at Gruzino and stayed at various abbeys,

---

[1] The disastrous interregnum in December 1825 need not be laid at Alexander's door. Philaret, the Metropolitan of Moscow, should have informed the Governor General, Prince Dimitry Golitzin, at once on receiving the news of Alexander's death. Philaret did not do so, acting on the assumption that the contents of the packet were known to the Prince. They were not.

visiting hermits and listening to their talk about the ways of God with a soul. In the summer Alexander returned to Tsarskoe Selo where his wife welcomed him with her customary warmth, though incessant family claims could not but interfere with her peace.

'*L'empereur . . . va journellement faire visite aux dames de sa famille,*' Elizabeth wrote to the Margravine of Baden in June 1823, '*sans égard aux distances; ici, cela lui fait une demi-heure pour aller à Pavlovsk, une demi-heure retour, total, une heure de chemin. Avec cela, un empire sur le bras et les intérêts de l'Europe, ce qui fait ici sa matinée suffit à peine . . . [il] est souvent bien touchant par le besoin que son coeur a de jouir des liens de famille*', but Elizabeth added that her husband, looking for the reality of such a link, often found nothing but its semblance.

In all truth, his constant attentions were born of an exaggerated sense of duty. He had little in common with his bustling, imperious and stupid mother, with Constantine, whose ideas went no further than barracks and battlefields, with his younger brothers, Nicholas and Michael, both spoilt sons of the Dowager Empress. The Emperor had not much feeling for any of his sisters, the late Grand Duchess Catherine excepted. Constantine's first wife, Anna, her marriage annulled but her rank left to her, often had cause to complain that her annual grant would fall into arrears when a single word from the Emperor would have been enough to ensure its regularity. Constantine's second wife was not at court, but there remained Grand Duchess Nicholas, a little too conscious of the glittering future in store for her, a little too ready to dance an acceptable measure under the roof of her mother-in-law. The family, as Elizabeth knew well, adored Alexander and had very little use for her. There were endless misunderstandings, finely tipped barbs at her and an unceasing avalanche of harassing demands on him. It was not really essential for the Empress Marie to see Alexander daily, but she insisted on that morning visit as though it were an indispensable detail of the business of state. All through his frequent absences, Marie wished him to write to her every day, and the Autocrat of All the Russias carried out his mother's wishes with an assiduity suggestive of a deep devotion. Not a single family decision could be made without Marie's approval, nor any state entertainment be given unless she were consulted about the details. Alexander endured rather than enjoyed it all, always remembering the extraordinary provisions made by the Emperor Paul for his wife.

Marie duly took note of the changed relations between Alexander and Elizabeth, and often discussed them in the family circle, expressing her hope that her daughter-in-law might yet come to do justice to her position. In Marie's opinion, a tranquil existence was hardly suitable for an Emperor's wife.

As to Alexander and Elizabeth, the process of reconciliation was gradual, unmarked by any dramatic episode, and such was the strength of Elizabeth's feeling for him that she found nothing to forgive in a past which would have wholly alienated most other women in her place. With Alexander, it was the growing recognition of a need no other woman could have answered. None better than Elizabeth knew the reason behind his tortured restlessness. Herself aloof from all extravagances in feeling and behaviour, she never criticized her husband's plunges into the world of pseudo-mysticism. It was enough for her to have him back. But her indignation against his family was an open secret. Blind to the Emperor's weariness, they continued troubling him about various court appointments, awards to those whom they distinguished by their favour, and a host of other matters all equally trivial.

In the summer of that year Alexander went to watch the manoeuvres near Grodno. An officer lost control of his horse, who reared, all but collided with the Emperor's mount and, swerving round, kicked Alexander's left leg so savagely that he had to be helped out of the saddle. Elizabeth's health had been anything but good for some time, and Alexander sent very clear instructions to the north that she was not to be told about the accident. But the Empress Marie, always avid for the dramatic, must needs drive over to Tsarskoe Selo 'to reassure' her daughter-in-law about the consequences of an incident to her wholly unknown. That did not improve Elizabeth's health.

On his way back, the Emperor made a brief stay in Moscow where such a tumultuous welcome met him that he felt as though his youth were coming back to him. Indeed, the occasion was like a streak of morning light across a midnight sky. Icy rain and sharp winds were of no moment to the crowds mobbing his carriage and shouting endearments and later keeping a bitterly cold vigil in the Red Square in the hope of catching a glimpse of him at a window.

From the Kremlin Palace the Emperor wrote to Elizabeth to tell her how he wished she were there. He hurried back to St Petersburg when he heard that her condition was worse.

The ladies at the court of the Dowager Empress were convinced that the Emperor had no affection for his wife. Younger than Alexander, Elizabeth looked an old woman at forty-five. The beauty which had once so enchanted everybody was gone. Her hair had lost its lustre, her eyes their starriness. She abhorred cosmetics, and her skin told its story. The lovely Psyche, in whose honour sonnets would be written, was an ailing, tired woman, the griefs of many years stamped on her face

In early January 1824 they were at the Winter Palace, but no season was kept that year. The court had been getting ready for heightened festivities, the daughter of Prince Paul of Württemberg having just arrived in Russia for her betrothal to Grand Duke Michael. But a slight mishap on a palace staircase caused the Emperor such pain that he made no protests when Elizabeth began persuading him to go to bed. Within a few days, the left leg, hurt at the manoeuvres at Grodno, was inflamed from knee to ankle, the Emperor's temperature was rising, and both Wylie and Tarassov were afraid of gangrene.

The hush fallen over the capital at the first news of the Emperor's grave illness greatly astonished many foreign residents who thought that Alexander's popularity had gone. 'Theatres are empty. There is no dancing. The crowd outside the palace keeps so quiet that you would think those men and women had no breath in them. The churches keep open day and night, and they are never wholly empty. Even beggars have been seen parting with a copper to have a small candle lit for the Emperor's recovery—' wrote a French governess to her people at Grenoble.

'C'est érysipèle sur toute la jambe,' the Empress Elizabeth said in her letter to Baden, '. . . jamais je n'ai vu l'Empereur aussi patient dans une maladie que cette fois . . . il m'a dit avant hier une chose bien douce à mon coeur: "Vous verrez que je vous devrai ma guérison . . ." '

Her own ailments forgotten, she nursed him devotedly, but she could not shield him from the family. Every morning and every evening, his mother and brothers appeared in the sick-room, filling it with their loud voices and laughter—until the doctors all but wrung their hands. The young men related the latest regimental gossip. The Dowager Empress fussed about Michael's wedding, his bride's jewellery and the appointments to her household. Once, having worn Alexander out by a long discussion of a mistress of the robes she had chosen for her future daughter-in-law, Marie made her way to Elizabeth's rooms, 'me dire avec satisfaction qu'elle l'a entretenu . . .' At that moment, in a passage outside, Elizabeth heard Wylie's voice insisting that the Emperor must be left in peace. His temperature had risen after all the noise made by the family in his room. For the first time in all the years Elizabeth did not control her tongue. She told her mother-in-law that such senseless behaviour must cease. Helen's ladies, her wedding dress and jewels were not important at the moment. The Emperor must have quiet, Elizabeth repeated, in such a voice that her boisterous brothers-in-law tiptoed down the stairs. The Dowager Empress looked as dumbfounded as though a cushion on a sofa had been aggressive to her, but the younger woman did not spare her. 'Do you wish him to die, Madam?' she asked in a stony voice, and Marie left the room without a word.

'Cela m'a valu humeur foudroyante pendant plusieurs jours,' Elizabeth admitted to her mother, but the doctors had cause to be grateful to their patient's wife: peace was no longer broken in the sick-room.

'L'humeur foudroyante' mattered little enough to her when Alexander was at last pronounced out of danger, when all the belfries in the capital and throughout the Empire pealed in thanksgiving for his recovery, when, her duties eased, she could sit down in her study and pour out her heart to her mother, happy to write about 'l'affection réelle que l'Empereur me témoigne, ainsi que le désir de m'avoir près de lui . . . il semblait recevoir volontiers mes petits services, il me permettait de veiller près de lui quand il dormait, de le servir à son petit dîner, et lorsqu'il était mieux et qu'il lisait de son côté, je lisais du mien, prête à m'interrompre quand il voulait causer pour se reposer . . .'

Absolute privacy was assured to them, no member of the household or servant daring to come in unless summoned by a bell. The convalescence once started, the family could not be altogether excluded, but the Empress Marie suffered yet another defeat. Her youngest son's wedding was neither postponed nor celebrated in the traditional manner. According to Alexander's wishes, Michael and

Helen were married in a room next to his own, the ceremony shorn of all superfluities so as not to tire the Emperor, who followed the service from a sofa in the adjoining room. The Empress Marie was allowed to give as many balls and banquets as she pleased, but none of the fuss invaded the Winter Palace. She accepted her son's decision with as much grace as she could muster, though her manner to Elizabeth scarcely improved.

'. . . *ces passions et les rivalités de la famille pour l'Empereur font que je suis reduite à me regarder quelquefois à son égard comme sa maîtresse, ou bien comme si nous étions mariés sécretement, et je n'ose pas parler de ce qui peut prouver de l'affection et de la familiarité entre nous, afin de ne pas exciter de l'aigreur, de l'humeur, et souvent un surcroît de tracas . . . parcequ'alors, de crainte de n'avoir pas l'air aussi rapproché de lui que moi, on l'obsède à la lettre . . .*'

So steady was Alexander's progress that at the end of March they could move him to Tsarskoe Selo, and Elizabeth was able to count on at least six weeks free from all family fret. Once in the country, the Emperor regained his strength rapidly, and the accustomed routine came back into its own. He would rise at seven and breakfast alone on green tea with cream and a few wheaten rusks; his secretaries came at eight and work went on till noon when he and the Empress went for a walk in the park, fed the swans by the edge of the great lake, and remarked the least stir of spring on tree and bush. Then Alexander rested till dinner, and she remained in the room, her quiet assuring an unbroken sleep for him. They dined *tête-à-tête* at four, and soon afterwards he left her, to be closeted in the study again. When the clock struck nine, the Empress felt it was 'the best time of the day'. She joined Alexander in the study. Once the tea equipage was cleared away, they belonged wholly to themselves in speech or in silence. Some time before midnight all the candles went out in their apartments.

That very long illness was a proof that in spite of all the burdens and horrors of the Arakcheev yoke, Alexander was still beloved by his people, still 'The Blessed One', whose danger plunged them into sorrow and whose recovery made them break into song.

In late autumn of 1824 General Wassilchikov, head of police in the capital, came to the Winter Palace with a detailed report about a momentous discovery made by his underlings. A great and daring conspiracy existed in the Empire. The authorities had stumbled on a clue which enabled them to build a clear picture of the whole organization and the ultimate aims of the two secret societies. No arrests had yet been made pending the Emperor's decision, said Wassilchikov.

The report, for all its length, was succinct enough. The Northern Society, headed by Nikita Mouravies-Apostol, Nicholas Turgenev and Constantine Ryleev, the poet, stood for a constitutional government and insisted that monarchy must at all costs be preserved. The Southern Society, led by Pavel Pestel, rejected the very idea of a constitution. They were determined to work for the establishment of a republic. A monarch and his immediate family in exile did not particularly appeal to them. They did not exclude from their plans the utter extinction of the dynasty.

The report read, Wassilchikov waited for comment. None came, and Alexander's face was impassive. The general ventured to ask when it would please the sovereign to make his will known to the authorities. The Emperor replied:

'*Mon cher Wassilchikov, vous qui êtes à mon service depuis le commencement de mon règne, vous savez que j'ai partagé et encouragé ces illusions. Ce n'est pas à moi à sévir.*'

These baffling words, which would have gladdened Parrott and La Harpe, were spoken some time after Photius and his gang had persuaded Alexander that the translation of the Bible into the vernacular should be stopped, when Prince Golitzin had fallen from grace, after Photius could write triumphantly to his 'maiden daughter': 'Rejoice with me. . . . The hosts of blasphemers will soon be scattered. . . . Pray for Alexey Arakcheev, God's servant and a true St George, now fighting the dragon in the name of the Holy Church, God preserve him . . .'

And the same Alexander, who had never tired of linking revolutionary outbursts with '*le génie du mal*' at work in Europe, could now, on learning that the same evil had found a lodgment in his own Empire, say that for him to show the least severity was impossible.

A contradiction leaps to the eye. In reality, there was no contradiction. No repressive measures could have laid the ghost of the Emperor's earlier days. It walked by his side, that Janus of a ghost, remorse for a crime committed by others, hatred of evil side by side with a tolerance towards evil.

The episode[1] has been called in question by some historians, but there exist facts to lend it substance. Wassilchikov did not go to Arakcheev but to the Emperor. The favourite was not permitted a voice in the matter. If he had any liberty of action, all the men concerned would have been imprisoned without delay, tried in camera, and summarily executed. A year later, one John Sherwood, an Englishman in Russian service, brought an even more revealing narrative to Arakcheev, who referred the man to the Emperor. Alexander received Sherwood, but the revelations neither impressed nor troubled him. It was to be left to Alexander's successor to bring down his iron-gloved fist upon all the critics and enemies of autocracy. To Alexander, the matter allowed of no other approach than that of recognising his own responsibility.

The flood which smote St Petersburg in November 1824 shook Alexander to the depths. Street rumours whispered that the catastrophe was God's angry answer to the Russian refusal of help to the persecuted Greeks. The Emperor, replacing one superstition by another, saw the disaster in terms of a personal retribution fallen upon his people for a transgression committed by himself.

The flood was the worst in the chronicle of the city. Within a few hours, the wrath of the Neva swept away all the innumerable bridges and brought down more than seven thousand houses. The exact number of human casualties was never established, but on the existing evidence it ran into four figures. Out of the nineteen islands, those to be smitten hardest were peopled by the poorest of the poor, and those who had escaped death were faced with homelessness and destitution. On 19th November Elizabeth wrote that they were at the Winter Palace '*comme sur un vaisseau.... L'Empereur a envoyé une grande chaloupe . . . je mourais de peur qu'un beau mouvement d'humanité ne lui donnât envie de s'y mettre lui-même . . .*' Alexander spared his wife such anxiety on the first day only. The very next morning found him making the rounds of the wrecked capital. He went by boat, two equerries accompanying him. 'I must see for myself,' he told the Governor General of the city, 'so as to be able to order immediate relief.' The rebuilding of the bridges was met out of the municipal funds. The succour of the homeless came from Alexander's private purse, the enormous donation enlarged by

[1] cf. Schilder, op. cit., Vol. IV, p. 236.

the Empress's share. St Michael's Castle and other Crown houses were open to give shelter to the dispossessed folk. Field kitchens were organized in all the squares. All entertainment ceased—much to Alexander's pleasure. A society woman, who had sent invitations to a ball, found her threshold forsaken for several months. At Christmas Elizabeth told her mother that the Emperor's birthday had been spent *'dans la plus grande retraite . . . il n'a pas voulu qu'on le fête . . . parcequ'il dit que, dans ce temps-ci, il y a tant de malheureux qu'il serait choquant de se faire fêter . . . comme je désirais aller à la messe pour ce jour, l'Empereur a fait placer la chapelle portative dans un de mes salons à deux chambres de mon cabinet de sorte que nous avons entendu la messe tout seuls à nous deux, ce qui m'a fait plaisir et à l'Empereur aussi . . .'*

The doctors were anxious about Elizabeth's lungs. She knew how ill she was, but she did not greatly care. Alexander surrounded her with every care and *'il me témoigne . . . une solicitude qui me prouve toute son amitié.'* He certainly did: he forbade members of his family to harass his wife by unnecessary visits, and he took her to Tsarskoe Selo. But the Empress's doctor, Stoffregen, must soon consult his colleagues about a patient whose condition did not improve. Fever began accompanying neuralgia and the cough meant broken nights. Those were admittedly remediable ills, but the nervous system asked for peace rather than pills, and the doctors knew that peace could hardly be enjoyed anywhere with the Dowager Empress almost round the corner. Herself robustly healthy, immune against mental irritation, Marie would have shown sympathy in the case of some infectious disease or a broken limb. Her *'cette pauvre Lise'* hinted at impatience, and the words *'mais il ne s'agit que de ses nerfs'* carried thinly disguised contempt. Such a state of health asked for a vinaigrette, a little self-control, and some pleasant relaxation. 'Your neuralgia would have left you if you had come to my *fête-champêtre*—there was such gaiety there,' such was the Dowager's remark in reply to Elizabeth's excuses for having missed an entertainment at Pavlovsk.

The doctors were in a quandary. Wylie, still remembering the tumultuous scenes at the Winter Palace during the Emperor's illness, could offer little advice. Alexander could and did veto the tempestuous visits of his brothers, but he could never exclude his mother. In the end it was decided that the Empress Elizabeth must not spend the winter in the north.

They were in the early summer of 1825. Marie was at Pavlovsk. Her favourite daughter-in-law, Grand Duchess Nicholas, was expecting another confinement, which, in the Dowager's opinion, afforded an excellent reason for an increased to and fro between Tsarskoe Selo and Pavlovsk. She paid surprise visits to her son and his wife to inform them that '*chère Alexandrine*' had eaten raspberries but could not endure an apple compôte, to consult them about the choice of godparents, to chatter fatuously about the sex of the infant, to choose one archbishop and to reject another for the christening, interlarding it all with gossip from Dresden, Vienna and London, and then flying back to '*chère Alexandrine*' whose '*cadeau de couches*' must be chosen without delay.

Elizabeth, all energy shredded, knew she must be reconciled. '*Le calme ne peut pas se rétablir tant qu'Alexandrine sera ici en couches . . . parceque c'est un motif pour l'Impératrice d'y venir fréquemment. [Ce soir] elle est venue avec Grande Duchesse Marie pour voir l'Empereur malgré qu'il avait passé hier deux heures à Pavlovsk et ce matin aussi. . . . Lorsque je le vois ainsi harassé comme un cerf aux abois . . . et qu'on lui enlève encore les petits moments de loisir qu'il pourrait avoir, il m'est difficile de me contenir. . . .*' In those days nothing sustained Elizabeth except the hope that the Emperor would accompany her whenever she went. '*[Cela] m'est déjà un point de tranquillité bien nécessaire . . .*'

In his own turn, Alexander longed to escape the court shackles even for a short time. When the doctors suggested some place on the Mediterranean coast, the Empress declared that she did not wish to leave Russia. To go anywhere abroad, she told her husband, would mean little more than exchanging one kind of fatigue for another. She wanted to be taken to the sea, to some secluded spot where real simplicity could be enjoyed and where no social occasions would be forced on her. Alexander, having left her full liberty of choice, remembered a quiet little town he had visited on his earlier travels in the south. It was Taganrog on the shores of the Sea of Azov. The idea pleased Elizabeth, and the departure was fixed for early autumn.

St Petersburg had barely heard the name of Taganrog, and the news led to a spate of fantastic rumours. People who had not even known of the town's existence now claimed a detailed knowledge of the place. It was called a town by mere courtesy, they said. It was little more than a village or else a garrison post. There certainly was not a house fit to receive a general's wife, let alone the Empress. The Sea of Azov was well known for its uncertain temper, and the neighbourhood of Taganrog was an immense marsh. The climate was so bad that every kind of infection could be feared. No Russians lived there, they said—the place teemed with Jews, Tartars and Turks. A drawing-room wit delighted his hostess by remarking that the climate of Taganrog being utterly vile, the houses there were not inhabited.

It is doubtful if any of that gossip came to Tsarskoe Selo. Even if it had, Elizabeth would not have felt troubled: she would have followed her husband into the very heart of the Siberian tundra. In sober reality, his reasons were perfectly sound: Taganrog offered seclusion and peace and, for all the calumnies spread about it, a good climate.

In the latter years, Alexander's dilatoriness had become almost a legend. Reports remained unread, letters unsigned, and audiences postponed for no better reason than that he seemed to regard any delay as a daily necessity. But he threw himself into all the arrangements for the journey and the stay at Taganrog with an ardour and an urgency which surprised everybody, including his wife. An army of couriers was posted to the south, and a decent house was found at Taganrog, some of its windows facing the sea. It was no palace: it numbered eleven rooms, eight of which were quite small, but the care with which they were appointed moved Elizabeth beyond all telling. Waggon after waggon left the north, all of them loaded according to lists drawn up by Alexander. Bedding, curtains, carpets, furniture, all the requisites for a chapel, china, silver, glass and mirrors, books and ornaments, everything was chosen in strict accord with the sick Empress's taste and preference, and Alexander left St Petersburg at an early date so that everything should be ready for her arrival. Every single stage of the long journey was arranged by himself—down to the special pillow cases, shades for the candles she liked, and the Dresden china for her breakfast and tea. She wrote to her mother from Borovichy on 17th September 1825:

'*L'Empereur compte à rester avec moi jusqu'a la nouvelle année.* . . . *Il est si bon pour moi encore sur ce voyage . . . il a prévu tout, arrangé*

*tout d'une manière dont je suis bien touchée . . . je voyage avec un luxe
de commodités que je n'ai jamais eu en route. Depuis mon départ . . .
j'ai déjà eu quatres lettres de l'Empereur. . . . Il me témoigne une
solicitude qui me touche et me pénètre . . .'*

The Empress travelled by easy stages, and Alexander met her
carriage at the last posting station before Taganrog. The unfamiliar
wild landscape of the steppes enchanted her, and the house prepared
by him with such obvious care pleased her greatly. '*Heimlich*', she
called it to her mother. The small terrace, the tiny garden, the
pleached apricot trees in the orchard, the dark green sea burning at
sunset, all of it was enjoyed all the more because she had Alexander
with her. The letters to Baden are triumphant with their unceasing
'*nous*': 'we have gone into the town . . . we have sat on the terrace
. . . we have walked in the orchard. . . . Our dinner came. . . . During
our drive . . .' '*ici, où on est si bien* . . .' 'The household,' said Dr
Tarassov in his memoirs, 'took heart to see them so happy together.'

They were. For all the smallness of the house, a most rewarding
amplitude entered their life. The cloying climate of court, the
wearying public occasions, the waspish interference of the family,
above all else the mask which must needs be worn lest an im-
moment word or look were to afford a foothold for malicious gossip,
all those were as though they had never been. Not all the members
of the small retinue accorded well one with another. Prince Peter
Volkonsky had good cause to dislike Dibitch, who had supplanted
him at the General Staff, and one of the two ladies-in-waiting,
Valueva, did not enjoy a great popularity. But all of them took care
to keep any signs of friction well in the background, and all, down to
the youngest footman, respected the imperial privacy.

Alexander and Elizabeth re-discovered each other at Taganrog.
Their pleasures were of the simplest. They drove along the sea-
shore and into the surrounding steppes, they went into the little
town, entered the humble little shops kept by Jews and Tartars, and
mingled with the people. The unimportant town could not quite
believe its honour. The Emperor had been there before, but
fleetingly, spending no more time than was needed for the rest of the
horses. But now Taganrog enroofed him; its people saw him daily,
its children learned to answer his smile with their own, and it was
something of a fairy tale to them all. In October the Empress wrote
glowingly to Baden:

'*Il n'est pas difficile de juger du bien partiel et général que l'Empereur fait par sa présence dans la contrée où il se trouve, celle-ci se ressent déjà . . .*'

She rested entirely—mentally and physically. He still had work to do, and couriers from the north arrived daily. He remained faithful to his filial duties, but the Dowager Empress could no longer enmesh them into her web. She detailed all kinds of daily trivialities in her letters, but Elizabeth could afford to read them, her peace unbroken.

Day by day, her health improved, though it is doubtful that her doctors had ever hoped for a complete recovery. Alexander was well and his leg gave him less and less trouble, and sometimes they joked together about the five doctors they had brought with them.

The small kitchen staff were occasionally in despair, so limited were the resources of the little market. But neither the Emperor nor his wife were troubled by the absence of delicacies. They often dined off pearl barley soup, fresh fish cutlets and lemon jelly, and the enforced monotony of menus was not even noticed by them. Day by day, Alexander's chivalrous care continued even in the smallest details. Elizabeth once regretted that the trees planted in the public square screened the view from the sea. 'People have so much further to walk to see it,' she said to Alexander, and within a few hours the trees were down—to the great pleasure of the elderly folk of Taganrog. A courier was sent to St Petersburg to fetch some French books she had left behind. Prott, the pharmacist, would be asked if he had enough ingredients for the cordial prescribed by Dr Stoffregen. The Empress felt as though she were caught up into a golden cloud. The sea air and the tranquillity certainly helped her, but Alexander's care meant infinitely more. Years of fret and worry slipped off Elizabeth's shoulders when she saw his smile, heard his laughter, watched him forestall some wish of hers. He was nearly forty-eight, she in her forty-sixth year. Taganrog gave them a second honeymoon.

To judge by the serenity of Elizabeth's letters written from Taganrog, it is doubtful that Alexander could have told her about an incident which deeply distressed him. Before leaving for the south, he, according to his custom, had left everything in Arakcheev's hands. A bare few days before the Empress's arrival at Taganrog, the Emperor received a hysterical letter from 'the serpent'. During his brief absence from Gruzino, some serfs in the house, goaded beyond endurance by his mistress's cruelties, had killed her, and now Arakcheev wrote that he 'was shattered to pieces', that the murder of 'the beloved friend' had robbed him of all reason, that he had relieved himself of all the offices he held and had sent a courier to State Secretary Mouraviev with a note to say that no papers of any kind were to be sent to Gruzino. He was fit for nothing except tears. He could not attend to any business.

'The beloved friend,' one Nastia Minkina, was a gross, evil-mouthed peasant woman, so deeply and constantly addicted to strong liquor that her lover had to keep her in the background during the Emperor's visits to Gruzino.

Alexander immediately asked his 'dear friend' to come to Taganrog and be comforted. Fortunately for Elizabeth's peace, Arakcheev never came, nor did he think of ever returning to his duties. Such was the return he made to his benefactor, and the Emperor's eyes may well have been 'opened', as Prince Volkonsky had once hoped.

He wrote again and yet again, but Arakcheev had no longer any room for either friendship or duty. Alexander concealed his distress, but no great imaginative effort is needed to understand what a blow had fallen on him.

The kindly autumn weather continued, and towards the end of October, Elizabeth's health no longer being a matter of immediate anxiety, Alexander decided to make a short excursion into the Crimea. Prince Volkonsky and a few others accompanied him. About ten days later, at St George's Abbey near Balaklava, the Emperor felt slightly feverish, refused his dinner, drank a glass of iced lemon water and, at Dr Tarassov's advice, decided to return to Taganrog.

Prince Volkonsky alone shared the carriage with the Emperor. Half-way down, Alexander sighed and said how much he liked the Crimea. 'I think I would like to live there—as a private individual. After all, my friend, I shall soon have done my twenty-five years of service when any soldier is free to claim his release.' On approaching Taganrog he forbade Volkonsky and the others to tell the Empress how seedy he had felt at Balaklava. But it was a futile command:

fever gripped the Emperor and he looked a very sick man when they reached Taganrog. Wylie at once diagnosed a sharp gastric disorder, but Alexander refused either to go to bed or to take any medicines. They were all fussing unnecessarily, he told Elizabeth over their usual evening meal of pearl barley soup, fish cutlets and lemon jelly. His appearance frightened her, but he did not refuse the food, and she felt slightly reassured.

Yet, a few days later, for once dispensing with his valet's services, the Emperor got up, started to shave himself, felt dizzy, and fell down in a faint. They carried him to bed, and the doctors were in despair over his obstinacy. Wylie, who knew him so well, wrote in his journal that he felt certain something occupied the Emperor's mind.

The next day Alexander felt better, but he could not get up. That afternoon husband and wife were closeted together for nearly four hours, none venturing to disturb them. The only clue to their conversation may be found in Elizabeth's letter to Baden written the same evening: *'Où est le repose dans cette vie? Lorsqu'on croit avoir tout arrangé pour le mieux et pouvoir le goûter, il survient une épreuve inattendue.'* The sentence was not followed by any explanation. It was grafted into the body of the letter, which dealt with the Emperor's illness. It is obvious that Alexander had pledged her to absolute secrecy in all that concerned their very last long conversation on earth. When we remember Alexander's words to Volkonsky on the way from Balaklava and so many of his earlier expressed wishes to hand the crown over to his successor during his lifetime, many obscure details gain in clarity. Arakcheev's shameful defection may or may not have accelerated the decision. *'L'épreuve inattendue'* could have been none other than the Emperor's resolve to leave the world on his recovery, and such a resolve could never have been carried out in Russia. His abdication as such could hardly have shaken Elizabeth. On the contrary, it would have sustained her by a promise of a tranquillity to last until death. But to have him living and gone from her into the silence of a hermit's cell would have been beyond her to endure.

Elizabeth had her faith, but the latter was of a kind which must express itself in charity to all. A violent renunciation, carried out in the name of the God of love, was something outside her nature. The deep feeling she had for Alexander made her accept his decision. But she could not see it in any other light than that of an '*épreuve* . . .'[1]

At Elizabeth's suggestion, the Emperor agreed to see a priest. The last sacraments administered, the priest begged him not to refuse his doctors' services, and the Emperor gave in. He felt slightly better that day, but Elizabeth dared not hope for a recovery. The fever hardly left him even by daytime and the weakness increased. She was hardly ever out of the room. When consciousness returned to him, Alexander looked at her and at no one else.

Late in the afternoon of 30th November Wylie went to rest and Tarassov was on duty, and it is in his diary that we find the details of Alexander's last night :[2] '. . . [he] was conscious of his wife's presence, took her hand, and kept it on his breast. . . . A little later the Empress retired. . . . About ten in the evening I noticed a change . . . Prince Volkonsky at once went to fetch the Empress . . . she came, sat down by the bed, her left hand holding his right . . . at times she cried very quietly. . . . The morning broke dull. . . . The square was crowded with people waiting for the news. . . . The Emperor grew weaker, but he kept opening his eyes . . . now looking at the Empress, now at the crucifix. . . . His last looks were of tranquillity and hope. . . . There was no suffering in his face. . . . At ten minutes to eleven his breathing ceased . . .'

The thirteen hours of the vigil were over. The Empress did not cry. She rose, bowed down to the ground, kissed Alexander's forehead, closed his eyes, bowed once again and left the room.

'*Notre ange est au ciel*,' she wrote a few days later to her mother. '*C'est presque au delà de mes forces* . . .' Almost it seemed as though the burden would have been easier to carry if she had not received so much tenderness until the very last moments. '. . . *il a fallu voir expirer cet être angélique, qui conservait la faculté d'aimer ayant perdu*

---

[1] I am aware that a totally different interpretation has been given to the above quotation from the Empress's letter. It has been suggested that it was precisely during that afternoon that Alexander discussed his plan of 'vanishing' from Taganrog and asked for her co-operation, and that, in effect, it happened (see below, Chapter XI, The Legend), but I would ask my readers first to remember the dates and then the number of people in the house. The conversation took place on 23rd November and all the records fully agree that the Emperor never left his bed again. All the members of the retinue and all the servants in and out of the house would have had to be taken into the Empress's confidence to ensure the success of a plan whereby the Emperor's 'disappearance' could be made possible.

[2] cf. Schilder, op. cit., Vol. IV, p. 384.

celle de comprendre. . . . Peu de monde ont connu cet âme, tout ce qu'elle valait, mais Dieu la connaissait bien. . . . Le premier jour [après la mort] il avait une expression de gaieté . . . si animée qu'il semblait qu'il allait se lever avec toute la vivacité habituelle de ses mouvements. . . . Il savait que je ne tenait qu'à lui. . . .' and again and again the Empress returned to the moment when he pressed her hand against his breast. *'Il savait tout ce qu'il m'était et que lui seul m'était tout,'* and she recalled all the instances when, as she thought, Alexander's soul *'semblait se centupler,'* when his entire business consisted in giving pleasure, comfort and happiness to so many. *'Il était mûr pour l'éternité.'*

The midnight had come for her. To live without him was something out of accord with nature. *'La rôle que j'y jouerais à la longue serait au dessous de la dignité qui doit toujours rester attachée à la mémoire de cet Empereur Alexandre, unique et incomparable aux yeux de l'Europe entière . . .'*

Elizabeth's desire was soon granted. The slight improvement in her health was undone by the weeks of that unremitting vigil. She was unable to follow her husband's body to the north. She stayed at Taganrog all through the winter, her strength waning every day. She left in the spring. One April evening in 1826 she reached Belev, a small town in the Kaluga Province. She was so ill that further travelling was impossible. There were no inns at Belev, and some makeshift arrangements must be made at a private house. Elizabeth's hope to join Alexander in the eternity she so firmly believed in was fulfilled that night.

Four tributes to the Emperor will be found in the Appendix. It is a truism to say that historical appraisals have some affinity with quicksands, and it may well be found impossible to echo every detail of those eulogies. Nor are all the details necessary today. Alexander I deserved well of posterity not only in spite of his many faults, mistakes and imperfections but also because of them. The very contradictions in his policy were salutary for a nation all too prone to pay homage to tradition and custom. Nor would it be just to wrench the last years of his reign out of their context, as it were, and let them colour the rest. The twilight came indeed, and it was grievous, its causes all but eluding analysis. That night in March 1801 was by no means the first dark doorway Alexander had to cross. Inwardly halved and impressionable as he was, he had the worst possible initiation into the part he had to play. A future autocrat educated by a republican, a man inclined to peace committed to an inexorable military pattern, his hunger for individual liberty answered by accents of tyranny, his desire for hidden corners turned into a mockery by the blinding lights of a public stage, at every turn in Alexander's youth, the design to be accepted warred against his needs and aims.

He came to the throne at a moment in history when mediocrity spelt a greater disaster than a total lack of ability, when vision was more valuable than keen eyesight, and yet the formative years of the reign bear hardly a hint of the glory to come. The man's peculiar genius had nothing in common with the bureaucracy which made daily and hourly demands on him and which he could, if he so wished, reform but never annihilate. The enthusiast in Alexander hurried towards reforms, their shape never clear in his thought. The dreamer shrank from the dusty alleys leading to the least administrative change, and once again a pattern crying against everything in him must needs be accepted. But now, unlimited power under his hand, Alexander could command, commit mistakes, veil his intentions by ambiguities, translate a hope into a realizable form, none questioning his judgment. Many mistakes were made, both at home and abroad, but in the end they suggest so many rungs of a ladder he found hard to scale.

Europe has remained in his debt to this day, not for his decision to carry the war to the end and not for the creation of the Holy Alliance, but rather for the fresh breath he brought to her counsels. Not many men in European chancelleries gave much thought to disinterestedness and still fewer admitted that such a policy could ever answer. Alexander's liberation of Europe was the act of a man dedicated to his neighbour's needs. It was the height of a moment that even a genius could not have sustained for long, and Alexander was no genius. But he gave that moment and the use he made of it to history, and those abide.

They have so often reproached him for his absorption in western Europe to the neglect of his own Empire, for granting a constitution to Poland and an autonomous status to Finland at a time when Russia was still far from the threshold of electoral franchise. They have accused him of a stubborn refusal to give room to the new ideas brought home by his own people. All those reproaches are not altogether unmerited. Alexander's handling of the Polish matter ended in dark tragedy after his death. His attitude to Finland exasperated many of his Russian subjects. His swerving away from the liberalism of his younger days paved the way to the iron gyves of his brother's reign. Yet even in his mistakes Alexander could not avoid redeeming contradictions. The words spoken to Wassilchikov, '*pas à moi à sévir*', tear at least one of the veils away. He could not punish those who worshipped at a shrine he had frequented. Even through the years of twilight his people could travel abroad, and whilst Alexander's ministers persecuted professors of humanities, young Russians were still free to sit at the feet of the day's celebrities at many a university in Europe.

Alexander's preoccupation with the other-worldly was disastrous for himself and in some degree for his people. His idea of expiation was little more than a desire to reach a self-satisfaction denied elsewhere. His private morality cannot be condoned, though all his infidelities were more of the body than of the heart and the thought, and his wife knew it well. His perfidies in friendship can infuriate. His dalliance with monks and lachrymose seers, his treatment of Parrott and La Harpe, his tolerance of his silly mother and his no less silly sister, and his unspeakable neglect of his wife: none of it makes pleasant reading, but none of it should be brushed away from the landscape. 'The Blessed' never reached the heights of saintliness. How could he? None the less, the nation kept the name to the very end, and Alexander's sins came to be forgiven even by those whom they most wounded.

A great-great uncle of mine, Constantine Poltorazky, an officer in the Semenovsky Guards regiment, was on duty at St Michael's Castle during the night of Paul's murder, and he left a record of all that he saw and heard. He ran to find the young Emperor because— '*j'adorais Alexandre . . .*' and the use of the word held true to the end. The brothers Rostov, both Nicholas and Petia, mirror an entire generation. Alexander had the quality of evoking the best, the most living elements in all he met. Something of that climate endured even during the years of twilight. To it is due much of the stubborn hope which conquered even on the scaffold during his brother's reign, and his nephew, the second Alexander, owed his uncle a debt few were prepared to admit at the time.

He infuriates and he puzzles. He never bores or disgusts. In Russian history, he stands undatable. With hardly any Russian blood in him, Alexander I seems to link centuries together, a Viking of Rus, a Grand Duke of Kiev, Dimitry Donskoy on the Kulikovo Field, Ivan the Terrible in the fair morning of his reign, Peter the Great, all but trapped by the Turks on the banks of the Pruth: the great exemplars seem crystallized in the man who fought and crushed Napoleon not out of revenge for the flames of Moscow but in the cause of Europe.

Alexander eludes. He always will. 'The Sphinx on the throne' had his secret buried with him, a secret which had nothing to do with any hermits in Siberia. Something of that secret remained to enchant poet and composer, stir a historian's imagination, feed a peasant's hunger for landscapes lovelier than his own, and establish a young man's hope for a world shaped in a clearer accord with an ideal rather than with an idea.

There was virtue in Alexander which was caught up into a great moment in history, and he answered the moment on all his pulses.

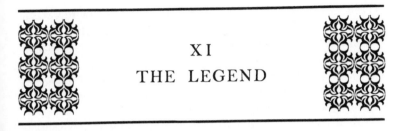

XI

THE LEGEND

ALEXANDER'S DEATH in a town as remote as Taganrog threw the household into indescribable confusion. Prince Volkonsky alone had the presence of mind to arrange for the immediate dispatch of couriers with letters to the Dowager Empress, Grand Duke Constantine and the Senate. The letter to the Grand Duke was addressed to 'His Imperial Majesty the Sovereign Lord and Emperor'. The contents of Alexander's Succession Manifesto were then still unknown, and for something like three weeks Constantine in Warsaw and Nicholas in St Petersburg exchanged letters until the manifesto came to light, Alexander's will was made known, and the oath of allegiance sworn to Nicholas as the Autocrat of All the Russias.

At Taganrog, priests and monks began chanting the appointed offices. The doctors were almost in despair since the essential materials for the embalming were anything but easy to find. The Empress Elizabeth either stayed in her room or attended the requiems. The improvement in her health gained since her arrival in the south had gone overnight. A bent-shouldered shadow, she moved from her room to the chapel and back again. Her ladies and Volkonsky saw to it that nobody harassed her with fussy and unnecessary inquiries. It was obvious to all that Elizabeth would not be able to leave for the north. So she stayed behind when soon after the New Year the cortège, carrying the indifferently embalmed body of her husband, started on its long journey to St Petersburg.

Long before that the Empire learned of its loss and of the uncertainty of the succession. Special precautions were taken all along the route, and they are easily understood when it is remembered how suddenly the Emperor had died and that the facts about a great planned conspiracy were in the hands of the authorities. By the time the funeral cortège reached the capital, the December mutiny was in the past and Nicholas I had ascended the throne, but the feeling of loss among the masses was heightened by the dearth of information. Taganrog was such a remote speck on an immense map. Few papers were then published in the Empire, what news they printed was meagre enough, and, in any case, such information would have been beyond reach of the illiterate masses.

Nobody can tell how it started, but almost immediately cautious whispers ran from one village to another. Little by little rumours left the countryside and reached the towns where the vague story began assuming clarity and shape. Now here, now there, men and women began remembering wisps of gossip once heard from those whose uncles and cousins had uncles and cousins of their own in various imperial households. The Emperor Alexander had meant to lay down the sceptre and to dedicate the remnant of his days to the service of God. Taganrog was at such a distance away, and could anyone be really sure of what happened there? Did 'The Blessed' die at all? Stitch after stitch, the wonderful tapestry came to be woven until some people were positive that a mysterious foreign yacht had entered the Sea of Azov just about that time. She was supposed to have come from England. Did 'The Blessed' embark on her for an unknown destination? He would hardly have gone to Mount Athos because of all that trouble over the Greek rebels. It must have been the Holy Land, and the people's imagination leapt at the idea of atonement to redeem 'The Blessed's' inexplicable refusal to come to the aid of the Orthodox Greeks.

Apart from its enduring grip on the people, the legend was not particularly original. Not to go further back, the eighteenth century carried quite a few examples of the reaches which the national fantasy could encompass. Not everybody at the time was certain that Peter the Great died in 1725. There were doubts about the fate of his grandson, Peter II, who, aged fifteen, died of smallpox in 1730, on the eve of his wedding day. The unfortunate Ivan VI, deposed as an infant and murdered in prison in 1764, had quite a number of adherents for some years after his death. The murder of Peter III in 1762 led to a bloody mutiny in the late seventies when a Cossack deserter, one Emelyan Pougachev, claimed to be the late Emperor 'miraculously rescued from his assassins', and untold thousands recognized the extravagant claim. Therefore the root of the legend was familiar enough to the people. In Alexander's case, however, it bore very different colours from those found in the earlier examples. No other Romanov had been as much loved as he was. No other Romanov had ever nursed a desire to give himself up to God's service. So there was no end to the rumours. They must needs all be whispered since it was not safe to have such things shouted about during the reign of Nicholas I.

That Alexander meant to abdicate is beyond doubt, but this raises a point ignored by all the partisans of the legend. Sovereigns had been deposed in Russia. None had abdicated. For Alexander to do so would have meant creating a precedent, and precedents of such a nature must needs be surrounded by a framework of law. Alexander's profound respect for the law rules out the very possibility that he could, as it were, vanish in the dark. The matter did not involve only himself and his possible successor. The oath of allegiance sworn by all men in his service, whether military or civil, was binding until the sovereign's death. For Alexander to disappear without having signed the formal instrument of abdication would have been an outrage against the law and against millions of consciences.

That he hoped to spend the remaining years in solitude may be inferred from Elizabeth's fateful letter to her mother with its words about '*l'épreuve*'. There are no actual proofs, but, if death had not intervened, he would most likely have abdicated in 1827, that is, on reaching his fiftieth year. Yet—and here is another vital point ignored by all the adherents of the legend—Alexander would never have stayed in Russia. For all the words alleged to have been said by him to Grand Duke Nicholas—'and I shall be among the crowds in Moscow at your coronation and join in the cheers'—Alexander's dynastic sense would have recoiled from the idea of causing the least embarrassment to his successor, and such embarrassment, to say no more, would certainly have been created if he had stayed on in the Empire. To remain there would have brought him into a thorny thicket of difficulties—noisome interference by authorities so long as the incognito was kept up and sickening servility in the very possible event of recognition. Alexander's secret would not have been kept in Russia for a year.

Yet, according to the theories put forward, that secret remained unbroken for eleven years.

It is altogether outside the scope of this book to give a minute account of the life of Fedor Kuzmich. Numerous works claiming and disclaiming that he and Alexander I were one and the same person have been written in Russian and some in French. Briefly the facts *known* about the Siberian hermit are as follows. In 1836, a peasant, surprisingly well mounted, appeared at Krasnoufimsk in the Perm Province. The horse having cast a shoe, he stopped at a forge, and the blacksmith got suspicious and reported him to the authorities. He refused to answer questions. They arrested him for a vagrant, flogged him, and deported him to Tomsk. From the moment of the man's appearance at Krasnoufimsk, everybody was convinced of 'a mystery'.

Now the very beginning of the legend is pure fantasy. In 1836, i.e. twenty-five years before emancipation, no peasant, still less a self-confessed vagrant, would have owned a good mount. Had he stolen one, he would never have ridden it into a populated district. To the incident at Krasnoufimsk is joined a story of a local inhabitant who alleged—several years later—that the Emperor Nicholas, on hearing about a vagrant refusing to give his name, had sent his younger brother, Grand Duke Michael, to Siberia. The Grand Duke is supposed to have read the riot act to the authorities, and the old man, still held in prison, had begged that the incident should be forgotten. Next we hear of him in a village near Tomsk. About 1865, i.e. a year after his death, his host's daughter related about some presents sent to the hermit in 1842—from the Dowager Empress Marie. She having died in 1828, it is odd that her gifts should have taken fourteen years to reach Siberia.

The man called himself Fedor Kuzmich; he wandered from one village to another, was known to possess the gift of healing and to devote whole hours to prayer. His charm, kindliness and saintliness began to attract thousands. It is known that members of the imperial family had a great respect for him, and some among them visited him. His manners were certainly those of a *grand seigneur*, and his habits did not suggest a peasant origin. He changed his linen very often and was most particular about the cleanliness of his little hut. Numbers of people claimed to have 'recognized' him, and all of them said that he had enjoined them to keep his secret. Quite obviously there was some mystery about Fedor's antecedents. He died at Tomsk in 1864, not having divulged his identity to anyone.

The first biography, written anonymously and claiming that

Alexander I and Fedor Kuzmich were one and the same person, appeared in St Petersburg in 1891, but no historian could possibly accept a theory which has not a shred of evidence to support it and which is wholly built on conjecture and coincidence.

It is alleged, *inter alia*, that Alexander's silence on the subject of the succession affords a solid 'proof'. The reasons for this silence have been discussed above and they are wholly irrelevant to the issue. It is also held that the increase of restlessness in Alexander all through 1825 can be explained by his having arrived at the decision to vanish at the end of that year. All irrelevance apart, the Emperor was no more restless during 1825 than he had been in the preceding year. He is supposed to have discussed it all with a hermit at the Alexander Abbey in St Petersburg on the eve of his departure for the south. It is perfectly true that he visited the Abbey that evening where a short service was held to wish him Godspeed for the journey. It is also true that he spent a little time in a hermit's cell, but it is difficult, to say the least, to see a link between a conversation of which not a detail is known and Alexander's supposed decision.

In point of fact, the picture drawn by Schilder of the Emperor leaving the capital, his mood 'heavy with melancholy and premonition', is quite untrue. The general evidence of contemporaries proves that the Emperor left for the south with his spirits high. The prospect of a few months away from the cacophony at court heartened him greatly. There is not a single note in a minor key in the letters written to his wife during his journey and hers. A shadow did indeed fall later. Alexander's departure from Taganrog broke the well-nigh miraculous harmony of those days and could not but trouble the Empress. It can be explained by more than a heightening of the habitual restlessness: Arakcheev's defection. He neither came to Taganrog nor recognized that to a man in his position state duty should have come before any personal loss. His replies to the Emperor's letters were brutal evidence of weakness, meanness and small-mindedness. The weakness would have been pardoned. The small-mindedness and the meanness deeply wounded the Emperor. For the firm rock of loyalty he now saw the shifting sands of treachery. Once again nothing but a conjecture may be offered, but Arakcheev's defection may well have pushed the Emperor a step nearer to the goal he desired.

The chief sources of information about his illness and death come from the eyewitnesses: the letters of Elizabeth to her mother and those of Prince Volkonsky to the Dowager Empress and to members of the Government. Finally come the memoirs, composed some time later, of the Prince and of Dr Wylie. There is also the diary kept by Dr Tarassov and the Empress's own journal. It must be admitted that there are discrepancies and contradictions in some of the letters, but the very suddenness of the Emperor's illness and his obduracy in refusing all medical help until it was too late for any remedies to be effective can explain the confusion reigning in the house. Some of the letters to Baden and to St Petersburg mention slight improvements and a worsening at one and the same time. Here again it should be remembered that the Emperor himself had given strict orders that his family should not be made 'unduly anxious' on his behalf. As to the discrepancies met with in the various memoirs, they were written some time after Alexander's death when a host of lesser details would have escaped the writer's memory.

15th November is a date particularly stressed in the pro-legend literature to prove that Alexander did not die at Taganrog. When analysed, the facts carry no such proof. Wylie noted that the patient had spent a bad night, but Elizabeth spoke of an improvement, and so did Prince Volkonsky, who, on inquiring if the Emperor had slept well, received an affirmative answer, but, added Volkonsky, 'son regard me parut affaibli et les yeux me semblèrent troublés.' The Empress does not seem to have spent the whole night in the sickroom. It may well be that she wrote about 'the improvement' on being assured by her husband about a better night he had had. The same discrepancy occurred a little later.

Now we come to 23rd November when all agree that husband and wife spent the afternoon together. In the evening of that day the Empress wrote to her mother about a great and unexpected trial to fall upon her, its nature left unspecified. On the strength of that sentence, a whole mountain of 'evidence' has been erected. Nothing being known of the subjects discussed in the afternoon, it is alleged that Alexander then confided in Elizabeth, telling her of his intention to disappear and making her promise to keep his secret inviolate. In the end we are asked to believe that a very sick man, his strength ebbing from day to day, walked out of the house at dead of night and made for the open steppes in the wild November weather, there to start his wanderings towards some remote region, a stranger, most conveniently resembling the Emperor in every feature, being left to die in his bed!

Another proof of 'a highly suspicious nature' is found in the fact that the Empress's diary ends rather abruptly at that date, i.e. a week before the Emperor's death. All the records agree that Elizabeth spent whole days and sometimes nights at her husband's bedside. What time, inclination, or energy would have been left to her to make entries in her journal? What very little leisure she had was devoted to writing to her mother.

Six people, Fedorov, the Emperor's faithful valet among them, were present in the room at the moment of death. According to the architects of the legend, all those people, including the Empress, 'knew' that the Emperor had left the house a few days before and that an unknown commoner was dying in his bed. Having herself closed the stranger's eyes, the Empress then proceeded to feign sorrow in many letters to her mother, and to appear in the chapel to pray for the eternal repose of the soul of a living man!

Another 'proof' offered is the fact that the Empress did not follow the body to St Petersburg—but lingered on 'for mysterious reasons' at Taganrog until the spring of 1826. 'The mysterious reason' was the shattered state of her health. Her death on the journey could hardly be considered sudden in view of her condition, but stubborn fantasy refused to accept such a disappointingly pedestrian fact, and we have the image of one 'Vera the hermit' settling down at some unnamed convent, having made a vow of perpetual silence. We also hear of 'Vera' receiving many visits from Countess Anna Orlova, Photius's 'maiden daughter', whom Elizabeth could hardly endure in her lifetime.

One of the best studies of Alexander was written by the late Grand Duke Nicholas.[1] His position gave him access to archives closed to a commoner and his great erudition enabled him to make fine use of the material. He devoted much time to the problem. He reached the conclusion that the identity of Fedor Kuzmich was insoluble. In the light of all the evidence, the Grand Duke was convinced that the Siberian hermit and Alexander I could not have been one and the same person. 'I confess,' says the Grand Duke in

---

[1] Younger son of Grand Duke Michael, grandson of the Emperor Nicholas I and great-nephew of Alexander I. The Grand Duke devoted all his life to historical research. He was murdered by the Soviet Government in January 1919 in Petrograd.

the last paragraph of his study of Alexander, 'that the story attracted me for several years. . . . I decided not to spare any efforts to unveil the mystery surrounding the name of Fedor Kuzmich. I learned everything about his life in Siberia. . . . One thing alone was clear: the hermit was not and he could not be Alexander I. After many years of study devoted to the Emperor's character, I came to the conclusion that such a metamorphosis was out of all question. . . . Let us remember that, according to his own story, the hermit had been a vagrant until 1836 when he was arrested and cruelly and publicly punished for his vagrancy. Can we for a moment admit that Alexander I would have submitted to any of it? One's imagination recoils from any such admission . . .'

Those words were written about 1911. In 1916 I happened to be at the British Embassy when the Grand Duke and Sir George Buchanan were discussing the legend, and I remember the Grand Duke saying that he was supposed to have discovered some documents proving the real identity of Fedor Kuzmich and that circumstances he could not mention prevented him from making it public, and he called the story a pure invention.

There exist many conjectures about the hermit's real identity. In 1919 the Cathedral of SS Peter and Paul in Petrograd was closed to the public for several months, and as usual fantastic rumours began creeping about. All the marble sarcophagi were then supposed to have been opened and that of Alexander I found to be empty. An old lady who was then still living in Petrograd and was a fund of fact and legend—Mademoiselle Rohmer, once maid-of-honour to the wife of the Emperor Alexander II, dismissed the idea that Alexander's tomb had been found empty, but said that she had heard from a lady-in-waiting to the wife of Nicholas I that Fedor Kuzmich was a great-grandson of Peter the Great and a cousin of Alexander I, and she gave me the man's pedigree. The story would have been utterly fantastic anywhere except in Russia.

One of Peter the Great's daughters, Elizabeth, who reigned from 1741 till 1761, was morganatically married to Count Razumovsky. She is supposed to have given birth to a daughter. Nobody had ever heard of the child until about 1772 when a young woman appeared in Paris and claimed to be the legitimate Empress of Russia. In 1773 she is supposed to have married Prince Radziwyl and had a son by him. Nobody knew what happened to the child, but the prince deserted her. She was kidnapped by the Russians in Italy, brought to St Petersburg, and imprisoned in the Fortress where she died in rather mysterious circumstances. She went down in legend as Princess Tarakanova. Her real identity was never established. It is a fact that all the documents relating to the case of '*la belle inconnue*' were destroyed and that Catherine the Great's agitation at the woman's appearance in Europe was out of all proportion if she were a mere adventuress of obscure origins. There remains one rather curious detail: a son of the Empress Elizabeth's daughter and of Prince Radziwyl would have been a pure Slav, about three years younger than Alexander I, who was born in 1777. There exists a photograph of Fedor Kuzmich towards the close of his life, and the features are undeniably Slav. The only Russian blood Alexander had in him came from his great-grandmother, Anna, Duchess of Holstein, daughter of Peter the Great. That unfailingly compelling '*je ne sais quoi*' about him was not a Russian quality.

The identity of Fedor Kuzmich promises fair to remain insoluble. As to the legend, it was born out of the imagination of a people always hungry for the mysterious and the unattainable. Reality weighed heavily on the Russian masses. It was comforting—particularly during the iron reign of Nicholas I—to believe that 'The Blessed' was still among them, dedicated to a life they all venerated. A belief informed with warmth and affection does not die easily, nor is there any harm in it so long as the consoling delusion is not grafted into the texture of legitimate history.

E. M. Almedingen

Somerset
August 1963

APPENDIX

APPENDIX

Some Opinions of Alexander:
One Englishwoman and Three Russians

(1) E. C. Disbrowe was appointed Minister Plenipotentiary to Russia early in 1825. The following extract is from a letter from Mrs Disbrowe to her family in England. It is quoted from *Original Letters from Russia, 1825-1828*, ed. by C. A. A. Disbrowe, London, 1878.

St Petersburg, 2/14 December 1825.

'. . . Never was a monarch so mourned; but it is not as their Emperor that they deplore him, it is as a common friend. Every individual weeps as for the loss of their dearest best friend. He was loved for himself, was so affable, so benevolent, interesting himself about his lowliest subjects, entered into the concerns of all around him in the most affectionate manner, and in short was completely identified with his people. . . . He won strangers by his amiable condescension, and it was impossible not to like him. Mr Law (the English chaplain in St Petersburg) gave us a most impressive sermon on Sunday, and passed a most beautiful eulogium on the late monarch. . . . The Empress Mother expresses great satisfaction at the way in which the English have solemnized the Emperor's death, and says: "*Remerciez ces bons Anglais pour moi.*" Since the sad news the taverns have been entirely deserted—a remarkable trait of the grief of the people.'

(2) Nicholas I. Turgenev.

'*La Russie et les russes*'. Paris, 1847. Vol. I, p. 519.

'C'est parceque son cœur ne lui permettait pas de rester entièrement inaccessible aux vœux dictés par le désir du bien général, qu'il a mérité les égards, l'estime et les respects des hommes bien intentionnés. Ce sentiment et son zèle pour le bien public, bien qu'ils n'aient pas été féconds en résultats utiles, n'en feront pas moins vivre avec honneur son nom dans l'histoire. Alexandre sans doute est mort despote, mais il était né pour être mieux que cela.'

(3) A. N. Pypin.

'*Social Movements in Russia under Alexander I*' (in Russian), St Petersburg, 1900, pp. 14 and 47. Extract translated by the author.

'His personality bewilders us by its many contradictions. Lack of stability was always evident, and today it is easy to understand why Alexander's instability, sometimes shown at the most critical moments of his reign, should have created an unpleasant impression on his contemporaries and even given rise to undisguised antipathy. . . . None the less, having examined all the different aspects of his life, we end by being reconciled to that baffling personality. . . . There was nothing intrinsically vicious in any of his faults. . . . His will had never been properly trained. . . . His ideals and aspirations had not been developed in healthy surroundings. All the complications of his earlier years served to separate his consciousness and his emotions. His education was broken off just when it had reached its most demanding and important stage. . . . We can value Alexander's merits all the more when we remember the pleasure evinced by his allies in dedicating themselves to reactionary policies. Not for them to share Alexander's doubts and anguish. . . .'

(4) Prince Peter Wiazemsky, Complete Works, ed. by Count C. D. Sheremetev, St Petersburg, 1882. The extract below, translated from the Russian by the author, is taken from '*Russky Arkhiv*', 1886, Vol. III, p. 401 *et seq*.

'During the last decade of his life Alexander I was not—and he could not be—the man he had been. He had gone through a hard school. The earlier liberalism was shaken and wounded by rude reality. Revolutionary movements abroad, the mutiny of the Semenovsky Guards regiment, unrest in the country, the arrogance of the Polish Diet, from whose members Alexander had hoped for so much, misgivings about something evil being shaped in the Empire, all of it together could not but influence his sensitive nature. His earlier energies were spent, his self-confidence was gone. He found himself compelled to admit that good is not always easy to do and that the very same people for whom such good is intended will paralyse its effects by the manner of their acceptance of the benefits bestowed. Alexander's disillusionment was bitter and hard. Ruthless critics would say that a man of strong will must keep himself above life's daily storms. It may well be so. But we do not feel that we have the right to echo such harsh judgments. We think that all the mistakes committed by Alexander were redeemed by his trials and his griefs. Here, we dare not sit in judgment. We can feel nothing but compassion. . . . Cheap and sceptical historiography all too often tries to erase the splendours of history. Those efforts are futile. A nation lives in its past glories. . . . Many pages of the chronicle stir the nation's pride and love . . . and Alexander I wrote one of the most splendid and unforgettable pages in the story of our land . . .'

SELECT BIBLIOGRAPHY

IN RUSSIAN

Grand Duke Nicholas Mikhailovich, *The Emperor Alexander I: an Essay in Interpretation*, two volumes, St Petersburg 1912.

Letters of the Emperor Alexander I to his Sister Catherine (ed. by the Grand Duke Nicholas Mikhailovich), St Petersburg 1910.

The Empress Elizabeth, three volumes, St Petersburg 1909.

Schilder, N. K., *The Emperor Alexander I, His Life and Reign*, four volumes, St Petersburg 1912.

Pypin, A. N., *Social Movements in Russia under Alexander I*, St Petersburg 1900.

Some Researches into the epoch of Alexander I, Petrograd 1917.

Afanassiev, G. E., *Napoleon and Alexander*, Kiev 1912.

Alekseev, E. N., *Alexander I—His Personality and Government*, London 1908 (very rare).

Zablotsky-Dessiatovsky, A. P., *Count P. D. Kisselev and his Times*, four volumes, St Petersburg 1889.

IN FRENCH

Vandal, Albert, *Napoléon et Alexandre*, Paris 1894.

Sorel, Albert, *L'Europe et la Révolution française*, Paris 1905.

Masson, F., *Relations diplomatiques entre la France et la Russie*, first volume only, Paris 1909.

TRANSLATION OF
FRENCH PASSAGES

p. 17: Despicable principles, shoddy tricks, never enter his mind. Great men do not dissimulate; they despise ignoble acts.

p. 23: That boy . . . is a combination of many contradictions.

p. 27: [The Grand Duke] gave me a hostile look.

p. 28: My dear friend, you tell me I hold the happiness of a certain person in my hand. Oh, if that is true, his happiness is assured forever. You can be sure that I love you more than I can ever express.

Her manner is cold, but courteous. She is not very talkative, so that very few people really know her.

p. 30: I shall be alone, absolutely alone, without anyone to whom I can tell my smallest thoughts.

pp. 30–31: When we know each other at very close quarters, you notice little nothings, really nothings, which, you might say, are a matter of taste, and there are some of those nothings that are not to my liking and that have put an end to the excessive fashion in which I loved him. I still love him very much, but with a difference. Those nothings are not concerned with his character, for on that side surely I believe he is beyond reproach, but rather they are in his attitude, in a something-or-other external.

p. 31: Dear Mamma, who told you I let the Grand Duke in through the window? I have never done that. I often talk to him at the window, I give him my hand through the window, but never has he come in through the window.

p. 33: His entire court is composed of rascals and fools. She loves her husband, but he is too young to occupy her fully.

. . . a devil incarnate with her everlasting intrigues.

A terrible thing for me is that I never dare to relax among the people around me. . . . Without my husband, the only one who makes me happy here, I should have died a thousand times. . . . If I find someone friendly, as there are a few women here, in particular, a certain Countess Golovina . . . I dare not show that I like her for the public here is insufferable.

p. 34: I am surprised she was not embarrassed the morning after her marriage. She is naturally shy. . . . As for me, I was so tormented by the Grand Duke's father and by the Grand Duchess, I thought I would sink into the ground.

p. 36: [I] owe everything to you but the daylight . . . and now I am alone at the Court I loathe, destined for a position the mere thought of which makes me shudder. . . .

To get rid of my burden . . . here everyone cheats. You almost never meet an honest man . . . it is frightful . . . but I am very lucky with my wife.

p. 37 in note: The minute details of military service and the habit of attaching extreme importance to them warp the Grand Duke's mind. At Gatchina he developed gout that he could not cure. During his entire reign he suffered from a mania for parades that wasted precious time when he was on the throne and, in his youth, prevented him from doing useful work and acquiring indispensable knowledge.

CHAPTER II

p. 41: Your Majesty's kindness in deigning to write with your own hand a document that will help to explain the other papers.

I hope that Your Majesty will see, by my zeal to win your precious favors, that I fully appreciate their value.

I shall never, it is true, be able to repay sufficiently, even with my blood, all that [Your Majesty] has deigned to do, and will still do, for me.

pp. 41–42: These papers clearly confirm all the reflections Your Majesty was kind enough to communicate to me a little while ago and that, if I may say so, cannot be more pertinent.

p. 44: You have no idea how everything, even down to the most insignificant matter, is turned completely upside down.

p. 45: That made such an ugly impression on me that I scarcely recognized myself.

Anne was my only consolation as I was hers . . . our husbands were almost never at home.

Anne and I did not know what to do with ourselves.

p. 46: You have no idea what a terrible emptiness there is.

Everyone is sad . . . except their new Majesties.

Not a word about his mother, except to blame her and to disapprove of everything that was done in her time.

[She] behaves on all rather serious occasions without any proper judgment. . . . You should see how angry my husband gets on those occasions. 'What foolish blunders Mamma makes! She has not the slightest idea how to behave.' He says these things only when we are alone . . . just between ourselves.

p. 47: That isn't appropriate.

[He] is extremely anxious to return, for it is difficult for him always having to sleep in the same room with the Emperor.

I was very happy to see my husband again . . . I was strangely moved when I embraced him.

p. 50: He orders today what a month later he countermands. He gives no thought to the happiness of the State . . . there is only one absolute power that does everything without rhyme or reason. . . . My poor country is in a condition impossible to describe. . . . Spending all my time on the duties of a petty official, not even having a moment to give to my studies.

It would be much better if I were to work to free my country and prevent it from becoming in the future the plaything of madmen. . . . That would be the best form of revolution, carried out by a legal authority that would cease to exist the moment the constitution was drawn up and the country had representatives.

. . . the outrages of despotism and tyranny.

. . . this goal so dear to me.

p. 52: We are so accustomed to telling each other everything, hiding nothing from each other.

p. 55: Every man is thinking only of feathering his own nest.

p. 56: You say to yourself, 'Tomorrow I must see that I am given something.'

. . . too imprudent . . . that is what I tell him constantly—just between us —listening to the advice of sensible people is not exactly a weakness of his . . . most of the time, and as much as he can, he has his own way and anything said to him on this subject he calls folly and cowardliness. . . . But, in spite of that, have no fear for him or for me.

p. 60: . . . their arms around each other, their foreheads pressed together, and both of them weeping so bitterly that they did not see me come in.

p. 61: During that night of anxiety and horror, Empress Elizabeth was, in a way, the only authority who, using her influence as a go-between welcomed by all, became a true mediator . . . between her husband, her mother-in-law and the conspirators.

What we have long feared, has come to pass.

Russia is about to breathe freely again after four years of oppression and, if a natural death had ended the Emperor's life, perhaps I would not have felt as I do at present, for the thought of a crime is horrible.

The Grand Duke Alexander, today the Emperor, was absolutely prostrated by his father's death, by the way in which he died . . . his sensitive soul will always be tortured by it . . . never would I have thought he would cost me so many dreadful moments . . . [he] did not know what he was doing. . . . In the end [he] went off to the Winter Palace in the hope that the crowd would follow him.

No other motive can give him firmness. And he needs it, for, great God, in what a condition is this Empire he has received!

CHAPTER III

p. 63: I must confess that, with all Russia, I breathe more freely.

p. 64: I am leaving for Russia because I believe that all honest men should rally around him and do their utmost to heal the infinite wounds his father inflicted on the country.

p. 65: Alas, things have not turned out as we thought they would.

p. 67: . . . [he] had hours of dejection, and to such an extent that we feared for his reason. . . . I tried to reconcile him with himself and with the great task that lay before him. . . . But remorse was still there.

p. 69: Nothing is definitely settled yet. . . . Despair was followed by delirious joy. . . . All that is a violent condition and one certainly needs a sense of proportion throughout the entire course of government.

p. 70: The Emperor had not made any plan. He was, so to speak, knocking at every door.

p. 74: . . . to sound out the situation.

The new Emperor is much beloved because he does all he can to make himself loved and after the constraint and tyranny the people suffered under Paul I, he has given them great freedom.

All I want is to contribute to the peace and quiet of Europe.

p. 75: . . . the impropriety of ruining the country that follows it too literally.

p. 76: The King of Prussia had written private letters to the Emperor of which the minister here had no knowledge.

p. 78: . . . one of the most infamous tyrants history has ever produced.

The good Empresses wept. The Grand Duke [Constantine] is furious and His Imperial Majesty is no less deeply disturbed. . . . The French Legation is no longer received.

The protest that [Russia] raises today leads to the question of whether, when England was pondering Paul I's assassination, she had known that the authors of the plot were within one league of the frontier, she would not have hastened to have them seized.

p. 80: His Majesty is firmly decided to go to war against Prussia.

They will receive the Russians with open arms, the inhabitants will cooperate to their utmost to aid our army against the Prussians. . . . The Russian army will be fed and supplemented with the greatest of ease and we shall be able to form new corps.

p. 83: We arrived here Saturday evening after a rough journey—which is why I have not yet recovered. . . . The Emperor was absolutely determined to get here on the fifth day, with the result that we rested only a few hours on chairs or on the floor as the beds did not arrive till the following morning.

p. 84: . . . [he] has an attack of laziness that is terrible for everyone. . . . All the next day one has to hear complaints because he went there. . . .

. . . break the monotonous life we lead although I do not think the Emperor will make much effort to entertain him.

I tell you on the whole . . . it is exactly like this winter . . . one must have patience . . . not to persevere in my opinion, which, for that matter, is unchangeable, but to endure with indifference many things that would undermine me if I did not try incessantly not to take them to heart . . . I remind myself constantly that we are in this world not to enjoy but to endure, but then I cannot help finding it a little unfair that I am obliged to suffer alone the penalty for something for which I am certainly not the only one to blame.

p. 85: She replied: 'I think I am pregnant.' She knew very well that I was fully aware of who was responsible for her pregnancy. . . . I don't know what will become of it all or how it will end.

p. 86: When I think about it, when I build up this daydream, my first thought is of the extreme pleasure it would give me to announce it to you.

. . . with his fondness for the military, [the Emperor] is in his element and when I see him content and in a good humor, I very quickly feel the same. . . . There is a limit to patience that is beyond human strength. . . . The Emperor is the first to ridicule modest behavior . . . by the way, he makes remarks that are really revolting from the lips of one who should keep an eye on order and morality, without which there would be no order at all. . . . This is what they cannot understand and this is what leads to reproaches.

p. 87: I have been extremely "gloomy" for several days.

It is a long time since I have been able to talk to you freely. . . . I don't know whether Amélie wrote to you about an occurrence that made a deep impression on me.

. . . I pitied the Emperor from the bottom of my heart . . . my share in his sorrow brought me almost tenderness on his part but for about two weeks only.

I doubt whether such a letter would have any effect.

CHAPTER IV

p. 90: . . . an impertinent whipper-snapper.

p. 92: . . . a wonderful event.

p. 93: . . . people rushed to kiss his hands, his feet, and even his clothing.

You remember my deep sorrow when he was appointed minister . . . it is for you to judge . . . whether it is in the interest of your service to let him contend with such fairly marked opinions . . . whether it is more useful to ask for the retirement he has requested.

p. 93 in note: The Russians have always suspected me of wanting to influence Russian policies in the direction of a close tie with Napoleon. This was very far from my thoughts, for it was obvious to me that any entente between the two Emperors could not fail to run counter to the interests of Poland. . . . The idea of its [Poland's] re-establishment was implicit in the very spirit of my work and in the trend I tried to give Russian policy.

p. 94: . . . because of the tender friendship he has shown me of late.

p. 95: . . . la Naryshkine flaunts her influence and obtains the most marked proofs of it; also anyone who solicits Court honors is on his knees before her. . . . This intrigue, which distresses and worries the Empress . . . contributes no less than the extremely fatal blunders of Austerlitz to diminishing respect for the Emperor, love of Russians, and the sort of adoration that is generally paid him.

p. 96: Your father's attachment to that very court [Berlin] was disastrous for him, and yours . . . has been disastrous enough so far.

p. 97: . . . the headlong march of the Russian Army flying to the aid of the Prussians.

It is clear . . . that you have taken up arms again to help and in the end to save Prussia, but it is equally true that, through that series of circumstances, we have seen our frontiers threatened and you have been obliged to ask your nation for aid in an amount so far unknown in the annals of Russia. In developing your policies, therefore, you will have to persuade the nation that you are acting for its glory and its peace and quiet; and that there is no Prussian influence involved.

p. 98: We are wrong to fight for the King of Prussia.

p. 99: It would be better for the Emperor to order every soldier to load his gun and kill himself.

Never has any situation been more critical. . . . In making peace, if we can still reach a suitable one, it can, unfortunately, only be a question of making the least onerous peace possible.

p. 100: . . . to draw back in order to make a leap.

p. 101: If only I had seen it sooner! The veil is torn and the time for mistakes is past. . . . God has saved us . . . we are coming out of this struggle with a sort of luster. But what do you say to all these events? Me—to spend my days with Bonaparte, to be whole hours with him in tête-à-tête!

Fortunately with all his genius, Bonaparte has a vulnerable side. It is his vanity, and I have decided to sacrifice my pride to the welfare of the Empire.

p. 102: It is the only profession Bonaparte knows.

Why did the Emperor Alexander reject at Tilsit the first plan I proposed to him?

. . . The Treaty of Peace and Friendship.

p. 104: The remarks one hears on all sides are frightening . . . in private groups and even in public assemblies there is often talk of a change of reign.

p. 105: I shall push Russia toward France as long as I can. Do you not see a motive in some unfortunate souls with whom I do not deal at all and who are too cowardly to start anything? I love my relatives very much, but I am the ruler and I demand respect and consideration. You see . . . I have a great deal of confidence in you to discuss family matters with you.

What is the magic upon which he draws to change opinion so abruptly and to such a degree? . . . She has succeeded in looking like a leader of the revolt. All the malcontents—and there are many of them—rally around her. . . . There are times when this good Emperor seems to me betrayed and sold out by his own family.

CHAPTER V

p. 115: The world is not big enough for us to come to an agreement over the affairs of that country.

p. 116: Sire, what have you come here to do? It is up to you to save Europe and you will do that only by standing up to Napoleon. The people of France are civilized, her sovereign is not. The sovereign of Russia is civilized, its people are not. The sovereign of Russia must therefore be the ally of the French people.

. . . stubborn . . . pretending to be deaf when he did not want to hear. . . . Bonaparte claims I am nothing but a fool. He laughs best who laughs last, and, as for me, I put my hope in God.

We'll make the Czar drain a glass of opium and, while he is asleep, we shall be busy elsewhere. . . . a nincompoop, a Greek from the Lower Empire.

p. 117: This alliance will end by being disgraceful.

. . . is reaching the point where I do not see much hope for a reconciliation that is so desirable.

You have developed a flightiness that is not natural to you. . . . You mourned for your children . . . that was the moment to return to your former self. . . . Let your true nature govern, cling to the only woman worthy of your full devotion. . . . Give up other liaisons . . . that your heart should condemn.

pp. 118–119: Amélie thinks as I do about your shocking decision, which, I hope, you will renounce. You are right not to tolerate such lack of respect . . . protest, and openly. You owe it to your honor and to the position you occupy. . . .

Louis is the only honest man among that crowd. . . . I shudder to think what that procedure might lead to. . . . That step would make you lose in one second a reputation justly earned over the years . . . what regrets and remorse you would have if you were the cause of an upheaval in the Empire . . . I fear [this plan] as the greatest misfortune. . . . Give it up, for the love of God.

p. 120: . . . to make itself strong and even stronger so that by negotiating it can shake off that state of tension which is useful only to France.

CHAPTER VI

p. 126: Do not think that [my faith] dates from these past days: I have been seeking this path now for several years. . . . Pray to the Supreme Being to give me the necessary power to finish my work for the nation, to make my country happy, but not in the vulgar sense; I stake all my glory on advancing the true kingdom of Jesus Christ.

p. 131: Monsieur my brother, I learned today that in spite of the loyalty with which I have kept my pledges to Your Majesty, your troops have crossed the borders of Russia, and at this very moment I receive a note from Petersburg in which, because of this act of aggression, Count Lauriston announces that Your Majesty has considered himself in a state of war with me from the moment Prince Kourakine asked for his passports. . . . As a matter of fact, that ambassador was never authorized to do so . . . and as soon as I was informed of it I expressed my disapproval by ordering him to remain at his post. If Your Majesty does not intend to shed the blood of our peoples over a misunderstanding of this sort and if you agree to withdraw your troops from Russian soil, I shall regard what has happened as never having happened and an amicable settlement between us will be possible. In the contrary event, Your Majesty, I shall be forced to repel an attack that I have done nothing to provoke. It depends on Your Majesty to avoid the disasters of a new war.

p. 136: The public wanted him to be appointed. I appointed him. As for me, I wash my hands of it.

p. 138: I see that I am the one who must pay the piper. I order the retreat.

p. 139: The farther Napoleon advances, the less he must think peace possible. This is the unanimous feeling of the whole nation. . . . This is what Napoleon did not count on. He was wrong in this as in many other things.

Napoleon or me—we cannot both continue to reign at the same time. I have learned to know him and he won't take me in again.

There is nothing in it but bluster and bragging.

p. 140: The occupation of Moscow is frightful; nevertheless, if it is possible to look at that disaster from an abstract military point of view, we will draw several comforting conclusions from it . . . [Napoleon] believed firmly . . . that Moscow was the ultimate goal, that from there he would set out, exalted, to subjugate those parts of Europe that were still holding out against him . . . [but] no one talks to him of peace and the moment we cannot defend Moscow any longer, we shall destroy it. . . . He is scarcely accustomed to such receptions in the other capitols of Europe; even Spain was more friendly.

p. 142: All of that will vanish without me.

CHAPTER VII

p. 146: If we failed to cooperate [with the Emperor Alexander], he would be discouraged and it would not be at all surprising if he were to abandon the powers to their own devices, convinced above all that he has done enough to consolidate public opinion in his favor.

p. 148: . . . to restore to every nation the full and complete possession of its rights and its institutions; to place all of them and ourselves as well under the safeguard of the general alliance and to preserve them from the ambitions of conquerors. Such are our premises. Providence has set us on the road that leads straight to our goal. We have covered part of it. The part we still have to cover bristles with tremendous obstacles. They must be removed.

Let me tell you that if, aside from the work of Providence, whatever perseverance and energy I have had occasion to display these past two years have been useful to the cause of the independence of Europe, I owe it to you and to your guidance . . . the desire to be worthy of your solicitude, to deserve your esteem, has sustained me.

p. 149: Metternich behaved abominably on the Swiss question. . . . He compromised himself, his Emperor and me with him. . . . If you have a chance to speak to the Swiss, make it clear that I am utterly against any violation of their territory.

p. 150: The presence of the Emperor electrified the cavalry to such an extent that nothing could stop them.

Tell . . . the Parisians that I do not enter their walls as an enemy and that it depends on them alone to have me as their friend, but tell them also that I have one single enemy in France, and that with him I shall never be reconciled.

p. 152: It was obvious that everything emanated from him, everything revolved around him . . . the King of Prussia passed unnoticed.

p. 153: The English nourished a swine, the French bought it for eighteen louis, but it isn't worth a napoleon.

p. 155: This visit did not pass without several annoyances. [The Emperor] was not in sympathy with the Prince Regent [and] left England little pleased with his sojourn but carrying with him an exalted idea of the prosperity and grandeur of that country.

The year has passed. . . . I thank heaven. . . . I have done no one any harm.

Why does that dear Emperor give you so few details and why is he so lavish with them to his mother? It is inconceivable. For, aside from being his wife, you are his best friend and share with the greatest warmth his fame and his success.

p. 157: . . . I felt in thinking over all that had happened in the past year and where Divine Providence had led us.

CHAPTER VIII

p. 159: The Congress dances, it does not walk.

p. 161: To re-establish Poland in order to hand it over to Russia would mean creating a danger for Europe.

In order to obtain Alexander's assent to the existence of Old Saxony, we had to give Poland to the Czar.

p. 162: There must never be any question between us on this matter. We have something else ahead of us now: Our alliance will be stronger than ever. . . . We are Christians . . . our holy law commands us to forgive offenses.

p. 163: Alone among the sovereigns [Alexander] walks toward posterity.

p. 163 in note: If in the great interest of general peace we have not made it possible for all Poles to be reunited under the same scepter, I have done my best to at least soften as much as I could the rigors of separation, and to obtain for them on all sides every possible enjoyment of their nationality.

p. 164: I have tremendous things to say to him, for I have suffered a great deal on his account.

p. 166: If you knew how much He loves you, you would not be able to resist Him in anything. . . . one of the elect and your heart was already prepared by great sacrifices and enormous sorrows to become the joy . . . of our God.

In our relations your reserve blocks everything. . . . You must become as a child. . . . No human power can teach you anything—you need the divine eye . . . you need that woman accustomed to living at the feet of Christ.

[I] cling to you like a tender mother anxiously watching over her child. . . . The ties of nature, those of the Empire, are merely secondary where Your Majesty is concerned. . . . Where would you find the soul who could be for you what I am? I tell you without fear you cannot go on without me so long as God wishes me to be the one.

p. 168: We were forced to leave Baden without a cent of money. . . . In the end one wonders what good the Holy Alliance is, and whether one dares to believe it is not just an empty sound. . . . Christians are asleep. We have pleaded the cause of the oppressed and we have been persecuted. . . . In Prussia they treated us like felons. . . . The King of Saxony was the only one who was humane toward us.

I proclaimed you to the people and to the nation as the Chosen of the Lord.

pp. 171–172: Alexander showed himself to be both what he really was and what he wished to appear, prudent and magnanimous. That greatness of soul of which he felt capable, which had been his ideal since his youth, he had made rather a show of, and, more than having given an exhibition of it in 1814, he had actually tested its effectiveness and achieved the desired result. In 1815, he saw loftily, he saw clearly, he saw far, and he acted with as much simplicity and uprightness as with energy and skill.

p. 172: That is what our Allies want to make of France. Only my signature is lacking, and I promise you it will always be lacking.

I am completely resigned, knowing how badgered, busy, overburdened with affairs he is.

p. 173: . . . the discontent resulting from it . . . if this smoke was cleared away, I do not know what would become of this great Empire. . . . The Emperor thinks himself strong enough with his army . . . to stand up against . . . any enemy at home. . . . The army is constantly the object of his attention.

p. 174: The demon of evil, crushed by the superior action of Providence . . . is apparently making new efforts.

p. 178: The Emperor's attitude toward me has become altogether friendly.

p. 179: . . . but not the slightest confidence—not in any case. For the Emperor, all respect, complete confidence and the greatest friendship. . . . the apple of the Dowager Empress's eye.

p. 180: France and Europe harbor a breed of dangerous men who have a horror of order . . . and who fit well into a regime that satisfies all low passions. . . . Your government, freed of surveillance by, the allied armies, must not close its eyes to these dangers.

CHAPTER IX

p. 184: Nicolas has only one idea in his head—to reign.

p. 186: They constantly attack the power that religious ideas exercise over the monarch. It is certain that Petersburg society has never been subjected to more privations than it has since those ideas gained the strength they exert today.

pp. 187–188: [Alexander] could not forbid what his brother represented to him as not only necessary to his happiness, but even to the tranquillity of his conscience; no longer wishing, he said, to lead a wild life.

p. 188: However, not everyone would judge the Emperor as I do: There will be a great deal of disapproval.

p. 189: His heart will always be torn asunder.

It is a question of finding a remedy for the evil that is spreading rapidly, and with every occult means that the satanic demon who directs it can use. The remedy we are seeking is, unfortunately, beyond our puny human power. . . . The Saviour alone . . . can furnish the means. . . . Let us call upon Him, therefore, with all the fervor of our hearts that He may deign to spread His Holy Spirit over us, and let us walk only in the path that can please Him and that alone can lead us to salvation.

p. 193: The present evil is even more dangerous than Napoleon's devastating despotism, for present-day doctrines are much more alluring to the masses than the military yoke under which he held them.

p. 194: The center is in France, the French revolutionaries stirred up the Greek affair.

I am deeply distressed at what is going on.

p. 196: Even I do not recognize myself; it is as if I were on a journey and had arrived at the house of a strange prince, as I have just told the Emperor. He has given so much thought and care to the attentions with which he is receiving me.

p. 197: . . . all that produces a tone that shocks one. It is only one of the thousand things you are obliged to see without being able to remedy it. . . . We groan about it often with the Emperor. . . . What I like so much in the Dowager Empress is that she keeps abreast of the spirit of the times. There is even no etiquette and constraint in her salon. Run and make haste—that is the motto of the imperial family—that's the way life goes on, without profit to anyone at all.

CHAPTER X

p. 201: . . . the abyss at the edge of which the Empire's state education stands, and which they go to so much trouble to hide from you.

p. 204: The Emperor pays daily visits to the ladies of his family regardless of distances; from here, it takes him half an hour to go to Pavlovsk, a half hour to return, altogether an hour on the way. With all that, an Empire on his hands and the interests of Europe, which means that the forenoon is scarcely enough time . . . [he] is often very touching in his heartfelt need to enjoy family ties.

p. 206: He has erysipelas over his whole leg. . . . Never have I seen the Emperor so patient in an illness as this time. . . . He said something very sweet to me, day before yesterday, that touched my heart: 'You will see, I shall owe my recovery to you.'

p. 207: . . . to tell me with marked satisfaction that she has talked with him. That put me in a terrible temper for several days.

The genuine affection the Emperor shows me, as well as his desire to have me always near him . . . he seemed to be glad to have the little things I could do for him . . . he allowed me to watch beside him when he slept, to serve him at his supper, and when he was better and he was reading, as was I, ready to break off when he wanted to have a rest and talk.

p. 208: The result of those passions and the family rivalries for the Emperor is that I am reduced to considering myself sometimes almost as his mistress, or as if we were secretly married; and I dare not mention anything that can show the affection and intimacies between us, in order not to stir up bitterness, bad temper, and often additional trouble . . . because then, afraid of not seeming to be as close to him as I am, they literally plague him.

p. 209: My dear Wassilchikov, you who have been in my service from the beginning of my reign, know that I have shared and encouraged these illusions: It is not up to me to be severe.

p. 210: . . . as on a ship. . . . The Emperor sent a large sloop . . . I was dying of fear lest a fine humanitarian impulse might make him want to take a hand in it himself.

p. 211: . . . in the greatest seclusion . . . he did not wish it to be celebrated . . . because he says that, in these times, there are so many unfortunate souls that it would be shocking to have a celebration. . . . As I wanted to go to mass that day, the Emperor had the portable chapel placed in one of my salons, two rooms from my study, so that we two heard mass by ourselves, which pleased me and the Emperor too.

He shows . . . a solicitude for me that proves all his affection.

p. 212: There can be no quiet again, as long as Alexandrine is here having a baby . . . because it is a reason for the Empress to come here frequently. [This evening] she came with the Grand Duchess Marie to see the Emperor, although he spent two hours at Pavlovsk yesterday and also today. . . . When I see him as exhausted as a deer at bay . . . and that they even rob him of the brief moment of leisure he might have, it is hard for me to control myself. . . . [That] is already a very necessary period of serenity for me.

p. 213: The Emperor expects to stay with me until the New Year. . . . He is so kind to me on this trip again . . . he has foreseen everything, arranged everything, in such a way that I am deeply touched . . . I am traveling in luxurious comfort such as I have never had en route. Since I left . . . I have already had four letters from the Emperor. . . . He shows a solicitude for me that touches me to the heart.

p. 215: It is easy to judge the personal and general good the Emperor does by his presence in this region; one can feel the effects already.

p. 217: Where can one find peace and quiet in this life? When you think you have arranged everything for the best and can enjoy it, an unexpected trial crops up.

pp. 218–219: Our angel is in heaven. It is almost more than I can bear. You should have seen the death of that angelic creature who, though he had lost the power to understand, still possessed the power to love. Few people have known that soul, all its worth, but God knew it well. . . . The first day [after his death] he looked happy . . . so alive that it seemed as though he were going to get up with his usual quick movement. . . . He knew that I cared only for him.

p. 219: He knew all he meant to me and that he only was everything to me. . . . seemed to be increased a hundredfold . . . he was ready for eternity.

The part I would play in the long run would be beneath the dignity that must always remain attached to the memory of that Emperor Alexander who was unique and incomparable in the eyes of all Europe.

CHAPTER XI

p. 228: I thought his glance seemed weakened and his eyes looked troubled.

APPENDIX

p. 235: It is because his heart would not let him remain wholly impervious to the vows dictated by his desire for the general good that he deserved the consideration, the esteem, and the respect of men of good will. That feeling and his zeal for the public welfare, though they may not have been fruitful in useful results, will none the less cause his name to live in history with honor. Alexander undoubtedly died a despot, but he was born to be better than that.

INDEX